THE REDEMPTION OF GOD

A Theology of Mutual Relation

Isabel Carter Heyward

UNIVERSITY
PRESS OF
AMERICA

LANHAM • NEW YORK • LONDON

Copyright © 1982 by
Isabel Carter Heyward

University Press of America,™ Inc.

4720 Boston Way
Lanham, MD 20706

3 Henrietta Street
London WC2E 8LU England

Printed in the United States of America

Library of Congress Cataloging in Publication Data
Heyward, Isabel Carter.
    The redemption of God.

    Bibliography: p.
    1. Theology–Miscellanea. I. Title.
BT75.2.H49   234   81–43706
ISBN 0–8191–2389–7   AACR2
ISBN 0–8191–2390–0 (pbk.)

To Bev

because we can count on so few
to go this hard way with us.*

*cf. Adrienne Rich, "Women and Honor: Some
Notes on Lying," On Lies, Secrets, and Silence: Selected Prose,
1966-1978. New York: W.W. Norton and Co., 1979, p. 188.

This book is an unrevised publication of my 1980 Doctoral dissertation. During the two years since the manuscript was submitted to the Faculty of Union Theological Seminary in New York, I have presented it to several publishers for consideration. Three times I have been told that it is "too academic" for general readership and "too general" for academics. One publisher suggested that I rewrite it so as to upgrade its marketability for either scholars or commonfolk. I have been unwilling, however, to rewrite or revise it, for I believe that its integrity belongs to the situation in which it was written: in a studio apartment, at a kitchen table, night after day/day after night/in unbroken succession for twelve months, by a liberal Christian woman--a graduate student--beginning to see the limits of, and alternatives to, "liberalism and individualism," and to articulate theologically this vision.

Certainly, the urgency of these times demands ever-sharper analysis, and ever-more-passionately-lived-and-preached commitments to justice by those of us in the "immoral minority." The emergence of the radical right in this country, with its broadside attack on "humanism" (read: humanity), has fostered a theological praxis for the rest of us which begs stronger collaboration, concerted action, and commitment to solidarity. If I were to re-write this book I would pay more explicit analytical attention to the issues of solidarity and struggle. It is not enough to proclaim that "'I love you' means 'Let the Revolution begin!'" (pp. 162 & 225); but it is important nonetheless to proclaim this here and now.

Hence, this book. It is "unfinished." No theology, no book, is ever enough. Only justice is enough, and if any book can help us along this common way, may it be read and taken to heart.

My appreciation to Helen Hudson, and others at the University Press of America, for their efforts in enabling this publication. Special thanks to Staley Hitchcock, who typed the manuscript for its presentation at Union Seminary and who typed it again as this book. His expertise, as well as his delight in this project, have been a source of pleasure for me! Finally, I am grateful for the support of the Dean and Faculty of the Episcopal Divinity School, who have underwritten the expenses for this publication.

Carter Heyward
Cambridge, Massachusetts
February 1, 1982

iv

ACKNOWLEDGMENTS

Many have been involved in the shaping of this volume. I can mention here only those whose contributions have been specific or whose involvement so thorough-going as to be immediately apparent to me.

The faculty of the Episcopal Divinity School gave me time to do my work, and extra time to do it well.

Groups of faithful people in Oberlin, Ohio; Charlotte, North Carolina; Denver; and New York City have helped me experience, and believe in, the power in relation. Struggling against ecclesiastical bondage to false gods, Alison Cheek, Bob DeWitt, and Sue Hiatt have encouraged me to do likewise--and to articulate something about this common struggle.

Throughout our time together at Union Theological Seminary, Sally Bentley's friendship has helped keep me in touch with what is most valuable: the elusive and compelling character of right-relation. Similarly, Emily Hewitt has fed me with a passion for justice.

For the past two years, Angela Askew, Connie Baugh, Muffy Burns, Katie Cannon, Linda Clark, Mary Glasspool, Sara Goold, Mary Pellauer, Tom Reese, Dorothee Soelle, and Virginia Wink have probed relational issues with me, often in depth. Jill Thompson and Karen Ziegler shared their M.Div. theses with me, thereby adding new dimensions to the work I have been about.

Eve Edmond sang about friendship; Bill Crawford mimed and raised serious questions; and the "Third Floor Ice Cream Coalition" in Van Dusen taught me much about the relation between play, celebration, simple sharing, and political effectiveness.

Bob Brown, Newton Dougherty, Anne Scheibner, and participants in the "Issues in Feminist Theology" class at Union read parts of this manuscript and have been generous in their responses. My mother

Mary Ann and Victor Schramm helped dig up several obscure references. My dog Tera lay on the floor and watched me write and took me to the park whenever I needed a break. Linda Clark, Christopher Morse, and Dick Norris served on my committee.

Staley Hitchcock produced a magnificently typed document as well as special gifts of banter, insight, and patience.

Brooke Leddy, Susan Savell, Fredrica Thompsett, and Janet Walton have pushed hard with me against stubborn boundaries of old assumptions and risked naming new relational/theological possibilities.

Finally, there are two without whom there would be no book: Bev Harrison's relation to me is a rare and remarkable resource of power and faith; and Tom Driver's unfettered mind, wise counsel, and non-confounding criticism has helped me keep going without losing my mind, my faith, or my friends.

All of these people and others have given "my" work an intense spirit of collaboration, suggesting that ... in the beginning is the relation, for which I am grateful.

Carter Heyward
May 23, 1980

vi

CONTENTS

Can we be like drops of water
falling on the stone
splashing, breaking, dispersing in air
weaker than stone by far
but be aware
as time goes by
the rock will wear away

and the water comes again*

*Holly Near and Meg Christian, "The
Rock Will Wear Away," on record album, Meg Christian,
Face the Music, ©1977 Olivia Records, Inc.

PROLOGUE

RE-MEMBERING OURSELVES

and what
 will David do without Jonathan
 and Karl Marx without Engels
 and Mary without Elizabeth
 and Che Gueverra without Fidel
 and Jesus without John
 and Dietrich without Eberhard?[1]

        And what will I do without you? With-
out you, I will do nothing. Without you, I have no
home. The night of the soul is long and dark because
it is lonely, an abyss entered on a promise that I am
alone and so are you. I wait to die and so do you,
yearning for release from alien residency in this
city.[2] To pray for death, to pray to "God," is all
that I can do to impose meaning upon this emptiness,
upon myself, upon you whom I do not know, and upon
"God." To pray is to construct a bridge to someone
who enjoys my loneliness. For my "God's" existence is
postulated on our separation and my despair and my
incessant search for relation with "God" in heaven
since I cannot find it with you on earth.

        You may protest. If you do, and if you
are a Christian, I will assume that you do not understand the Christian faith. I will remind you of the
fathers and the martyrs and the faithful yearners who
knew better than to love themselves and each other too
much.[3]

        I remember. I have not forgotten the
fall, 1967. St. Luke's Hospital, Clark 8 Psychiatric
Unit. First year seminarian: "confused." I kept a
journal and a Bible and that was it. Seeking alone a
vocation, I had come to New York City to work things
out for myself. It was between "God" and me, and my
confusion was simply the lot of a person seeking self-
affirmation, yet attached fast to a narcissistic "God"
who demands her self-negation.

xv

In my journal I wrote: "God calls us to be alone. He calls us to be harrassed, spat upon, mocked, beaten--emotionally, mentally, physically, spiritually ... He calls us to be crucified."[4] All relationships, all <u>Christian</u> relationships, I noted, "are those in which we say to others, 'You are my master.'"[5]

I wrote poetry:

There is a God.
I know that He exists
because without Him
I know that I could no longer exist.

. . .

But I continue to seek
and I begin to realize
that I am making my own hell
because I want to know too much.

. . .

Yes, hell is manmade ...
hell is the desire,
my desire,
to be creator and not simply creature.

. . .

But the pain, the agony, of hell
convinces me
that I must die to my own sin.

. . .

Ultimately comes my acceptance,
like Jesus':
<u>Thy</u> will be done--on earth.
Do as must be done with me.
Convince me that I am not creator!
Help me accept my imperfection!
Show me that I am man!
Make me willing to accept
        my badness
        my suffering
        my manness.

                Let me reach not to other men
                    but to Thee, my God!
                Help me reach up, not down,
                    but up, up, up
                    and touch Thee![6]

        You may still protest, as many sensitive
apologists would, that this is not Christian teaching
but rather only a faulty hermeneutic given zealous
voice by one confused young woman. Faulty hermeneutic?
Indeed. But it is not simply the confused voice of one
person. It is a recurrent voice of orthodox Christians, from Augustine to Barth, and the target of the
dissent of the heretics and heterodox Christians, from
Pelagius to the final testimonies of Bonhoeffer.[7]

        It is a narcissistic love story between
a lonely "God" and a lonely creature; a story about a
spiritual affection--or preference--that I, and I [8]
alone, can experience for myself, by myself, alone.
To ask for more is to damn myself because it is to ask
that humanity, my humanity, be taken seriously, a possibility that "God" must reject if "He" is to be "God."

        I remember. I have not forgotten
either myself or you: you who are patient, you who
feel guilty, you who know how to confess but not to
celebrate, you who despise your sexuality, you who
believe that other persons are your masters, you who
pray to "God" for a peace that is always promised but
never forthcoming.

                        . . .

                We starve
                look at one another
                short of breath
                walking proudly
                in our winter coats
                wearing smells of laboratories
                facing a dying nation
                a moving paper fantasy
                listening to the new told lies
                the supreme visions
                of lonely tunes.[9]

        Remember the 1960s in the United States:
a dying nation, a dying "God," the dying of a loneliness that did not quite die. But the process is worth

the remembering of this period as an effort toward relation and against the alienation and isolation constructed socially upon ordered and distanced ranks of humanity: white over black, old generals over young combattants, government over people, large economically secure nations over a small poor country in Southeast Asia, men over women, you over and against me, you in your world and me in my world over and against us in our world. People untouched by people.[10]

     Struggling for the power to effect--create, accomplish--anything worthwhile in the world, blacks, civil rights activists, draft resisters, students, farm workers and exploited laborers, other restless troubled citizens, and by the end of the decade women and gays, demonstrated our refusals to go further as bodyselves isolated from one another and thus structurally invisible to those who understood themselves to be guardians of our isolation as well as their own.

     In those times the experience of power in collectivity was taken seriously as the solution to the problem of injustice--that is, the structural inhibition of love rooted in the assumption that loneliness, disguised as "privacy" and "individualism," is the human condition.[11] In those times human needs, human feelings, human work, human dreams were taken to heart by human beings who had begun to imagine that in the beginning is the relation: we, not simply I; involved, not merely observing; on earth, not simply in heaven. The dying of a lonely "God" signalled the ultimacy of the human experience of relation.

     But gods do not die easily because the human experience which finds and names them is always stubborn.[12] So it is with the experience of wanting to secure a promise that I will not dis-integrate in the chaos of a world that frightens me among people whom I do not know; the experience of seeking assurance that even among people whom I do know, there is something less fearful, and less fleeting, than the ambiguities and tension in relation. I want something. I want "God." And I will hold onto "God" until you and I touch, until we are able to realize our power in intimate and immediate relation.[13]

     We are untouched and untouching until we realize our <u>intimacy</u>; until we know a fundamental bond between our innermost senses of who we are.

Intimacy is the deepest quality of relation, the realization of ourselves, generically, as <u>humanity</u>--people
with something in common--rather than as alien pieces
of flesh and blood playing our separate parts in an
absurd drama of loneliness.

We are unmoved and unmoving until we
realize our power <u>immediately</u>: now, not later;
directly, not circuitously; a straightforward, not a
manipulative, power; you and I together, without need
of a mediator to warn us falsely that we cannot co-
operate.

We do not reach or touch. We are left
alone, untouched, until we choose to take ourselves--
our humanity--more seriously than we have taken our
"God."

Dare we press fiercely against the
boundaries of isolation? Does something burn between
us? Have we intimations of ourselves together? And
whereas we cannot bear easily the death of "God," can
we leave forever unexhumed the dream of what we will
do together, you and I, if we dare?

. . .

No one lives in this room
without confronting the whiteness of the wall
behind the poems, planks of books,
photographs of dead heroines.
Without contemplating last and late
the true nature of poetry. The drive
to connect. The dream of a
common language.[14]

Yes, there is a dream, a vision. I
have dreamt it, I have seen it. You are in it. You
have told me. Together, we are at home, alive, in
the world. There is nothing still in the movement
between us. No apathy.[15] No security to dull our
senses to change. We will transvaluate values, con-
verting the minimal benefits of isolation to the possibilities of love.[16] We will see that philia, eros,
and agape are different words for a single act of
love.[17] We will co-create the world, for in the
beginning is the relation.[18]

xix

FOOTNOTES: PROLOGUE

[1]Dorothee Soelle, part of a poem written for
Sydney and Robert McAfee Brown, New York, N.Y., May 18, 1979.

[2]For Augustine, the chosen people of God are
alien residents of the human city, sojourners in this world,
until they leave this mortal life: "Since then, the supreme good
of the city of God in perfect and eternal peace, not such as mor-
tals pass into and out of by birth and death, but the peace of
freedom from all evil, in which the immortals ever abide, who can
deny that that future life is most blessed, or that, in compari-
son with it, this life which we now live is most wretched ...?"
The City of God in Great Books of the Western World, Vol. 18
(Chicago: Encyclopedia Britannica, 1952), XIX:20, pp. 523-4.

[3]Consider these men's assumptions about the
worthlessness of the human body, women, and sexual relations in
the following examples of patristic thought:

"Continence is an ignoring of the body in
accordance with the confession of faith in God." Clement of
Alexandria, "On Marriage," or Stromateis, Book III, ed. J. Oulten
and H. Chadwick, Alexandrian Christianity in Library of Christian
Classics, Vol. II, eds. Baillie, McNeill, & Van Dusen (Philadelphia: Westminster Press, 1954), p. 41. "The human ideal of continence, I mean that which is set forth by Greek philosophers,
teaches that we should fight desire and not be subservient to it
so as to bring it to practical effect. But our ideal is not to
experience desire at all. Our aim is not that while a man feels
desire he should get the better of it, but that he should be con-
tinent even respecting desire itself." Ibid., p. 66.

"Men marry, indeed, so as to get a manager for
the house, to solace weariness, to banish solitude; but a faithful slave is a far better manager, more submissive to the master
... than a wife ... if she does what pleases her, not what she is
commanded .... A wise man can never be alone. He has with him
the good men of all time, and turns his mind freely wherever he
chooses. What is inaccessible to him in person he can embrace in
thought. And, if men are scarce, he converses with God. He is
never less alone than when alone." Jerome, Against Jovinianus,
Book I, eds. Schaff and Wace, A Select Library of Nicene and
Post-Nicene Fathers, Vol. 6 (Grand Rapids: Eerdmans, 1955), p.
383.

And from The Desert Fathers, trans. with introduction by Helen Waddell (Ann Arbor: University of Michigan Press, 1957): "The abbot Antony said, 'Who sits in solitude and is quiet hath escaped from three wars: hearing, speaking, seeing: yet against one thing shall be continually battle: that is, his own heart,'" from Book II, "On Quiet," p. 63.

"At one time a priest from Scete went up to visit the bishop of Alexandria. And when he came back to Scete, the brethren questioned of him, 'How fares the city?' But he answered them, 'Believe me, my brothers, I saw no man's face there, not even the face of the bishop ... I wrested away my soul, that I might not look upon the face of man.' And the brothers profited by the story, and guarded themselves against lifting up their eyes," from Book IV, "On Self-Restraint," p. 72.

"A certain brother was going on a journey, and he had his mother with him, and she was old. They came to a certain river, and the old woman could not cross it. And her son took off his cloak and wrapped it about his hands, lest he should in any wise touch the body of his mother, and so carrying her, he set her on the other side of the stream. Then said his mother to him, 'Why didst thou so cover thy hands, my son?' He answered, 'Because the body of a woman is fire. And even from my touching thee, came the memory of other women in my soul,'" Ibid., p. 74.

[4]From my journal, November 18, 1967.

[5]Ibid.

[6]Excerpts from poem, "Random Thoughts," my journal, November 20, 1967.

[7]This needs to be understood primarily in terms of emphasis. Augustine and Barth, for example, emphasize human pride and fall, whereas Pelagius and Bonhoeffer, in his Letters and Papers, emphasize humanity's natural possibility for goodness. None of the Christian theologians to whom I refer has maintained that humanity is divinity and thus morally responsible only to itself. Still, in laying emphasis on humanity's alienation from divinity, theologians such as Barth draw our attention toward the legitimate primacy of our experiences of guilt and, thus, a felt need to negate, rather than affirm, our humanity. There is tension in Barth's own work between the sin of pride (Church Dogmatics, IV:1, pp. 413-78) and the sloth of man [sic] (Ibid., IV:2, pp. 403-83). On the one hand, "Sin in its unity and totality is always pride ..., the disobedience of man ..., the unbelief of man" (IV:1, pp. 413-14); furthermore, "man is the being whose attitude not only does not correspond to the attitude of God as revealed and active in Jesus Christ, but

contradicts it and actively opposes it, that the two attitudes move in a diametrically opposite direction, and that no other view seems to be possible than that they never seem to coincide ... [T]he meaning and character, therefore, of sin, is in fact the pride of man in contrast to what in the light of the being and activity of Jesus Christ we can only call the humility of God" (Ibid., p. 418). On the other hand, Barth makes an eloquent case for "humanity," which "means to be bound [not only to God but also] to other men" (IV:2, p. 432). This, of course, is planted in Barth's christological anthropology. In [Jesus Christ], a person lives for all other persons. "Among all ... for whom [Jesus Christ] is a Fellow and Neighbor and Brother as we are ... we remain in our isolation and seclusion and self-will and unwillingness ... in relation to them; in a word in our inhumanity" (Ibid., p. 433). While Barth makes christo-logical sense theoretically, it is difficult for me to imagine in what actual anthropo-logical sense it is possible, on the one hand, for human beings to turn away from and reject a condition--the human condition--which we experience as "diametrically opposed" to God; and on the other hand, to be bound affirmatively to this same human condition as encountered in other persons. What does it mean to love our neighbors as ourselves if we experience ourselves as beings whose "attitude" contradicts and opposes that of God?

In short, Barth emphasizes the goodness of God in contrast to the sin of humanity, which may leave us stuck--both in a salvation wrought by God and as persons who cannot look to other persons for the help we need. Bonhoeffer charged his mentor-friend, Barth, with a positivism which makes no sense in "a world come of age." Bonhoeffer asked, "How do we speak of God--without religion ...? How do we speak (or perhaps we cannot now even 'speak' as we used to) in a 'secular' way about 'God'? In what way are we 'religionless-secular' Christians ... those who are called forth ... as belonging wholly to the world?" Letters and Papers From Prison, ed. Eberhard Bethge (New York: Macmillan, 1953; First Macmillan Paperback, 1972), pp. 280-1.

This is a tension in emphasis between God's and humanity's activity in the world.

[8]For discussion of Augustine's "preference" for the spiritual, see Chapter IV, pp. 150f.

[9]Lyrics of the song, "The Flesh Failures/Let the Sunshine In," by Gerome Ragni and James Rado, from the record album Hair; United Artists Corp., 1979.

[10]This reference is to the "Death of God" movement in theology in the United States in the late 1960s. Citing Bonhoeffer appreciatively as "the most decisive theological

influence on the younger generation of Protestants today" in Rad-ical Theology and the Death of God (Indianapolis: Bobbs-Merrill, 1966), p. 113, William Hamilton and Thomas J. J. Altizer pub-lished, together and separately, several works in which they her-alded the dawning of "Christian atheism" as an affirmative recog-nition that God "does not make himself known [to us], even as an enemy. This is more than the old protest against natural theo-logy or metaphysics; more than the usual assurance that before the holy God all our language gets broken and diffracted into paradox. It is really that we do not know, do not adore, do not possess, do not believe in God .... We are not talking about the absence of the experience of God, but about the experience of the absence of God." Ibid., pp. 27-8.

[11]See Dorothee Soelle's Political Theology, trans. with introduction by John Shelley (Philadelphia: Fortress Press, 1974), pp. 83-92, for a relational and political interpre-tation of "sin" as "collaboration [with] and apathy [toward]" injustice. ["W]e shall adhere to the Old Testament content of the word sin, which in all of its diverse meanings refers 'pri-marily ... not to individual, private sentiments, but to the con-nection between the deed that disturbs the divinely willed union of brotherhood and the resulting punishment.'" W. D. Marsch, "Is Consciousness of Sin False Consciousness?" in Moral Evil Under Challenge, ed. J. B. Metz, Concilium (New York: Herder & Herder, 1970), p. 30, n. 5, quoted by Soelle in Political Theology, p.91.

[12]Peter L. Berger and Thomas Luckmann discuss the "symbolic universe" as "bodies of theoretical tradition that integrate different provinces of meaning and encompass the insti-tutional order in a symbolic totality ..." in The Social Con-struction of Reality: A Treatise in the Sociology of Knowledge (Garden City, N.Y.: Doubleday & Co., 1966; Anchor Books, 1967), p. 95. They describe the function of the symbolic universe as that of ordering and legitimating "a whole world" (p. 96), in both its "objective" and "subjective" aspects. What is extremely interesting to me is Berger and Luckmann's recognition of the symbolic universe's social significance in "protecting" its sub-jects against "terror": "It is in the legitimation of death that the transcending potency of symbolic universe manifests itself most clearly, and the fundamental terror-assuaging character of the ultimate legitimations of the paramount reality of everyday life is revealed. The primacy of the social objectivations of everyday life can retain its subjective plausibility only if it is constantly protected against terror. On the level of meaning, the institutional order represents a shield against terror. To be anomic ... means to be deprived of this shield ... while the horror of aloneness is probably already given in the constitu-tional sociality of man, it manifests itself on the level of meaning in man's incapacity to sustain a meaningful existence in

isolation from the nomic construction of society. The symbolic universe shelters the individual from ultimate terror by bestowing ultimate legitimation upon the protective structures of the institutional order ... [T]he social (as against the just discussed individual) significance of symbolic universes [is in their function as] sheltering canopies over the institutional order ..." (pp. 101-02). This theme is explored more fully by Berger in The Sacred Canopy: Elements of a Sociological Theory of Religion (Garden City, N.Y.: Doubleday & Co., 1967), which includes a consideration of the social bases of theodicy ("the religious legitimation of anomic phenomena," p. 55). One such basis, Berger suggests, is the self-denying surrender to society, or "masochism," upon which a person declares, "'I am nothing--He is everything--and therein is my ultimate bliss.'" (pp. 55-6).

Berger continues, "The sadistic god ... remains invulnerable, infinite, immortal by definition. The surrender to him is ipso facto protected from the contingencies and uncertainties of merely social masochism--for ever" (p. 57). It is from this sociological perspective that I make the claims I do about the experience of self-in-relation as being the ultimately "nomic" experience, against which--and within which--the anomic terror and denial brought on by the experience of loneliness ("aloneness") serve in the construction of "God." See also Chapter V, pp. 153-163.

[13]I became fascinated with "intimate" and "immediate" and their etymology when I read the following:

> [There is a] mystery [in] subatomic-particle behavior--namely, how two particles that are separated in space and moving apart at the speed of light seem to know instantaneously what each other is doing (this is puzzling because "almost all physics rests upon the assumption that nothing in the universe can travel faster than the speed of light") ...

> [T]he solution to this mystery [was] proposed in 1964 by a Swiss physicist named J. S. Bell. According to Bell's theorem ..., "all the 'parts' of the universe are connected in an intimate and immediate way previously claimed only by mystics and other scientifically objectionable people."

See New York Times, Wednesday, March 28, 1979; Christopher Lehmann-Haupt's review of The Dancing Wu Li Masters: An Overview of the New Physics by Gary Zukar (Morrow), 1979.

"Intimate" and "immediate" need to be understood etymologically: The word "intimate" is derived from the Latin verb *intimare* (to put or bring into; to drive or press into) and from the adjective *intimus* (inmost, deepest). It may be used as a verb, a noun, and most often in my work as an adjective, meaning "inmost, most inward, deep-seated; pertaining to or connected with the inmost nature or fundamental character of a thing; concerning or affecting one's inmost self." It is critical to what I am doing that "intimate" ("intimacy," "intimately") be read not as simply a personal feeling, or as a designation of a romantic or private attachment. It is meant to convey a profound quality of relation which is seated in the depth of human character.

The word "immediate" has its roots in the Latin adjective *immediatus*. Both in Latin and in English, "immediate" has a dual meaning: (1) without mediation or interposition; without an intervening agent; that is, in actual direct personal relation; and (2) present or next adjacent time; current; now. The former meaning pertains to the *modus* *operandi* of relation; the latter refers to time. The word "immediate" ("immediacy," "immediately") may designate both of its meanings in a single usage, dependent upon context. *A* *New* *English* *Dictionary* *on* *Historical* *Principles*, ed. James A. H. Murray, Vol. V:H-K, Pt. II:1, J, K (Oxford: Clarendon Press, 1901); pp. 427-8 (intimate); pp. 62-3 (immediate).

[14] Adrienne Rich, from "Origins and History of Consciousness," *The* *Dream* *of* *a* *Common* *Language* (New York: W. W. Norton & Co., Inc., 1978), pp. 7-9.

[15] Dorothee Soelle points out that *apatheia* "literally means nonsuffering ... Apathy is a form of the inability to suffer. It is understood [here] as a social condition in which people are dominated by the goal of avoiding suffering that it becomes a goal to avoid human relationships and contacts altogether." *Suffering*, trans. Everett R. Kalin (Philadelphia: Fortress, 1975), p. 36. See the following chapter for my own explorations of passion as suffering.

[16] A "transvaluation of values" involves a *radical* departure from pervasive social values, such as the value, for women, of being "feminine"; or, for Christians, of being "patient"; or, for institutional administrations, of being ordered, paid, and regarded hierarchically. In other words, to "transvaluate" love is not simply "to love" more fully but rather to re-define love on the basis of an experience of mutual relation that in no way resembles a self-denying or self-effacing "love." Mary Daly is insightful on the transvaluation of patriarchal values in *Beyond* *God* *the* *Father:* *Toward* *a* *Philosophy* *of*

Women's Liberation (Boston: Beacon, 1973), especially pp. 98-131.

[17]In _Agape: An Ethical Analysis_ (New Haven: Yale University Press, 1972), Gene Outka, while concentrating his analysis on _agape_, or "Christian love," notes that both _philia_ ("mutual relation," or "friendship") and _eros_ ("sexual love" or _epithymia_) are important "conditions" for agape, and vice-versa. In the case of eros, Outka writes, "No love-relation is ever devoid of epithymia: love would be impoverished without it" (p. 288).   Outka's point is that, from an ethical perspective, there is no contradiction or competition between agape, philia, and eros.   My point is that an _act_ of love as distinguished from _concepts_ and even _feelings_), involves an agapic, philial, and erotic _integrity_.   It is a single act--between or among persons--in which agape, philia, and eros are experienced and manifest as one relational bonding.   Put otherwise, the Christian love of one's neighbor as self, the mutuality of friendship, and the sexual dynamic that draws us into relation are revealed, _in practice_, as one act of love.   While Outka does not draw this identification, he comes closer to doing so than, for example, Paul Tillich, for whom agape is the "quality of love [that] cuts into the _libido_, _eros_, and _philia_ qualities of love and elevates them beyond the ambiguities of their self-centeredness." _Love, Power, and Justice: Ontological Analyses and Ethical Applications_ (London: Oxford University Press, 1954), p. 116.   The issue I take with Tillich (and less with Outka) is suggested in the sub-title of Tillich's book: "Ontological Analyses and Ethical Applications." If we begin, like Tillich, with an idea of an essential quality of love--ontologically and conceptually distinct from human activity--we will inevitably construct an ideal "love," beside which all other qualities of love fall short.   Thus, ontology contributes to a concept of _agape_ as "something" better than _philia_ and _eros_.

[18]See Appendix A for a discussion of "relation" in liberal Protestantism.

CHAPTER I

IN THE BEGINNING IS THE RELATION

> Relation is reciprocity .... We
> live in the currents of universal reci-
> procity .... Whoever hates directly is
> closer to a relation than those who are
> without love and hate .... In the begin-
> ning is the relation.[1]

This book has its origin in my search
for the answer to a single question: to what extent
are we responsible for our own redemption in history?
The operative theo-logical assumption throughout is
that God and humanity need to be understood as relational and co-operative, rather than as monistic
(synonymous) or dualistic (antithetical). This being
so, to what extent do we participate also in the
redemption of God?

The Prologue is meant to demonstrate
the theological problem in which my question is
rooted: Christian theologies have tended to foster
"loneliness" (separation, division, estrangement)
as the human condition. Our underlying assumption has
been that human bonding in the world is less good than
our worship of a lofty deity who "needs" our isolation
if "He" is to be "God." That is, in order to be
wholly other than "His" creatures, yet a deity in
whose image we are made, "God" requires that we--like
"Him"--be set above the world, apart from our own
humanity, over and against each other. In such a
schema, "redemption" is God's act of lifting us above
ourselves, a process of divine deliverance from the
human condition.

My own theological assumptions--in con-
trast to those articulated above--are suggested in the
Prologue's final pages and elaborated in the present
chapter: namely, that the experience of relation is
fundamental and constitutive of human being; that it
is good and powerful; and that it is only within this
experience--as it is happening here and now--that we

1

may realize that the power in relation is God. The possibility of naming God as power in relation is so foreign to most traditional Christian thought that to explore this possibility theologically necessitates an insistent hermeneutical bias (love of neighbor as self--rather than love of God--as the norm for Chris- tian life and theology), as well as new symbols, or images, by which we might express the value of our shared power.

Exploring certain characteristics of the power in relation, Chapter Two "re-images" Jesus of Nazareth as someone who chose to make God incarnate and in whose life this power was co-operative and effective. Set in opposition to the story of Jesus, the third chapter bears ugly witness to moral evil, or the violation of relation. Human and divine life was exterminated when the Nazis--abetted by the silence of church and Allies--implemented a "Final Solution" to rid the earth of any trace, even memory, of Jews. Two major Christian responses to the problem of moral evil are presented in Chapter Four. In an assessment of the theodicies of Irenaeus and Augustine, I attempt to show the serious inadequacy--moral irresponsibility-- of Christian calls to fasten our attention on the future "beyond" history (Irenaeus) or on heaven "above" the world (Augustine) rather than to involve ourselves passionately in the present world at the present time.

A theology of mutual relation is sug- gested in Chapter Five. Simply because we are human, we are able to be co-creative agents of redemption. Our vocation is to take seriously the creative char- acter of who we are--both in relation to one another (humanity) and to the power of relation itself (God). Our evil is seated in our sin (the fear and denial of the power we share, hence of one another). The redemption of the world--of human and divine life, ourselves and the transpersonal bond among us--is dependent upon our willingness to make love/justice in the world. In so doing, we co-operate with each other and with God in a process of mutual redemption-- that is, in the deliverance of both God and humanity from evil.

Love of Our Power in Relation

What happened to our common experience of ourselves as co-creative (co-redemptive) friends of

2

God and one other? How did we lose touch with our
power in our relation?

        Martin Buber's "ich und du" sums up
what is central to Jewish faith: the relation between
God and humanity in history, specifically the relational covenant between Yahweh and Israel. Yahweh
speaks. Israel responds. Yahweh acts. Israel acts
with Yahweh. Herein is righteousness, right-relation
between creator and creature, which is reflected in
justice between and among human beings. In relation
to God, we are responsible for creating a just world.
What is remarkable in Jewish faith is the voluntary
character of the relation, including the human
response. The stories of the people of Israel are
stories about people in relation to a God who is the
constant source and re-source of relational power in
the world, a power which we choose to claim or not.

        The God of Israel is fundamentally a
God of righteousness, or justice.[2] In his theological
assessment of the Old Testament, von Rad suggests that
God's righteousness had nothing to do with the establishment of an absolute ethical norm, but rather was
God's character as revealed in God's acts.[3] Similarly,
human righteousness was manifest in activity on behalf
of the human community formed around the covenant, a
voluntary relational contract in which both parties
agreed to act in a righteous way. It was on the basis
of the covenant that the people of Israel understood
the meaning of the law of love (Deuteronomy 6:4) and
of the other commandments of God (Deuteronomy 5:1-21)
as implicit in the doing of justice within the Hebrew
community. The same covenant of justice served as the
basis for Jesus of Nazareth's work toward "the fulfillment" of the law of love (Matthew 5:17; 7:12;
22:36-40). The fulfillment of righteousness between
God and humanity was made in-carnate in right-relation
between and among human beings. This was a matter of
choice and action on the parts of both God and humanity.
                    . . .

        In the development of Greek christology,
Christians lost the ultimacy of the voluntary character of the divine-human covenant.[4] In order to pre-
serve the unity of divinity and humanity in Jesus
Christ, Chalcedon (451 A.D.) compromised the plausibility of a voluntary (moral) conjunction between the
human Jesus and the divine God (a possibility sug-

3

gested in Antiochene christology), opting instead for
a hypostatic (essential) union of the two natures.
The possibility of Jesus' actual human choice (a function of human nature) was eliminated by the eternality
of his divine nature. Relation to God gave way to an
inner union of God and humanity. The Jewish tradition
of voluntary activity between God and humanity collapsed in orthodox Christianity under the weight of
Greek metaphysics, in which human and divine natures
were conceptualized as being so distinctly "other" as
to disallow the possibility of any voluntary cooperation between them. In Jesus, divinity and humanity do
not love one another; they are "without confusion,
without change, without division, without separation"
--united in a divine prosopon (identity of something
as experienced) and hypostasis (a real, concrete
thing).

What is lost here is the voluntary
character of a God of justice who chooses to act in
relation to people who choose to act in relation to
God in the world. Rather, there is a God whose relation to humanity is that of overcoming human nature.
There is no voluntary relation at all but rather a
domination of humanity by God. An active relation
between God and humanity succumbs to an eternal negation of humanity by a God whose "love" must be understood as self-love, because where there is no voluntary relation, there is no love for another.

In this way, Christians raised a new
covenant above the realm of on-going voluntary decision and situated it in a "spiritual" realm of right-
relation between God and humanity, a relation already
effected by the Messiah, a relation marked primarily
by faith, not works:

> What shall we say, then? That Gen-
> tiles who did not pursue righteous-
> ness have attained it, that is,
> righteousness through faith; but
> that Israel who pursued the right-
> eousness which is based on law did
> not succeed in fulfilling that law.
> Why? Because they did not pursue
> it through faith, but as if it were
> based on works. (Romans 9:30-32a)

Right-relationship between God and
humanity--achieved once and for all by Jesus Christ--

4

is to be enjoyed in the spiritual realm which extends
into an afterlife. For the Jews, history was the
realm of righteousness. For Christians, history
became a waiting room for some other world, in which
the righteousness achieved by Jesus would be fully
revealed. As Jews had worked for a Messiah, Christians waited for the parousia.

        This early doctrinal development sig-
nalled a critical shift in the understanding of how
justice is established and by whom: a shift from work
in history to faith in that which lies beyond history;
a shift from humanity's responsibility for creating
justice to God's gift of a "natural" justice; a shift
from the love of one's neighbor in the world to the
love of one's God above the world.

        Thus, "ich und du" becomes easily for
Christians a mystical religious formula for the
expression of an invisible, intangible, and immaterial
relation between God and humanity and between and
among human beings. Visible, tangible, material relations in the world are of less importance than the
relation which has been established by God as natural,
right, and eternal in a spiritual realm.[5]

        But the experience of evil and suffer-
ing may push us--both Christian and non-Christian--
beyond making an easy peace with God's justice as a
sacred mystery and spiritual reality which is natural
and right in the ways of God. Rather, we may ask, if
God's justice has been achieved already, what then of
human justice on the earth? When will God save the
people?

Re-membering Our Power in Relation

God knows,
That is enough.
God wills,
That is enough.
God takes,
And God gives back,
God breaks
And God consoles,
That is enough.

No, it is not enough![6]

It is not enough to affirm that God knows, wills, takes, gives back, breaks and consoles. It is not enough to believe that we are pawns in a divine board-game, even if it be a game of paternal "love." If God loves us, the human-divine relation is reciprocal, dynamic, and of benefit to both parties. No lover is completely autonomous, wholly untouched, finally unmoved by the loved one.

We know God only insofar as we know ourselves, our own humanity. All knowledge is grounded in human experience and in our reflection on this experience. This is as true of "sacred" knowledge as it is of knowing each other, knowing how to cook, or knowing how to ride a horse. While doctrines of God and humanity can be understood most adequately as relational, interdependent, doctrines, my point of entry in seeking to understand God is by taking human experience seriously. Here I stand close to Elie Wiesel (Chapter III) who elaborates the vitality, even necessity, of approaching all theological inquiry through an intense interest in humanity. Like Wiesel, I think to do otherwise is wrong--both methodologically and ethically.

Still, it is important for me to acknowledge here, in the beginning, that I believe in God, and that this faith-claim is rooted in my experience of humanity. I believe that God is our power in relation to each other, all humanity, and creation itself. God is creative power, that which effects justice--right-relation--in history. God is the bond which connects us in such a way that each of us is em-powered to grow, work, play, love and be loved. God makes this justice, our justice. God is not only our immediate power in relation, but is also our immediate re-source of power: that from which we draw power to realize actively who we are in relation. It is to this God that we pray. It is this resourceful God "whom" we "love" and "who," we may believe, "loves" us--our Mother or Sister or Brother or Father or Friend.

To "believe in God" is a possibility rooted in our experience of--and serious respect for--our own relational power: that which en-livens us, together: God's presence in the world; God's invest-ment in the world, in the flesh, in humanity; God with us, here, now; God in-carnate. To believe in God is to believe that God and humanity are together in the

6

world, intimately and immediately connected. "That you need God more than anything, you know at all times in your heart. But don't you also know that God needs you--in the fullness of his eternity, you?"7 If God loves us, God needs us. A lover needs relation--if for no other reason, in order to love.

If God is not incarnate; if "He" is set apart from human experience (physical, tangible, sexual, painful, humorous, delightful, terrible experience in the world) by the nature of "His" impassivity, then God is completely useless to us. Such a "God" is a destructive controlling-device, manufactured in the minds of men who have bent themselves low before ideals of changeless Truth, deathless Life, pure Spirit, perfect Reason, and other qualities often associated with the patriarchal "God." Even the divine attribute of love is sterilized, spiritualized, in Christian thought, to the effect that divine love is held to be completely other than human love. Divine love is qualitatively, quantitatively, essentially, and morally superior to human love, which is believed to be in need of redemption, or the spiritual transcendence of flesh, body, human being, and the world.8

I have not needed, wanted, or been willing any longer to tolerate this divinity. The theology which postulates this "God" denigrates humanity and that which is ultimately most meaningful, to us in the world: God in-carnate. I have wanted to help loosen the grip we have allowed a false "God" to hold on us in order that we might be better able to experience God in-carnate as friend and lover. I have wanted to probe human experience--ourselves, values, choices, the ultimacy of who we are together--rather than the idea of a "God" who is that which we are not, always some wholly other than human experience.

Fifteen years ago, in my sophomore theology class in college, I developed an unfocused antipathy toward the tenets of Karl Barth and his neo-orthodox confrères. I have since imagined that my distaste was fastened, first, in boredom with what seemed to me to be theological jargon devoid of existential substance; and only later, in a more sophisticated theological and feminist perception that neo-orthodoxy provides a paradigm for the legitimation of an "over-and-against" relation, in which the higher possesses a Truth with which it penetrates the lower, who receives it with great thanksgiving.

I wrote my senior thesis in college on "The Radical Christologies of Altizer, Hamilton, and Van Buren," names which may evoke recollections of "the death of God"--the death of an impassive, thoroughly spiritual and untouched "God," a wholly other Platonic reservoir of unearthly purity. I took the death of "God" quite seriously, not as a metaphysical event, but rather as an affirmation of what has been true all along: that there is no impassive, wholly other, deity in charge of the world.

Had I at the time selected a contemporary patron-saint, it would have been Dietrich Bonhoeffer, who excited and puzzled me in his manifesto that

> our coming of age leads us to a true
> recognition of our situation before
> God. God would have us know that we
> must live as men who manage our lives
> without him. The God who is with us
> is the God who forsakes us (Mark 15:
> 34). The God who lets us live in the
> world without the working hypothesis
> of God is the God before whom we stand
> continually. Before God and with God
> we live without God.[9]

In 1967, I did not understand what Bonhoeffer meant, but it moved me. Something rang true for me. Still now, I make no claim to understand fully Bonhoeffer's paradoxical affirmation of a God both with us and absent. But I know there is something here, something that has hounded me for years, something that has sought articulation and serious, active, attention. Hence, this book.

With Bonhoeffer, I know that we must learn to live without "the working hypothesis of God." With Bonhoeffer, I believe that God is with us in the world, as a moving spirit, which creates, liberates, and blesses the world. God's relation to us creates us as relational characters: we are created in relation, immediately and intimately bound to "something" that is neither our possession as individuals nor our capacity apart from others. The "something" is the power we experience in relation to parents, plants, animals, air, food, and even to our selves--that is, in our ability to know what "our selves" need or want (for example, to eat, cry, speak, touch, walk, and so forth).

8

God is who God is (Exodus 3:14) in relation to creation. Without creation, without humanity, our God-in-relation does not exist. What does exist is an image of a "working hypothesis"--a lonely, remote, and gnostic deity who has no need of friends. Our God is so actually in-carnate--in flesh, in humanity, in the world--that we are never without the option of choosing to befriend God in the creation, liberation, and blessing of the world.

From an experiential standpoint--that is, from within the experience of being human, our only standpoint--our voluntary participation in making right-relation among ourselves constitutes our love of God. To love humanity is to befriend God. The human act of love, befriending, making justice is our act of making God incarnate in the world.

In relation to God, as in any relation, God is affected by humanity and creation, just as we are affected by God. With us, by us, through us, God lives, God becomes, God changes, God speaks, God acts, God suffers and God dies in the world. To say that God dies is not to speak "merely" metaphorically. It is to suggest, for example, that in the death of each of six million Jews, a creating, liberating, and sanctifying presence was, in fact, exterminated from the world. Destroyed. Killed. Literally--actually, physically, emotionally, mentally, spiritually--removed from the world--forever. God died in Auschwitz, which is not to say that God was not active in the liberation of Auschwitz by the Allies in 1945. The constancy of God is the activity of God in the world wherever, whenever, and for whatever reason, humanity acts to create, liberate, and bless humanity.

God of Jesus

But is this God the God of Israel and of Christianity? There is a sense in which I do not, and cannot, know. This is true of anyone attempting to give fresh articulation to theological experience. Every particular theological expression is peculiar to the theologian and to the community, time, and place which she represents. I can suggest, however, a qualified identification between the God of whom I speak and the God of Jewish and Christian traditions. If Yahweh--God of the Bible and of Jesus--is humanity's friend, a God who in relation to the people of the

9

earth both moves and is moved, gives birth and is born, gives and receives, needs and is needed, then this Yahweh is the same God whom I affirm: "the changer and the changed."10

Such a God is not a projected construct of hierarchical power, control, possession and jealousy. Such a God does not demand obedience for the sake of obedience. Such a God does not obliterate Canaanites, denigrate sexuality, and despise women—in Israel, in the church, or in the so-called "pagan" glorifications of female power through the image of the Goddess. Such a God is as truly the Goddess as she is God, she who bears a close a resemblance, for example, to Asherah (Canaanite Goddess of sexuality) as to the Hebrew God of righteousness, Yahweh.11

Scripture presents different, sometimes contrasting, images of God. Each of us selects images that coincide with or expand our own experiences of God. Western religious traditions have highlighted images which are planted deep in the collective human experiences of the "God" (ultimate meaning) of patriarchal social structures. I am, happily, not a patriarch, and I do not wish to affirm male property rights that extend into areas of sexuality, the role of women and children, a competitive economy, and the construction of a jealous and possessive male deity. As a feminist, my images for God include those of sister, lover, amazon, wisdom, mother, and brother more often than those of king, victor, husband, judge and father.

The God I wish to affirm is God of relation and friendship (see, for example, Exodus 3; John 15:9-15; and Psalms 4, 16, 18, 23, 33, 41, 46, 57, 63, 65, 68, 71, 100, 104, 105, 106, 107, 121, 133, 137, 138, 145, 146); God of justice for the poor (see Jeremiah 2-5; Amos 5:24; Matthew 25:31-46; Luke 6:17-27); justice for women (see Mark 14:3-9; Luke 10:38-42; John 4:5-26; Galatians 3:28); justice for the outcast and "the other" (see Matthew 25:31-46; Luke 10:25-37; John 4:5-26; Acts 10:44-11:18); and God of sexuality (see Song of Songs).12

I have no interest, except an angry one, in an other-worldly "God" who sets "Himself" above and against human experiences of suffering, work, play, sexuality, doubt, humor, questions, physicality, and material needs. I am not interested in the "God" who batters like a ramrod through the priestly pages of

Leviticus and on into the misogynist diatribes of
Jerome, Martin Luther, and John Paul II. If this is
the "God" of Jews and of Christians, then I must
reject Christianity's "God" and the Church that pays
"Him" homage.

I base my identification of God with
Yahweh on my understanding of Jesus' experience of
Yahweh as God, one with whom he was in intimate,
immediate relation. I take Jesus seriously enough as
one who knew God to believe that his relation to God
bears implications for all who know God; thus, that
Jesus' experiences of God cannot be comprehended or
expounded fully within the limits of any particular
cultural situation--including the patriarchal limits
which Jesus shared in his own time and place. Jesus'
Abba may not be the "daddy" of women or men who--in a
different time and place--have begun to experience not
only the reality of female power but also the power
and intimacy in mutual relation rather than in dominating, hierarchical, relation. Jesus' "daddy" may be
our "mama": more powerfully yet, our sister or brother, our friend and lover, our advocate and soulmate
in the world.

Methodological Consideration

Two methodological considerations have
been basic to my work: (1) Because language is
intrinsically relational, a matter of bridging self to
other on the basis of common assumptions, the importance of the words with which we express our experiences of God (our theological imagery) cannot be over-
stated. (2) The hermeneutical norm of my work--that
is, the authority by which I interpret which materials
to use and how to use them--is the love of one's
neighbor as oneself.

Power in Theo-logical Imaging

To shape an image of God, to image the
world, is to affirm one's humanity. "To exist humanly
is to name the self, the world, and God."[13] Aware of
the power of words, Mary Daly undertakes a process of
re-naming a reality that has been denigrated, dis-
torted, or denied altogether by male theologians:
women's experience. Her remarkable audacity in claiming the power to re-name "sacred" reality has awakened

11

many a sleepy-feminist-consciousness-waiting-to-be-
"sparked."14 Daly understands that words can hurt us
just as they can help us. They are a relational tool
used to convey meaning from person to person. If I
mean to be above you, below you, or at your side,
close to you or distant from you, the words I choose
to express who you are to me are tools that will help
sharpen or dull our experiences of our relationship.
Human bondings are constantly clarified, confused,
abrogated, or reconstructed by the words we use, abuse,
or refuse to use.

          Christian theology may be described as
an effort on the parts of Christian people to communicate what it means to be Christian. Christian theology may be described also as the Christian's attempt
to give meaning, by words or other symbols, to the
human-divine relation as she experiences it. All
theology--the systems of Aquinas, Calvin, and Barth,
as well as the sermons of seminarians--expresses symbolically the human-divine relation insofar as it is a
meaningful human experience. Christian theology is an
effort to show in what way this experience is Christian, rather than, for example, Jewish or Islamic or
post-Christian, experience.

          All theologians depend to some extent
upon assumptions which are shared by those to whom we
address ourselves. But what these common assumptions
are is difficult to determine. It is impossible prior
to our experience of Christian praxis--that is, our
shared-life and shared-reflections on what we do
together. Credal formulations not withstanding,
"Christian experience" is claimed by theists and
atheists; transcendentalists and humanists; trinitar-
ians and unitarians; armed fighters and pacifists;
capitalists and socialists; gay groups and homophobic
organizers; feminists and those who espouse "total
womanhood"; totalitarians and anarchists; black
preachers and white racists.

          The theologian's on-going constructive
task is to discern common assumptions which are emerging in the praxis out of which and to which she
speaks. Her task is not to determine which assumptions "have always been" Christian. No common understanding of such words as "God," "humanity," and
"Jesus Christ" can be assumed as a priori to the theological task, because there is no universal agreement
among Christians on the meaning or importance of these
linguistic symbols.

I have begun my work by calling attention to the human experience of relation, which is
where I believe it all begins--theology as well as
life. In so doing, I make a methodological and sub-
stantive claim which is not shared by all (or perhaps
many) Christians. I am seeking points of empathy and
identification with some readers, as many as possible.
I am seeking solidarity--good strong relation--in
Christian praxis, if not in theological language.
What we do together is more critical than whether we
recite the same creed.

But language is a primary vehicle of
communicating values and commitments, ourselves in
relation to each other and to that which we may call
God. To speak or write, to frame and utter a word, is
to carry responsibility for what we do and do not do
in our relations. It is to reveal, make visible or
audible, that which needs expression among us. To
form a word is to in-carnate something that is real
for us. Language should not be used lightly, without
recognition of its power to sustain or break human
relations. Theological language is no exception. To
the contrary, if theological language is symbolically
revelatory of that which we value most highly, it must
be used carefully, in recognition of the power we and
others grant it in our lives.

I am attempting to respond to the human
need for good--empowering, mutual--relation among ourselves. I seek linguistic images appropriate to this
concern, words to convey symbolically the experience
of relation. As a theologian re-searching Christian
thought, I have been unwilling to throw away the corpus of symbolism that has provided the coherence and
continuity constitutive of "Christian tradition"--
linguistic symbols such as "God," "Jesus Christ,"
"church," "crucifixion" and "resurrection," "omnipotence," "good" and "evil." At the same time, I am
persuaded that the "symbolic universe"[15] constructed
by the Christian Church is not meaningless to contemporary persons but is rather often a gross impedi-
ment--heavy with meaning--to our realizations of who
we are and of what we might do together. Mainline
church dogmatics--both Catholic and Protestant--have
tended to dissuade Christians from claiming our selves
as sacred, proactive participants in the liberation of
humanity from injustice and despair.

Believing this, I have undertaken a

13

task of re-naming--re-imaging--various Christian sym-
bols--giving new meanings to old words, such as "God"
and "passion" and "intimacy" and "sexuality." In each
case, I do so because I have participated in some common experience which begs new language. In what I
write, I am attempting to elicit imaginative license
on the part of the reader to join in the re-naming of
what is what in our life together. As Daly notes,
"The liberation of language is rooted in the liberation of ourselves."[16] This re-naming is steeped in an
emerging, on-going and shared experience of liberation,
or redemption--of women from bondage to male-estab-
lished definitions of reality, including women's
senses of ourselves; of lesbian and gay men from
heterosexist assumptions about the "natural" order of
both creation and society; and of privileged white
United States of American capitalist competitors from
the illusion that our way of being in the world coin-
cides with the manifest destiny of all that is good
and hence of God Himself [sic].

I am re-imaging humanity, God, and
Jesus in order to speak my truth, to do some justice
to an experience I cannot call "my own" without
acknowledging that my life is in relation to others.
I write out of this shared life, a common experience.
The new meanings bestowed upon old words are fruits of
corporate search and struggle. If these new words
release some power, it is not because they are mine.
It is because they are ours.

Hermeneutics and the Norm

How do I interpret the material from
which I draw? Why do I choose to admit certain biblical, historical, or other data and not others? These
are the hermeneutical choices, made upon the values
implicit or implicit in my work. The values form the
interpretive framework within which I make whatever
claims I do to theological knowledge. For a Christian
to omit major reference to the Pauline epistles or
theology is of hermeneutical significance. The omission can be interpreted as an oversight or as intentional. If an oversight, the theologian is not careful; if intentional, the theologian is not "traditional"; in either case, how is the reader to interpret this omission? I regard the teachings of Jesus
as more fundamental to Christian theology than the
teachings of Paul, hence, of greater value in laying

14

the groundwork for theological construction. This
opinion--my hermeneutical bias--is rooted in values
which I bring to Christian theology, among which the
most compelling is love. Love is the act of making
right relation.

The Norm of my Work: Love of Neighbor as Self

The theological norm is the primary
hermeneutical principle. It serves as the center of
the theology that is constructed around it. All theological assertions are to be interpreted as they
relate to the norm. To state the norm is to present
the single most important clue to the theologian's
values, in this case to my own. The theological norm
operative for me is right-relation or the love of
one's neighbor as oneself. In Old and New Testaments,
this is referred to as the "second commandment":

> And one of the scribes came up and
> heard them disputing with one ano-
> ther, and seeing that he answered
> them well, asked him, "Which com-
> mandment is the first of all?"
> Jesus answered, "The first is,
> 'Hear, O Israel, the Lord our God,
> the Lord is one; and you shall love
> the Lord your God with all your
> heart, and with all your soul, and
> with all your mind, and with all
> your strength.' The second is this,
> 'You shall love your neighbor as
> yourself.' There is no other com-
> mandment greater than these."
> (Mark 12:28-31)

The principle upon which I am attempting to establish what is "of God" and what is not,
what is "good" and what is "evil," is limited intentionally to the "second" commandment. We begin with
humanity--human life, human body, human experience in
relation--as the focus of primary concern. Historically, there has been for Christians a normative ethical distinction between the love of God and the love
of neighbor as self. That Jesus did not hold these
two commandments as separate-and-unequal is instructive and will be examined in the following chapter.
In Christian thought, the higher, more spiritual value
has been ascribed to the love of God, thereby positing

15

it alone as the operative norm in Christian life.
Only when the love of humanity has been deemed in conformity with the "spirituality" (immateriality and
non-physicality) of the love of God has it been
acceptable as a normal standard by which to assess the
quality of Christian life.

I believe that an attempt is in order
to work from the opposite direction--that is, to take
seriously our physicality in the world and to examine
love as it is present in the forms we are able to see,
touch, recognize, and cultivate among ourselves.
Hence, I am purposely limiting the scope of my theological vision to human experience of human love. I
am not suggesting necessarily that "divine love" does
not act independently of human experience. I am suggesting that it is necessary for human beings--includ-
ing Christian theologians--to take with ultimate seriousness our own experiences of human love and of human
lack of love. I am suggesting also that our liberation
from injustice in the world is dependent upon the theological value we give to our shared humanity. As Gustavo Gutiérrez writes, "We are dealing with a real
love of man for his own sake, and not 'for the love of
God.'"[17] In order to do this, we must grant the
"second" commandment its precedence over the "first."

Tillich speaks of love as "the moving
power of life.[18] "Love is the drive towards the unity
of the separated ... love cannot be described as the
union of the strange but as the reunion of the
estranged."[19] Tillich grounds his definition in an
ontology of being within which human essence and existence is rooted. This enables him to presuppose a
monistic oneness which has been broken apart, and
toward which the separate parts are moved by love.

I think that we cannot assume philo-
sophically a monistic unity as either source or goal
of human relation. We can assume only that which we
know already: the experience of love between and
among human beings, an experience characterized by a
recognition of differentiation between and among persons. We give the name "love" to a particular human
experience of bridging differences, of reaching and
being reached by persons beyond ourselves, or in
Tillich's words, of "that which drives toward the
unity of the separated ... the moving power of life."
Human love refers to a creative trans-action between
and among ourselves. As a theological norm, human

16

love for humanity is the act of out-reach on which
depend "all the law and the prophets," including the
commandment to love God.

But what does it mean, to love our
neighbors as ourselves? Various criteria might be
helpful in determining what it means to love. I offer
only two, which I believe, taken together, constitute
an experiential and descriptive basis for knowing what
is loving and what is not: (1) Love is justice. It
is not necessarily a happy feeling or a romantic
attachment. Love is a way of being in the world, not
necessarily an emotional affect. (2) Love can, and
does, occur here and now, in this world, at this time.
It is important that love be experienced among human
beings here on earth. My interest is not in any
notion of a "love" or "justice" which is "postponed"
or "withheld" or "veiled" as characteristic of a sacred realm to which we have no immediate access.

Justice

> There is absolutely no concept in
> the Old Testament with so central
> a significance for all the rela-
> tionships of human life as that of
> **צדקה** [German translation: Ger-
> echtigkeit; English translation:
> justice or righteousness]. It is
> the standard not only for man's
> relationship to God, but also for
> his relationships to his fellows
> ... indeed, it is even the standard
> for man's relationship to the ani-
> mals and to his natural environment.
> [Justice and righteousness] can be
> described ... as the highest value
> in life, that upon which all life
> rests when it is properly ordered.[20]

Justice is a forensic metaphor for the
ethical establishment of love in human life. In Jewish and Christian theologies, human justice reflects
the justice, or righteousness, of the relation between
God and humanity.[21] In both Jewish and Pauline theology, justice denotes also an eschatological ideal,
but this motif is stronger in Paul than in Israel's
prophetic literature. In Israel's history, justice
refers primarily to the correct ordering of human

17

relationships on the earth. It is "the highest value
in life."22

        Although evocative of a collective
image, justice is applicable as well to the relation
between two persons.23 Justice is the moral act of
love. Love is <u>actually</u> justice. Justice can be
established, however, without "feelings" of love (emotional affect), such as in litigation. The existence
of legal systems suggests that the moral act of love
supercedes friendly or conciliatory affections. Where
there is no moral act of love, no justice, there is an
evil situation. <u>Evil is an act</u>, not a metaphysical
principle or a passive absence of good. Evil is the
act of un-love or in-justice. It is the doing of
moral wrong, specifically of breaking the relational
bond between and among ourselves in such a way that
one, both, or many parties are disempowered to grow,
love, and/or live.

Temporal History

        As the Greek philosophers remind us,
time is related to change. That which is in time
changes. That which is not in time does not change.
God is conceptualized as creator of time itself. God
is outside of time, e-ternal: God does not change.

> ... although you are before time, it
> is not in time that you precede it.
> If this were so, you would not be
> before all time. It is in eternity,
> which is supreme over time because
> it is a never-ending present, that
> you are at once before all past and
> after all future time .... Your
> years neither go nor come, but our
> years pass and others come after
> them .... Your years are completely
> present to you all at once, because
> they are at a permanent standstill.24

        In the <u>Confessions</u>, Augustine begins to
construct the dualistic theology which he develops
more fully in <u>The City of God</u>. The "city of God" is
the eternal realm of right-relationship between God
and humanity, and between and among those human beings
whom God has selected as inhabitants of the spiritual
"city." This chosen segment of humanity lives con-

currently in the city of God and as "resident aliens"
in "the city of men" while they are still on earth.

The philosophical/theological dualism
exhibited by Augustine has roots deep in humanity's
experiential question about time and eternity: Is
this all there is? We yearn for transcendence, for
some crossing over from "this" which we can see and
hear and touch to "that" which we cannot. Our minds
stretch toward mindless possibilities of eternal being,
immortality. Martyrs, saints, mystics, and poets bid
us to reach, grasp, even die for, an assurance of
timelessness, implying that there are two "worlds" (at
least) in relation to time: one _in_ time (the present
world) and one _above_ or _beyond_ time (some other world).
The present world is to some degree always less valuable than the e-ternal world.

To speak of time and eternity is to
speak of the historical and the non-historical, a-his-
torical, or supra-historical. History and change take
place in time. That which is non-historical and
unchanging takes place outside of time--eternally.
Philosophical theologians struggle with the relation
of time and history to the eternal and non-historical
"dimensions of the Spirit" (Tillich). What is at
stake is the seriousness with which Christians take
human history--this world and this time--as a locus of
ultimately meaningful activity.

As a criterion for what is loving, _it_
is only in history and in time that human beings can
realize who we are as lovers of humanity and of God
as well. I believe that there are eternal and transcendent dimensions of reality, and that their wellspring is human history and time. This is why we must
begin with humanity--in history, in time--in order to
be able to realize even what we mean by "God," "eternity," or "transcendence." I am attempting to sketch
an image of one world, not two, as the arena of _ulti-_
mately meaningful activity. It is _here_, and it _is_
now, that we will learn all we will ever need to know
about the meaning of love. We need not look to the
heavens--to an afterlife, to the "city of God," or to
projections of our own ideals of perfect justice, in
order to know what it means to love. To turn away
from humanity in this world at this time toward a
higher "God" is to avert ourselves from the possibility of loving neighbor as self and also from the possibility of loving God.

19

In his "Eleventh Thesis," Marx repudi-
ated the "abstract humanism" of Feuerbach.[25] Marx
held that the purpose of philosophy (in our case,
theology) is not to understand the world, but to
change it. It is not an either-or, but Marx's point
is well-taken: That which does not bear directly upon
human life and move toward the creation of justice in
society is not worth our bother. Theology is not a
cerebral exercise; it is a passionate effort to
express and evoke human activity. Its appropriate
focus is earth, not heaven. And it is not about God
as God is in Godself, but rather about us as we
experience God in this world at this time among ourselves.

FOOTNOTES: CHAPTER I

¹Martin Buber, I and Thou, a new translation with a prologue and notes by Walter Kaufmann (New York: Charles Scribner's Sons, 1970), pp. 67-9.

²Gerhard von Rad, Old Testament Theology, Vol. I: The Theology of Israel's Historical Traditions, trans. D. M. G. Stalker (New York: Harper & Row, 1962), pp. 370ff.

³Ibid.

⁴See Appendix B for discussion of Chalcedon's significance.

⁵It is hardly surprising that the concrete social value of human relation, as articulated by Buber in Ich und Du was lost in translation from Jewish existentialism to popular Christianity.

> "The recurrent "Thou" in the first translation [trans. Ronald Gregor Smith, Scribner's, 1937] mesmerized people to the point where it was widely assumed that Buber was a theologian. In fact, the book deals centrally with man's relationships to other men ....
>
> The aim of the book is not to disseminate knowledge about God but, at least in large measure, to diagnose certain tendencies in modern society ... and to indicate how the quality of life might be changed radically by the development of a new sense of community.
>
> The book will survive the death of theology, for it appeals to that religiousness which finds no home in organized religion, and it speaks to those whose primary concern is not at all with religion but rather with social change."

Walter Kaufmann, Prologue to I and Thou, p. 38.

⁶Elie Wiesel, Ani Maamin: A Song Lost and Found Again (New York: Random House, 1973), p. 71.

⁷Buber, I and Thou, p. 130.

21

[8]See Prologue, p.xxvi, note 17 on love; also Chapter IV, pp. 116f, on Augustine's spiritualization of human life.

[9]Dietrich Bonhoeffer, _Letters and Papers from Prison_, ed. Eberhard Bethge (New York: Macmillan, 1953; First Macmillan Paperback, 1972), p. 360.

[10]This reference is to lyrics of a song, "Waterfall," by Chris Williamson, Bird Ankles Music BMI, 1975, which is available on her album, _The Changer and the Changed_, Olivia Records, Inc., 1975. Chris Williamson is one of a number of contemporary lesbian feminist artists whose works suggest their buoyant, spirit-filled, awareness of a relational power (sister God? Goddess?) in women's bonding which is both personal and political in its effects, and which is both "the changer and the changed" in the so-called "natural" world and in historical process.

[11]In addition to Yahweh and Asherah, there are many Gods and Goddesses. I draw attention to Asherah here for two reasons: (1) she was the major Goddess of Canaan (the mother of Baal) and hence is usually considered to be a principle which Yahwists opposed. (2) she was specifically the Goddess of sexuality and procreation, powers which were attributed to the male (via patrilinear patriarchalism) in Hebrew religion and, at the same time, were excluded from the divine image: Yahweh is said to create _ex nihilo_ rather than with a sexual consort. Asherah symbolizes _sexual divinity_, which I--unlike the Hebrews (and later, Christians)--wish to affirm.

[12]In the following chapter, in which I attempt to "re-image" Jesus, I will be further developing images of God, especially as they are intimated in Mark's gospel.

[13]Mary Daly, _Beyond God the Father: Toward a Philosophy of Women's Liberation_ (Boston: Beacon, 1973), p. 8.

[14]See Mary Daly's _Gyn/Ecology: The Metaethics of Radical Feminism_ (Boston: Beacon, 1978), her most recent book, in which she presents an almost altogether new lexicon for the emerging radical feminist experience.

[15]See Prologue, p. xviii, on Berger and Luckmann's discussion of "symbolic universe."

[16]Daly, _Beyond God the Father_, p. 8.

[17]Gustavo Gutiérrez, _A Theology of Liberation: History, Politics, and Salvation_ (Maryknoll, N.Y.: Orbis Books, 1973), p. 202.

[18]Paul Tillich, Love, Power, and Justice (London: Oxford University Press, 1954), p. 25.

[19]Ibid.

[20]Gerhard von Rad, Old Testament Theology, Vol. I: The Theology of Israel's Historical Traditions, p. 370.

[21]I use the word "justice" because "righteousness" is employed more often to denote right-relationship between humanity and God.

[22]Rudolf Bultmann, Theology of the New Testament, Vol. I, trans. by Kendrick Grobel (New York: Charles Scribner's Sons, 1951), p. 273ff.

[23]See Chapter IV, pp. 132-8.

[24]Augustine, Confessions, trans. by R. S. Pine-Coffin (New York: Penguin Press, 1961), Bk. XI, p. 263.

[25]Dirk J. Struik, Introduction to Karl Marx's The Economic and Philosophic Manuscripts of 1844, trans. by Martin Milligan, ed. by Struik (New York: International Publishers, 1964), p. 19.

24

CHAPTER II

RE-IMAGING JESUS: POWER IN RELATION

> [I]t is at the level of _imagina-
> tion_ that contemporary Christianity
> is most weak. Men find it hard to
> believe in God because they do not
> have available to them any lively
> imaginative picture of the way a God
> and the world as they know it are
> related. What they need most is a
> story, a picture, a myth, that will
> capture their imagination, while
> meshing in with the rest of their
> sensibility in the way that messianic
> terms linked with the sensibility of
> first-century Jews, or Nicene symbol-
> ism with the sensibility of philosoph-
> ically-minded fourth-century Greeks.[1]

Imaging

Metaphysical poet Richard Crashaw
(1613?-1649) wrote imaginatively of Jesus' miracle at
Cana of Galilee (John 2:1-11): "Nympha pudica Deum
vidit, et erubit." Crashaw's own translation of the
poem was, "The conscious water saw its God, and
blushed."[2]

The poem _images_ a relation between the
water and its God. The effect of the image is to
evoke a sense of the miraculous as a powerful "happening" between the so-called natural and supernatural.
The process of imaging becomes a tool for expressing
relational dynamics which are difficult, perhaps
impossible, to comprehend or express literally. Crashaw imaged also his own relation to the Johannine
story and, we might reasonably assume, to the "characters" of Jesus, God, and even water, as Crashaw knew
these characters.

I am using the term "imaging" in much
the same way Dorothee Soelle employs the term
Phantasie:

25

In German, Phantasie has a potentially far more positive value than the word "fantasy" has in English. Its meaning includes the dimensions of imagination, inspiration, inventiveness, flexibility, freedom and creativity .... Its derivation from the Greek phantazein, to make visible, is significant. Divorced from the bizarre accretions of history, the word "phantasy" may be defined as "the free play of creative imagination as it affects perception and productivity"; it is closer perhaps to Shelly's definition: "The creative faculty to imagine that which we know."[3]

To image is not to "imagine" or "fantasize" in the popular sense of creating reality in one's mind. Rather, imaging is a process of exploring and expressing something about reality--namely, about a relation that we know already between ourselves and that which we image; in the case of Crashaw, between the poet's self-knowledge and his knowledge of the relational character of the natural world, in which both human beings and water participate. To image is to portray reality as relational. In every poem, picture, musical bar, drama, even in prose, verbal and non-verbal images denote and evoke a sense of relational dynamics between water and its creator, person and person, note and note, line and line, motion and motion, what is seen and what is unseen, what is said and what is left unsaid. In the beginning is the relation, movement, becoming. To image is to find a way of expressing relation.

Like art, theology is a process of imaging relation. The most creative theology is that in which the imaged-quality of the work is realized candidly and with pride. I do not pretend to be able to dissect empirically the corpus of either human or divine nature. I do not want to do this. I do not want to lose the relational quality of what I experience by stuffing pieces of reality into conceptual boxes and concocting a stasis of differentiation by labels and definitions. With H. R. Niebuhr, I too would choose to take my place among the poets.[4] To envision water looking at its creator and blushing is to be inspired playfully (and far more seriously) than to ponder the probability of divine intervention in the natural order. With Soelle, I want to "play"

freely, creatively, imaginatively; to image myself,
other persons, God in the world, and the character of
Jesus as he may be helpful in our realization of what
it means to make God incarnate, or to god, in the
world.

Imaging the Jesus of Geschichte

The publication in 1906 of Albert
Schweitzer's Von Reimarus zu Wrede (English translation: The Quest of the Historical Jesus) signaled the
end of the movement among Biblical scholars to
research and reconstruct the history (Historie) of
Jesus of Nazareth.[5] Subsequent New Testament theology
has been instructed by Schweitzer's insight that the
brief canonical documents we call the gospels, especially the synoptics, were composed in a climate of
eschatological expectation, and that Jesus is por-
trayed--imaged--in them as a Jew who shared with other
Jews an apocalyptic anticipation of a nearing eschaton.
The effect of Schweitzer's point was to demonstrate
that, even if we had access to a great many details of
Jesus' life (which we do not), we would be unable to
draw meaningful parallels between his words and acts
and our own today.[6] We do not share Jesus' urgent
sense of a rapidly-approaching end of time (at least
not in terms of divine intervention); hence, we cannot
imitate, or appropriate, the specifics of his attitudes and life. We cannot transpose his Historie upon
our own as a model for Christian life. Schweitzer
concluded that the so-called "historical Jesus" is
virtually useless to us now and that it is "the spirit
which goes forth from Him" which enables contemporary
Christians to live in right relation to God.

> [I]t is not Jesus as historically
> known, but Jesus as spiritually arisen
> within men, who is significant for our
> time and can help it. Not the histori-
> cal Jesus, but the spirit which goes
> forth from Him and in the spirits of
> men strives for new influence and rule,
> is that which overcomes the world.[7]

Four decades later, Rudolf Bultmann
suggested a means whereby contemporary persons might
understand "the historical event" of Jesus as an
eschatological event with meaning for us in our own
time. Taking seriously Schweitzer's insistence that

27

the hermeneutic of the gospels was grounded in the
myth of a tiered universe nearing its end and is hence
existentially unintelligible to modern humanity, Bultmann proposed that the gospel be "demythologized,"
whereby its "deeper meaning" might be uncovered.[8]
Basing his method on an existentialist understanding
of reality, Bultmann held that the motivation for all
theology is to be better able to comprehend our own
existence.[9] Such comprehension cannot be obtained
apart from God's address to us (God's Word), which is
Christ, and our response, which is faith. Bultmann
sought to show that the kerygmatic Christ is the historical event of Jesus, and that Jesus Christ is to be
understood as neither simply a first-century person
nor a timeless truth, but rather as the event of God's
acting in history.[10] Christ is the inexplicable entry
of the extraordinary into our ordinary lives. Christ
must be demythologized in order to be heard as God's
address to us here and now. For Bultmann, Jesus
Christ is "hidden from every eye except the eye of
faith."[11] "To live in faith is to live an eschatological existence, to live beyond the world, to have
passed from death to life."[12]

Bultmann understood that the on-going
vitality of Scripture is its capacity to enhance the
depth and quality of human existence. Like Schweitzer, he realized that the Historie of Jesus is not,
and cannot be, our history. Jesus' experiences were
not, and cannot be, ours. Yet Bultmann went beyond
Schweitzer by insisting that, still today, Jesus'
eschatological faith can be meaningful if understood
as a dimension of authentic human existence--that is,
as human life having faith "beyond the world." Bultmann helped us understand history theologically not as
Historie, or the biographical details of human life
that can be brought under empirical scrutiny, but
rather as Geschichte, or events in history as they
"assume a direct significance for the present."[13]
Unlike Historie, Geschichte includes the meaning of
events as the meaning is granted by persons who have
participated in, or otherwise been affected by, the
events. As Geschichte,

an historical event is not something
hypothetical and unrecoverable which
lies before or behind the experience
of the persons to whom and among whom
it occurred; an historical event is
this "something" as it was received

28

and responded to, as it was remembered
and interpreted, as it became creative
in history.[14]

The Geschichte of Jesus is, thus, an
array of images, or a compilation of stories. It is
not the literal biography of this person, and it does
not pretend to be. Any aspect of the history or story
(Geschichte) of Jesus is, as Bultmann saw, an image of
the kerygmatic Christ, whose meaning has been realized
from the outset by people in relation to Jesus--
through personal acquaintance with him while he was
alive, and through memory, oral tradition, and written
tradition as these various pieces of historical development have been, and continue to be, woven into the
expanding tapestry of Christian theologies. The
Geschichte of Jesus is shaped from generation to generation and persons to persons as a broad panoply of
images that are meaningful to contemporary human existence.

Dennis Nineham makes the rather start-
ling claim that "whatever is the necessary presupposition of our present Christian existence or experience
must have occurred."[15] He supports this claim with
the following observation about the character of theology itself, in this instance christology:

> During and after the Arian controversy,
> when the full divinity of Christ was
> called in question, the reply was, in
> essence, that the Christians knew them-
> selves to enjoy a condition--call it
> "divinization" or what you will--which
> would have been impossible unless full
> divine ousia had been present in Jesus;
> therefore such full divinity must have
> been present in him. Even more inter-
> esting in some ways is the counter-argu-
> ment put forward by the Cappadocian
> Fathers when Apollinarius denied the
> presence of a genuine human mind in Jesus:
> τὸ γὰρ ἀπρόσληπτον ἀθεράπευτόν. Christian
> experience proved incontestably that the
> human mind was included in the scope of
> salvation; this could not have been the
> case unless Jesus had a human mind; there-
> fore he must have had a human mind.[16]

Nineham is saying that Christian theo-

29

logians have always imaged Jesus in relation to known
Christian experience. Common sense suggests to me
that he right. Moreover, I see this not as cause for
alarm or apology, but rather as an epistemological
confession of what is, in fact, our opportunity as
Christian theologians to re-work, re-consider, re-
image Jesus in such a way as to make a positive, creative contribution to the church and, in so doing, to
the larger world.

           There is always, many will maintain,
the "danger" of "subjectivism" in assuming the authority of our own experience in doing theology. Of
course. There is a danger in assuming the authority
to do anything, a danger of becoming self-absorbed,
limited, parochial, dogmatic, irrational, and so
forth. But if theology is to be worth its doing, we
do it at some risk, both boldly and with a humble
awareness that our perceptions and images are limited
by the boundaries of our own experiences in the world,
which are always, to some extent, parochial, irrational, and infused with a certain dogmatic sense that
we are "onto something" important that seeks expression. The danger we incur is inherent in the opportunity. It is less a danger, I believe, than that
which is inherent in a theologian's refusal to admit
that she is both subject and authority of her own
work.

           To re-image Jesus is to claim the
authority to play freely with both Scripture and subsequent tradition in order to comprehend our own
existence. To re-image Jesus may involve letting go
of old images, "letting the dead bury the dead" and
bringing Jesus to life--that is, to our life together.
It is to sketch images of Jesus within, and for the
benefit, of our communities--of seminarians, women,
gay people, black people, poor people, whoever our
people are. Our images do not necessarily reflect
Mark's image, or John's, or Augustine's, or Luther's.
Our images of Jesus will never fully coincide with any
single image of Jesus in scripture or elsewhere in the
history of Christian thought. Jesus cannot be for us
who he was for the Twelve, Mary Magdalene, or Mary and
Martha of Bethany. We are not they. Our time is not
theirs. And Jesus is not with us in the same ways he
was with them. That Jesus is dead, however encouraging the memory of him, however inspiring the spirit
which moved both him and us. The most and least we
can do if Jesus is to be anything for us--other than

30

an idol which lures us away from the world--is to re-
image Jesus on the basis of what we know already about
ourselves in relation to the Jesus-figure about whom
we have heard, to each other, and to that which we
believe to be God. Our christology becomes an image
of our relational experience, just as, I believe,
incarnation was an image of Jesus' relational experience.

Why Jesus?

          Jesus matters only if he was fully, and
only, human. Otherwise we are speaking of something/
someone who bore no fully and only human relation to
God or his sisters and brothers. Jesus matters
because, for good or for ill, the titular name "Jesus
Christ" occupies center-stage in the religious (and, I
think, political) consciousness of the larger portion
of the Western world. We cannot simply shift Jesus
from center-stage and replace him with humanity or God
by wishing it were so. We need to re-image Jesus from
the perspective of our own experiences in the world
and, in so doing, image his most creative place in our
consciousness.

          Jesus matters for me, a woman, because
his name has been wielded as a bludgeon against my
sisters and me:

          "Jesus didn't choose any women disciples."
          "Jesus wasn't married."
          "And, after all, Jesus was a man."

          I am always tempted to respond, "Who
cares?" But I do care--not as much about the acclama-
tions or defamations laid upon this particular Naza-
rene as about women and men who live in the world
today and about what we do to one another, often in
the name of Jesus Christ. We need to act differently,
not in order to uphold Jesus, but rather in order to
uphold--support--ourselves. Only in this way does
incarnation--God's active presence in and with the
world, the flesh, humanity--make sense to me.

          Relational theology is incarnational.
It has to be. Relation is in-carnate, between us, in
the physicality of all that we do: breathe, move,
think, feel, reach, touch. The God of whom I speak,
the resource and power of relation, that with whom we

31

image ourselves in relation, is in flesh (<u>sarx</u>), alive
in human being, active in human life, on earth, in
history.

Christians have believed that God
<u>became</u> human in Jesus of Nazareth; that God descended
to earth and joined humanity--physically, tangibly,
for the duration of Jesus' life in the world. Orthodox Christians have emphasized incarnation as an act
of God. The role of humanity has been downplayed.
The centrality of Jesus' place in Christianity has
resulted from a mis-conception of Jesus as a divine
person rather than as a human being who knew and loved
God.

Nicea's (325 A.D.) and Chalcedon's (451
A.D.) Hellinization of Jesus evolved from, and
resulted further in, a spiritualization of the human
Jesus. The councils located Jesus' primary significance in <u>who he was</u> (the eternal Logos, consubstantial
with the <u>Father</u>, in two natures: fully human, fully
divine) rather than in <u>what he did</u> (preached, prayed,
taught, healed, befriended, and so forth). In establishing Jesus' <u>essence</u> as central to Christian faith,
the church relegated his <u>actions</u> to a place of deriva-
tive and rather unremarkable significance. There is
nothing remarkable about a divine man's capacity to
effect miraculous change. It is perfectly natural for
one who is divine to do such things. What is remarkable, for conciliar Christians, is who Jesus was: the
embodiment of a God who lowered Himself [sic] to
become human. Such terms as "scandal" and "humiliation" pepper orthodoxy's treatment of God's "condescension" to become human.[17] The only surprise here,
the only remarkable dimension of incarnation, is that
<u>God</u> chose to act in such a way. The role of <u>human</u>
choice and activity remains unattended.[18] Nicea and
Chalcedon produced a Platonic image of a divine man
whose humanity is incredible. Following Chalcedon, we
know that we cannot do what Jesus did (divine acts in
history) because we are not who Jesus was (divine).

The "quest of the historical Jesus"
challenged this line of ontological reasoning by suggesting that we can do what Jesus did (human acts in
relation to the divine) if we can discover what, in
fact, he did. The questers diverted attention from
christological dogma of divinization toward the activities of human Jesus, thereby deposing the metaphysical centrality of Jesus' divine <u>ousia</u> and putting in

32

its place the details of Jesus' life and work in the world.[19] This effort collapsed, as we have seen, under the weight of the fact that the historical (geschichtlich) Jesus is the theologically-interpreted Jesus Christ of whom we read in the New Testament. A history of Jesus is a hermeneutic of Jesus--whether in the gospel of Mark or in contemporary theology. To image Jesus' humanity, however, is not necessarily to deny his kerygmatic Geschichte. Provided we acknowledge the hermeneutical bias of any image of Jesus and admit that we cannot and need not know in detail what Jesus did, we may proceed to weave images of Jesus out of the threads of the New Testament as these threads may help strengthen the fabric of our experience.

Still, the question may be asked, why Jesus? Why not Socrates? Sappho? Sojourner Truth? Martin Luther King? Camilo Torres? Mother Theresa? I do not call attention to Jesus simply because of my own Christian heritage, although it is my Christian heritage that has provided me many occasions to wrestle with what Jesus means to me. I invite attention to Jesus at this point because I believe that what he did may be instructive in our understanding of the power in relational experience, a power discernable not only in Jesus' life, but also in the lives of Socrates, Sappho, Sojourner Truth, King, Torres, Mother Theresa, and countless other women and men in history, in whose relations a compelling and creative power has been operative and strong.

I want to re-image Jesus because I see in what he did the human capacity to make God incarnate in the world, a capacity no less ours than his. If Jesus was not the Son of God, or God the Son--as these titles have been applied to his essential set-apartness from us--what was Jesus' relation to God?[20] And what did Jesus do in relation to other people that may make any difference to us?

Legitimate critiques can be brought to bear on traditional christological images of Jesus, among them the critique of the authority bestowed upon a male figure. While I appreciate and share this weighty grievance, my purpose here is not to recapitulate the specific problems involved in sexist idolatry.[21] My interest here is in combatting the unique and essential Lordship put upon a particular human figure, thereby lifting him above human experience and

33

stripping us of our responsibility to make God incarnate in the world.

Relation of Jesus to "Christ"

Unless we begin emphatically in history, in the world, on the earth, with humanity, we will wind up with our feet off the ground. Unless we begin at an intersection of our own experiences as we live in the world and an image as he lived in the world--rather than with an ahistorical concept of eternal God-manhood [sic] (Tillich)--we will float in abstractions, universals, and ontic absolutes that may or may not bear any relation to human life.[22] Granted, in our imaging, we cannot locate a Jesus who is separate from the Christ-image. We cannot upwrap the Jesus of history from his layers of kerygmatic, christological, blankets. With critical tools, such as those that enable us to understand the Fourth Gospel differently from the synoptics, we can produce images of Jesus Christ that may or may not correspond with those of the authors themselves. Whether or not they do is unimportant, I believe. What is important is whether we can come to some better understanding of who we are in relation to God and each other. To this end, the image of Jesus is itself a tool.

To image what Jesus did instead of who he was is to lay emphasis on Jesus of Nazareth rather than on the eternal Christ. It is a way of beginning to lay the groundwork for a functional christology. This is important if one believes, as I do, that even if ontology must be the end-result of christology (which I doubt), there is no way to understand what something is until we have seen what it does. There is no way to any definition at all except through function, movement, relation. To begin with function is to begin with activity, verbs, what is said, what is done, what happens, rather than with the presupposition that the doer is more important than the deed. The latter epistemological image undergirds the notion of an eternal Logos, rather than the co-operation between Jesus and God, as ultimately responsible for in-carnation.

What relation might Jesus of Nazareth have to the kerygmatic Christ? There is a relation, often an identity. Yet we cannot answer this question with any degree of satisfaction until we have an image

34

of Jesus, a re-image of what Jesus did as a person in
his own time and place. Only then might we be able to
image the relation of Jesus to Christ, the Messiah,
the Anointed One. We (those of us who are, or have
been, Christians) cannot pretend that "Christ" is a
meaningless term for us without falsely denying ways
in which we have been helped or hindered by "Christ"
in comprehending our own existence. But we must
attempt to hold this concept and its overlay of images
at a distance in order to re-image Jesus of Nazareth.
Re-imaging Jesus becomes a first step in re-imaging
Christ, or christology.

Image of Jesus in Mark

        I have chosen to re-image Jesus as he
is portrayed in Mark's gospel. In order to re-image
Jesus, I have needed an image of Jesus off which to
bounce my own perceptions of what was happening in his
life. In other words, re-imaging occurs in relation
to an image.

        Mark presents an image of Jesus that is
distinct from those presented in Matthew, Luke, and
John. The Marcan Jesus stands closer to my own than
any of the other Biblical portraits of Jesus. In particular, Mark's Jesus is imaged in the prophetic tradition of Israel. Thus, I have chosen to explore more
fully my own anthropological/theological hermeneutic
by re-imaging a prophetic Jesus in whose life a certain enigmatic tension grips both Jesus and others:
tension between the present and future "kingdom"
(realm) of God; between the hiddenness and visibility
of Jesus' special role in relation to this community;
and between old (Jewish apocalyptic) and new images of
messianism.

        Howard Kee suggests that Mark "modi-
fies" Old Testament materials "to meet the new
[eschatological] situation in the interpreter's
[Mark's] own time."[23] Mark is "reworking prophetic
tradition in the light of the immediate, critical
needs of his community."[24] I am attempting something
similar. I am attempting to "rework," re-image, the
Marcan Jesus in the light of "the immediate, critical
needs" of people who are seeking to comprehend ourselves in a world in which relation is broken vio-
lently. How may Jesus help us comprehend ourselves--

35

that is, help us realize what we do together in the world?

Re-imaging Jesus

> And Jesus went on with his
> disciples, to the villages of
> Caesarea Philippi; and on the way
> he asked his disciples, "Who do
> men say that I am?" And they
> told him, "John the Baptist; and
> others say, Elijah; and others
> one of the prophets." And he
> asked them, "But who do you say
> that I am?" (Mark 8:27-29a)[25]

Image: They said, "You are the Christ." (8:29b)

Re-image: I say, you are someone in whose way of being I see power, the power of justice, right-relation. I say, you can help us see the power, love the power, claim the power, use the power.

To re-image a Jesus who can help us is to image relation: intimate and immediate relation between self and other, deed and doer, present and future, an image of Jesus and a knowledge of ourselves. To re-image a Jesus who can help us is to re-image the ordinary human and the extraordinary power in relation. Voluntary relation. Right relation. To re-image a Jesus who can help us is to leave Jesus where he was, to realize ourselves in another place and time, and to seek in the tension between then and now, there and here, Jesus and us, some glimpse—image—of relation between what Jesus did and what we are doing. To re-image a Jesus who can help us is to acknowledge our search for relation in the past, to Jesus, to each other, to a power that transcends cultural bounds yet is realized only in history—that is, in human experience. To re-image a Jesus who can help us is to acknowledge already the activity of something extraordinary, something of ultimate value, someting good, some God, in human life. To re-image a Jesus who can help us is to image Jesus in relation to God.

. . .

Image: "And a voice came from heaven,
'Thou art my beloved Son; with thee I am well pleased."
(1:11)

Re-image: And they heard God's voice,
"Jesus loves, and I am pleased." If Jesus loved, he
knew and loved his own power to love (God). God was
the source and resource of his love, that with which
he grew in love. His relation to God was like that
between a growing child and a parent, whose power is
appropriated in friendship by the younger generation--
naturally, organically, in such a way that the maturing Jesus is able to baptize the world with God.

> And [John] preached, saying, "After me
> comes he who is mightier than I, the
> thong of whose sandals I am not worthy
> to stoop down and untie. I have bap-
> tized you with water; but he will bap-
> tize you with the Holy Spirit." (1:7-8)

This parent-child relation is one in which each knows
an intimate and immediate bond with the other, a bond
upon which the very young child may be absolutely
dependent, but in which the child grows, along with
the parent, into friendship, or voluntary and mutual
dependence.[26]

The parent-child image which I invoke
is not intended to reflect an experience of nuclear
family, but rather an image of extended family, in
which children have many parents and parents many
children, in addition to or instead of the bloodline
relation between a mother, a father, and a child.
The parent-child relation in the nuclear family is
often neither voluntary nor mutual: the parent
teaches, the child learns; the parent gives, the child
receives; the parent disciplines, the child is disci-
plined; the parent is the changer, the child is the
changed; the parent is grown, the child grows. The
child is the property of the parent, and the parent
belongs to the child. In interpersonal psychoanalyti-
cal theory (H. S. Sullivan), this situation creates a
dynamic of "hostile integration," whereby each person
contributes to the other's inhibition of growth and
change.[27]

In the extended family, all members may
be adults or they may be both children and adults.
Where there is less a sense of private possession

37

between adult and adult, and parent and child, the various members may assume the functions of parenting (helping to grow) and being parented (growing with help) in relation to each other. The basic difference between nuclear and extended family is that while the former is constructed upon assumptions of privatism, possession, and fixed roles, the latter is built upon values of community, sharing, and roles that shift according to need.

In Jesus' relation to God, Jesus grows with God in love. It is a relation in which each gives and receives and stands out as distinct from the other. Jesus is not God's little boy, the offspring of a private--if miraculous--affair between God and Mary. Rather, Jesus is God's child who grows in relation to God and becomes God's friend in a voluntary and mutual relation. God is parent in that God is resource for Jesus' growth in power. But it may be equally appropriate (and I believe it is) to image God as Jesus' child, whose growth in the world Jesus facilitates.

Consider Jesus' relation to God as one in which each was aware of the other's way of being in the world and whose relation embraced occasions for chosen, rather than symbiotic, attachment and co-operation. The relational dynamic manifest in Jesus' life was a chosen relation, of common benefit, between the divine (God) and the human (Jesus), a relation which was absolutely dependent upon Jesus' on-going decision to love and co-operate with God, a decision first confirmed at Jesus' baptism and underscored by Jesus' own sense of right familial relation. Whoever does the will of God loves God and is God's extended family in the world.

And his mother and his brothers
came; and standing outside they sent
to him and called him. And a crowd
was sitting about him; and they said
to him, "Your mother and your brothers
are outside, asking for you." And he
replied, "Who are my mother and my
brothers?" And looking around on those
who sat about him, he said, "Here are
my mother and my brothers! Whoever
does the will of God is my brother, and
sister, and mother." (3:31-35)

38

A Christian theology which purports to take seriously the responsibility of human beings for acting to effect what is right and good in the world will be predicated on the assumption that Jesus was responsible for his action in relation to God. To ignore Jesus' voluntary capacity, the fully and only human freedom of his will, is to contribute to a docetic christology which disregards voluntary co-operation between the human and the divine and thereby relieves Jesus, and with him us, from any ultimately serious role in redemption.

It is no co-incidence that the current theology of liberation in Latin America lays heavy emphasis on the human Jesus' chosen and active identification with the poor. In Liberation Theology, as in any theology that speaks directly out of and to the human struggle for liberation from evil, christology and ethics will coincide on the basis of Jesus' moral act of self-assertion in relation to God.[28]

His "personal Abba experience" (Schillebeeckx), a relation to a God he may have experienced as "daddy," suggests an awareness of organic connection between Jesus and his own creative source of being in the world.[29] Jesus is not operating on a religious theorem. He is co-operating in an experience of close, natural relation between himself and that which he knows to be Yahweh, God of Israel, of righteousness, of justice. In Jesus we see that what is moral--right, just--is what is natural in the sense of the organic and deep relation that characterizes creation itself: in the beginning is the relation. Moreover, we see that moral choice and "human nature" are not in opposition, but rather that the human refusal to co-operate, or act, with God is that which is immoral and unnatural, an assault upon both humanity and God.

In Jesus, we see that the human-divine relation is so intimate (in which one's knowledge of the other is assumed) and so immediate (without need of mediation) that Jesus' choice to co-operate with the power that moves him into relation and keeps him there is his choice to do God's activity, or to god, in the world. By God, with God, for God, Jesus claims his own authority of possibility in the world. By Jesus, with Jesus, through Jesus, God acts.

39

There is a sense in which Jesus is representative of both God and humanity in the world.[30]
To both God and his sisters and brothers, Jesus re-
presents--re-images--the voluntary capacity (posse) of
the other to act in relation. To women and men, Jesus
represents God's capacity to touch and heal and rebuke
and comfort humanity. To God, Jesus represents humanity's capacity to co-operate in the touching and healing and teaching and rebuking and comforting of human-
ity--and perhaps God as well. Re-image a God who is
touched, healed, instructed, rebuked, and comforted by
Jesus.[31] An extraordinary power is re-leased, re-
vived, re-presented in and for the world. God is
strengthened by human cooperation. The co-operation
rests upon the willing character of both the divine
and the human to effect justice, right relation, in
the world. Each is dependent upon the other's capacity for good will.

Jesus' ousia is not divine, but is
rather the "essence" of the human capacity to choose
to act with God. In relation, both God and humanity
find their posse to effect justice. The divine and
the human are potent in co-operation. If Jesus is to
be understood as "divine," "divinity" must be understood in the functional terms of choice and activity.
A person who chooses to act with God in the world
chooses to act "divinely." The person is human. God
is God, a transpersonal power. But on the basis of
co-operation, the person may carry the weight of God's
authority on earth.

> And they came again to Jerusalem. And
> as he was walking in the temple, the
> chief priests and the scribes and the
> elders came to him, and they said to
> him, "By what authority (exousia) are
> you doing these things, or who gave you
> the authority to do them?" Jesus said
> to them, "I will ask you a question;
> answer me, and I will tell you by what
> authority I do these things. Was the
> baptism of John from heaven or from
> men? Answer me." And they argued
> with one another, "If we say, 'From
> heaven,' he will say, 'Why then did
> you not believe him?' But shall we
> say, 'From men?'"--they were afraid
> of the people, for all held that John
> was a real prophet. So they answered

40

Jesus, "We do not know." And Jesus
said to them, "Neither will I tell you
by what authority I do these things."
(11:27-33)

"Authority" (exousia) is power that has
been granted, power that is socially-licensed or
allowed. A person with exousia has been granted the
right to power. Occasionally, a person manifests a
different kind of authority. Not having been granted
exousia within the social order, she nonetheless manifests power--dunamis: a power unmediated by official
social legitimation. Dunamis is experienced by others
as raw power, spontaneous, uncontrollable, and often
fearful.

Re-image a Jesus whose "authority" was
not exousia, but rather dunamis: raw power, self-
attributed, socially illegitimate; a Jesus who was
granted authority by that which he knew to be God on
the basis of his realization of his power (dunamis); a
Jesus whose authority among human beings was unmediated and unlicensed. The cryptic exchange between the
religious leaders and Jesus, whose authority was not
exousia, points to the enigmatic character of Jesus'
authority.

Jesus could not answer the question put
to him. He and his interrogators were operating and
speaking on the basis of different assumptions. The
interrogators were interested in exousia. Jesus was
interested in dunamis. Their point of reference was
authority. His was power. His refusal to answer corresponds with his skirting of messianic self-identifi-
cation (8:30; 9:9) and with his silence before Pilate
(15:5). Having claimed the authority of dunamis,
Jesus displayed an authoritative power that was
incomprehensible to those around him. Jesus' authority could not be comprehended by persons seeking to
locate authority (exousia) outside and above the realm
of human power (dunamis). Jesus' authority could be
neither understood nor accepted by those who equated
authority with religious or civil government.

The bind in which the Jewish leaders
were caught by Jesus' question about John the Baptist
was the very bind in which they placed Jesus with
their question, "By what exousia--permission--are you
doing these things?" The interrogators, like Jesus,
understood only too well the nature of this riddle:

41

Neither of the two answers Jesus had proposed could locate satisfactorily the source of either John's or Jesus' authority. For Jesus to have claimed either God or humanity (including himself) as the source of his authority would have been for him to have issued a slap in the face of the Jewish leaders, who located all exousia in the religious government in which they themselves had the exousia. Jesus was no fool. He knew that in their eyes, he had no legitimate authority, no exousia, and certainly no way of being accepted among people whose livelihoods and deep convictions compelled them to locate all authority outside the realm of human dunamis--which was, in fact, the only authority Jesus had.

This may be why the synoptic accounts of Jesus' life portray an elusive character who liked better to ask questions about exousia than to answer them. Driven by dunamis, personally unable to be rightly identified or contrasted with God, and regardless of how he understood hiw own role in the context of Jewish history and religion, Jesus could make no public claim for or about his authority without being held in contempt by those who knew no authority except exousia.

Jesus was attempting to give exousia to relational dunamis; permission, license, authority to relational power, or God in-carnate. He was not attempting to undo Judaism, but rather to re-image it. The authority of Judaism, the God of Israel, source of all exousia, had been understood in terms of relational power. God's capacity to act and human dunamis, or human capacity, were necessary correlates. God's justice was effected in human justice. This was the character of the covenant. Human love for both God and humanity was the foundation for all the law and the prophets (Mk. 12:28-31; cf. Deut. 6:4-5 and Lev. 19:18). To all of this, Jesus said yes. He was not trying to negate the covenant, but rather to radicalize it. What was new in Jesus' realization of the covenant was the intimacy and immediacy of God's activity through human dunamis. In the power of relation, God is here, God is now. God is not simply in the memory of mighty acts or in the hope for salvation.

But where is God, what is God, who is God in terms of human dunamis? These were questions springing from Jesus' ministry. The scandalous questions. Re-image a Jesus whose dilemma is ours as

42

well: how to incarnate God in the world without either identifying ourselves with God or contrasting ourselves to God as not-God, even anti-God; a Jesus whose way of being in the world--his dunamis--was conceptually limited by categories constructed to differentiate everything from what it was not: exousia from dunamis, Jew from Samaritan, male from female, light from dark, us from them, life from death, divine from human. In the beginning is not the relation, but rather the opposition, separation, negation. In such a worldview, a person who claims the authority of dunamis is experienced as either mad, bad, or God. In any case, the authority of Jesus' dunamis flies in the face of the assumption that God is most surely not human and that no human being has the exousia to act as if he were God.

Re-image a Jesus whose dunamis pushed him toward a very different worldview, in which there was no occasion for absolute opposition; a Jesus whose relation to God was the resource of his movement into ambiguity and tension between self and other, the law and its re-imaging, heaven and earth, dunamis and exousia, past and present and future; a Jesus who was fully and only human and, as such, fully able (dunamai) to incarnate God in the world; a Jesus in whose acts dunamis was immediately human and divine.

Re-image our own humanity, in which our relation to God is the wellspring of our movement into and through ambiguity and tension toward an emerging sense of what it means to be human: to have dunamis, to relate, to claim exousia. Re-image a world in which there is no wholly other, no up-and-againstness between person and person, subject and object, but rather co-subjects, co-operating, co-creating. No more God and humanity defined by opposition: one up, the other down; one good, the other not-good; one with power, the other without; one giving, the other receiving; one in heaven, the other on earth, but rather a constellation of relation in which God is nothing other than the resource of relational dunamis, unable to be wholly contrasted or identified with any one person in any time or place.

This was, I believe, Jesus' image of the "kingdom (realm) of God."[32] And Jesus said, "The time is fulfilled, and the kingdom of God is at hand." (1:15a) And again he said, "There are some ... here who will not taste death before they see the kingdom

43

of God come with power." (9:1b) Most Christians, like Jesus' Jewish colleagues (both friends and enemies) do not realize the emerging realm of God among us. In our attempts to establish the nature of Jesus' relation to God on the basis of non-relational (ontological) categories, Christians fail not only to image a Jesus who grounded his own humanity in relation to God but, more importantly, to image ourselves as those who can go and do likewise. Jesus was not God. Jesus was moved by God to love and, in so doing, to make God incarnate in the world. Re-image the "kingdom of God" as the realm of human-divine co-operation in which humanity is bound by only one commandment: to love God, which is to love one's neighbor as oneself; or to love one's neighbor as oneself, which is to love God.

. . .

What were the features of Jesus' love? What may characterize an act of God in history?

Intimacy

Intimacy is the deepest quality of relation.[33] It is not a "personal feeling," an act of romantic endearment, a sentiment of exclusive attachment between two people. Intimacy refers to a fundamental bonding between persons' innermost senses of identity. It is the centering of relation in the depth of human being. To be intimate is to know and be known by others in such a way that we are assured, confident, that the mutuality of our relation is real, creative, co-operative.

I do not have to be your personal acquaintance, your close friend, or your sexual partner to know and be known by you intimately. My own files are abundant with letters from "strangers" who have known me intimately enough to realize a strong bond between who they are and who I am, simply on the basis of their having read a short piece by me or having heard something I said somewhere. When such a person writes me and communicates something to me from her own depth of being, then I realize my own intimate connection with her even though she is a "stranger." In such a way, a public ministry may be grounded in intimacy; a confidence in mutuality; an expectation that relational power will always be transpersonal; a sense of bonding that sometimes exceeds in depth and quality our day-to-day relationships with friends and lovers.

Re-image the ministry of Jesus as a ministry of intimacy, of persons knowing and being known by Jesus--intuitively? insightfully? spontaneously?--at such depth that they and he were affected.

> And there was a woman who had had a
> flow of blood for twelve years, and
> who had suffered much under many
> physicians, and had spent all that
> she had, and was no better but worse.
> She had heard the reports about Jesus,
> and came up behind him in the crowd
> and touched his garments. For she
> said, "If I touch even his garments,
> I shall be made well." (5:25-28)

Image: Jesus does not know this woman. She has "heard the reports" that Jesus has a magical power to make her well.

Re-image: Jesus knows this woman intimately, because he knows himself as a human being who, like all human beings, is seeking to touch and be touched, move and be moved, heal and be healed. He, like she, needs dunamis: the power to be able to do what we can. When someone reaches to touch Jesus, he knows exactly what it means: that she is seeking to be healed and has sought out Jesus in particular because she has "heard the reports" that people are touched, moved, and healed by Jesus. Jesus knows her. And she knows Jesus well enough to know that through him there may flow a transpersonal dunamis that will make her well. In this case, as in most cases recorded in the gospels, she, not Jesus, took the initiative in acknowledging the relation. She did so by coming up "behind him in the crowd" and touching his garments. To touch is to signify a relation that exists already. It is an expression of confidence in dunamis, the power in relation.

> And immediately her hemorrhage ceased;
> and she felt in her body that she was
> healed of her disease. And Jesus,
> perceiving in himself that power (du-
> namis) had gone forth from him, imme-
> diately turned about in the crowd,

45

and said, "Who touched my garments?"
(5:29-30)

Image: Jesus is diminished. His power
has left him. He is taken aback and reproaches the
crowd with his question.

Re-image: Jesus is moved, because
power has "gone forth from him." Someone else has
been empowered. He asks who.

The woman signalled, by touch, the
relation that she assumed existed already between
Jesus and those in need of healing. The dunamis
released by the woman's assumption of intimacy was
sparked by Jesus' reputation but was re-leased by the
woman herself who reached to touch him. The healing
was enabled not by Jesus "in himself," but by Jesus in
relation. Healing, and the intimacy that grounds it
in relation, is a reciprocal process in which the
healer is affected by the healed, so remarkably in
this case that Jesus turned "immediately" and asked
who touched him; who enabled the dunamis to go forth
from him.

And his disciples said to him, "You
see the crowd pressing around you,
and yet you say, 'Who touched me?'"
And he looked around to see who had
done it. But the woman, knowing
what had been done to her, came in
fear and trembling and fell down
before him, and told him the whole
truth. And he said to her, "Daughter, your faith has made you well;
go in peace, and be healed of your
disease." (5:31-34)

Image: Jesus heals the woman.

Re-image: Her faith heals her. Faith
is for the woman, as for Jesus, the claiming of
dunamis, power in relation. Whether or not the woman
comprehends what has happened, Jesus knows that the
dunamis is God incarnate, and that faith in this power
is, in fact, faith in God--that is, the claiming,
reaching for and taking not Jesus, but rather the
dunamis: "the power that has gone forth from him."
In relation, dunamis is divine power, God embodied,
what a person "can do" (dunamai). In relation to

46

Jesus, it is a person's faith that makes her well (see, for example, 7:24-30; 9:17-29; 10:52; 11:22-23). Faith is the affirmation of the dunamis stirred manifestly in Jesus which draws into intimacy with him those who are seeking and open to the dunamis that draws them close. Faith in this relational dunamis manifests itself as authority, that which Jesus is perceived to possess and which faithless persons perceive rightly that they lack.

Intimacy is the vital condition for Jesus' ministry. Those who know neither themselves nor God cannot be healed; nor can they appreciate what he is doing with them. Such persons as the religious leaders, the rich young ruler, and often even his own disciples, do not relate intimately to Jesus or one another. They do not grasp the significance of what is happening. (See 3:1-6; 10:17-22; 6:45-52) Their hearts are hardened: closed, invulnerable to dunamis as it spills over between persons and persons.

Jesus holds no monopoly on dunamis. He cannot, because dunamis is relational, denoting a dynamic of exchange between and among persons. Jesus is not a peculiarity, someone who "possesses" God, someone who "has" the power in relation as his own. Jesus willingly facilitates the revelation, or making-known, of God as the creative dunamis in intimate relation between the among human beings. God is no "one," but rather is the spirit which drives Jesus both into the wilderness (1:12) and into human community in order to reveal to human beings the possibility of their own godding.

To the extent that Jesus is perceived by others as superior to them, set-apart from them, one with authority over them, Jesus must live in an ambivalence between a knowledge of himself as someone with authority among people, and hence a special role in community, and a knowledge of himself as someone who, like all persons, needs mutual relation, friendship, love, help, counsel, support. Herein is an image of ambivalence between Jesus' particularity and his universality, an ambivalence shared to some extent by all persons who know both themselves and God.

No one is God. No one is without the possibility of active relation to God. Everyone can incarnate God: the disciples, the woman with the flow of blood, the scribes and pharisees. Everyone can,

47

but not everyone does. There are people who deny God and the intimacy that grounds God in human experience; people who do, and always will, reject God in order to cling to the comforts we find in religious tradition, material possession, familial ties, and political stability (see 7:8-9; 10:17-22; 3:31-35; 15:15).

The rejection and, finally, the crucifixion of Jesus was the denial and death of God not because Jesus was God, but rather because his dunamis disrupted so radically the good order of social and religious structures as to alarm those whose high institutional stakes were cemented in conformity, expediency, and the shallow secularity promised by established exousia. The rejection and crucifixion of Jesus signaled the extent to which human beings will go to avoid our own relational possibilities. God dies when a person is put to death because he loves humanity too intimately, too powerfully, too well.

> And one of the scribes came up and heard them disputing with one another, and seeing that he answered them well, asked him, "Which commandment is the first of all?" Jesus answered, "The first is, 'Hear, O Israel, the Lord our God, the Lord is one; and you shall love the Lord your God with all your heart, and with all your soul, and with all your mind, and with all your strength.' The second is this, 'You shall love your neighbor as yourself.' There is no other commandment greater than these." (12:28-31)

Image: The first, and most important, commandment is to love God. The second is to love our neighbors as ourselves.

Re-image: The two commandments are, in Christian faith and praxis, one--indivisible and inseparable. Jesus' pronouncement of love as the great commandment illuminates his experience of God and of what it means to make God incarnate in the world. Love is the active realization of relation. God is love. Love is God. To god is to love. The lover is aware that she is not alone, but rather that she is bound from the beginning to others; and that there is no greater good than this.

48

In Jewish, as in Christian, tradition, it is usual to speak of a commandment to love God as separate and distinct from a commandment to love humanity. This differentiation was an element of Jesus' tradition. This was the conceptual system and language common to Jesus and others in his time and place. These images of reality both enabled Jesus to communicate and hindered the transformation of a worldview in which God and humanity were experienced and conceptualized as higher and lower, more and less important, and virtually unable to be experienced together in a single motive, choice, or act.

But re-image a Jesus whose love for God was his love for humanity; a Jesus whose ethical norm was that to love God is to love our neighbors as ourselves. To love God is to effect right relation, justice, among human beings. To act with God, by God, and for God is to act with humanity, for humanity, by human choice. To love God is to love humanity so intimately that the realm of God is known to be here and now among lovers of humanity.

The shift on the part of Christian theologians from an image of Jesus' own knowledge of the in-breaking of God's realm among lovers of humanity to an image of Jesus himself as Lord of an otherworldly realm is tantamount to a movement from God to idolatry, or the making of Jesus into an image of all that he did not re-present in the world.[34]

. . .

Immediacy

There is some recognition that Jesus was proclaiming the realm of God as at hand--present and coming--among humanity, rather than himself as its unique head.[35] If this was so, as I believe, Jesus' life may be best characterized by its immediacy: an urgent sense of investment in the present. Jesus' own sense of urgency was undoubtedly steeped in his sense of the approaching eschaton. Re-image the relation between future and present, in which the present--present choice, present act--images the future, which is to say that what is coming is "at hand" in what is already. And it is always and only where we are, in time and space, that we are able to make God incarnate.

Re-image a Jesus whose urgency was motivated by a sense
of the power in present relation to effect the coming
realm of God. Re-image a Jesus who spoke and acted
directly, not circuitously, to effect the present and,
through it, the future. Re-image a Jesus whose
authority was experienced by others as his own, rather
than an authority in need of mediation; a Jesus whose
power was experienced immediately.

> And when [Jesus] came up out of the
> water, immediately he saw the heavens
> opened (1:10a) .... And the Spirit
> immediately drove him out into the
> wilderness (1:12) .... And immedi-
> ately they left their nets and fol-
> lowed him (1:18).... And immediately
> on the sabbath he entered the syna-
> gogue and taught (1:21b) .... And
> immediately there was in their syna-
> gogue a man with an unclean spirit
> (1:23) .... And immediately he left
> the synagogue (1:29) ....
> [underlinings mine]

These early Marcan passages abound in
description of the activities surrounding Jesus as
bearing an immediacy. There is no sense of delay, no
procrastination, no "let's wait and see," no "let's
consider other alternatives." This Jesus is not
imaged as one who hesitated before acting, or as one
who sat down to discuss the pros and cons of his sense
of mission with prospective disciples before telling
them to follow him. This Jesus did not consult or
negotiate with the religious leaders before claiming
the power to act on the sabbath. We see no indication
that this Jesus stopped to consider seriously whether
his present activity might prove counterproductive to
some greater future possibility which even he might
better accomplish further down the road. The immediacy of Jesus' godding immerses him in the present, in
intimacy with people around him, rather than allowing
him to be distracted either by memory, into a reac-
tionary attachment to the past, or by promise, into an
anticipation of a future unrelated to present incarnation. What happens between Jesus and others happens
immediately.

The experiences of death, loss of rela-
tion, separation, grief, and loneliness may well constitute the basic challenge to a person's immediate

sense of self as a creative agent, lover of humanity, one able to incarnate God in the world. These experiences induce in us a dreadful hesitation to realize our power to make any difference in the world.

> While he was still speaking, there came from the ruler's house some who said, "Your daughter is dead. Why trouble the Teacher any further?" But ignoring what they said, Jesus said to the ruler of the synagogue, "Do not fear, only believe." And he allowed no one to follow him except Peter and James and John the brother of James. When they came to the house of the ruler of the synagogue, he saw a tumult, and people weeping and wailing loudly. And when he had entered, he said to them, "Why do you make a tumult and weep? The child is not dead but sleeping." And they laughed at him. But he put them all outside, and took the child's father and mother and those who were with him, and went in where the child was. Taking her by the hand he said to her, "Talitha cumi"; which means, "Little girl, I say to you, arise." And immediately the girl got up and walked; for she was twelve years old. And immediately they were overcome with amazement. And he strictly charged that no one should know this, and told them to give her something to eat. (5:35-43)

Image: Jesus raises the child from the dead.

Re-image: The people's faith brings them away death to life.

In this story, Jesus "ignores" the reports of the girl's death and says to her father, "Do not fear, only believe." The fear unharnessed by death and grief becomes an obstacle to an authoritative realization of power in relation. Jesus is asking for faith. Only when the people realize their power can they escape the deathtrap of fear. Jesus sees that the people are overcome by grief and asks them why, noting that the child is not dead, but rather asleep. He may be suggesting that, in any

51

case, there is no power in death except that which is
given to it by people who have no faith.

Re-image death. It makes us fools,
tricking us into denial of God, the power in present
relation, including the power in our present relation
to the dead, a power that drives us into enlivened
awareness that, though the dead be dead, the power in
our relation to this person is not dead. The power in
the relation is alive. It is not broken except in our
denial of its present movement within and among us.

And Jesus takes the girl by the hand
and tells her to arise. And she does--immediately.
We may sweep away such miracles, enumerating many possible explanations, such as Jesus' own: that the
child was only asleep.[36] I do not think we need "miracle stories" to appreciate the power in relation.
Yet to deny even the possibility of the miraculous in
such a tale seems to me to deny, by limitation, God's
capacity to break death's grip and create life so
immediately as to revolutionize our commonplace
assumptions of what it means to be "dead" or "alive"
in the world.

Re-image a Jesus who had faith in his
own dunamis to topple common perceptions of what is
possible and what is not; of what can happen and what
cannot. A Jesus who knew his power to facilitate a
transformation from death to life, grief to amazement,
fearful impotence to the realization of power--immedi-
ately, in the present, physical, tangible world.
Jesus' attitude toward death may prefigure the subsequent attitude of his most faithful friends toward
Jesus' death. What is remarkable is Jesus' sense of
the immediate power in relation to cut through weeping
and wailing and drive toward a redefinition of human
reality: Faith is human power, and human power is
divine power in the world, and divine power raises the
dead to life, and a re-vived humanity breaks death's
hold and goes forth in amazement.

And Jesus "strictly charged that no one
should know this." Re-image a Jesus who did not want
to be set-apart from other people; a Jesus with no
essential claim to special mana; a Jesus who tried to
divert attention from himself and focus people on
their own capacities to incarnate God. Re-image "messianic secrecy" as implicit in Jesus' and his friends'

emerging experiences of what it really means to be messiah.[37]

　　　　　　　Image:　Jesus was a mediator between God and humanity.

　　　　　　　Re-image:　Neither God nor humanity needs mediation.　As Jesus acted immediately--without interposition--in relation to his <u>Abba</u> and to his sisters and brothers, so too could his friends act immediately in the world.

> And one of the crowd answered him, "Teacher, I brought my son to you, for he has a dumb spirit, and whenever it seizes him, it dashes him down; and he foams and grinds his teeth and becomes rigid:　and I asked your disciples to cast it out, and they were not able."　And Jesus answered them, "O faithless generation, how long am I to be with you? How long am I to bear with you? Bring him to me." (9:17-19)

　　　　　　　It may be that even Jesus' own disciples were unable to comprehend, during his lifetime, the radicality of the immediacy in their midst.　They were unable to realize that the immediate power was not only his, but also theirs.　Christian tradition, in imposing upon Jesus the role of mediator, bears witness to our on-going hesitation to claim our power, our <u>dunamis</u>, our capacity to make God incarnate-- immediately.[38]

　　　　　　　　. . .

　　　　　　　　Passion

> Some have an easy answer
> Buy a lock and live in a cage
> But my fear is turning to anger
> And my anger is turning to rage
> And I won't live my life in a cage.[39]

　　　　　　　In Christian ecclesiology, "the passion" refers to Jesus' last days of suffering, which were initiated by his triumphal entry into Jerusalem and culminated in his death on the cross five days later.

53

Terrified by the intimacy of Jesus' relational knowledge, unable to grasp the immediacy of what was happening among them, thus blinded by Jesus' image of
God, Jesus' antagonists--abetted by his friends' con-
fusion--decided to kill him.

But the passion of Jesus must be considered in a far broader sense than that which is
denoted by the common ecclesiastical usage of the
term. "Passion" is synonymous to "suffering" only in
the most all-inclusive meaning of the verb "to suffer"
--that is, "to bear up" or "to sustain"; in the case
of Jesus, to bear up God in the world.[40] It follows
that Jesus' entire public ministry is marked by his
passion, or suffering, which involves pain and
finally death.

Passion and Pain

To sustain power in relation is to suf-
fer pain in broken relation, including one's own. To
suffer the possibility of effecting good in the world
is to suffer also the evil of broken relational power
in human life. A person of passion endures both the
power and ecstacy of relation and the pain and trauma
of broken relation whenever she witnesses, or is
involved in, the destruction of human relation. There
is no way to avoid pain. There is only the choice
between pain steeped in passion and pain incurred
through dispassionate invulnerability to relation.

Re-image a Jesus whose experience of
God drove him into painful knowledge that this same
God, this relational power, was denied and broken--
vehemently, indifferently, or out of confusion--among
the religious leaders, secular leaders, in his own
hometown, among persons unwilling to follow him, among
his disciples, and even within himself--that is, in
his experience of doubting the constancy of God with
him. (15:34)[41]

Re-image a Jesus who was an intense,
purposeful lover of humanity and who bore up this love.
Re-image his pain and the possibility of his joy, of
which we see no trace in the gospel of Mark. The gospel authors did not write about the mutuality of Jesus'
friendships, the very quality of relation that provides the surest basis for joy in friendship. The
authors of the gospels missed the point, I believe, of

Jesus' passion—that is to say, its roots in relation. Re-image a Jesus whose pain was fastened in the perceptions of those around him that he was either demonic or divine; a Jesus who may have been joyful in relation to those who knew him, as they did themselves, to be fully human and driven toward intimacy in the world.

Re-image the passion as the intense suffering of both pain and joy, a passion which Jesus chose, rather than as something that was done to him. Jesus suffered pain not because he was perceived to be too radical, but rather because he was too radical to be accommodated into the present order. Jesus was persecuted and executed not because he was wrongly-held to pose a threat to Jewish and Roman stability, but rather because he was rightly-held to be planting revolutionary seeds which, if cultivated, promised to contribute to a transvaluation of values and to undercut basic religious assumptions, beginning with the idolatrous worship of a wholly other deity set above the world.

Pain and Anger

"And he looked around at them with anger, grieved at their hardness of heart." (3:5a)   In Mark there are several explicit accounts of Jesus' anger—indignation and rage—as well as numerous images of his no-nonsense rebukes of both friends and enemies for their hardness of heart (see 3:1-5; 4:40; 6:6; 7:9; 8:21; 9:19; 10:14; 11:15-19, 27-33; 12:38-40; 14:6). Even such an innocuous remark as "He who has ears to hear, let him hear" (for example, 4:9), may be read as a tempered challenge, with an indignant edge, to people whom Jesus expects will not hear.

Although there are images of Jesus' sorrow, or sadness, at peoples' refusal to appreciate what is happening among them, Jesus' anger—whether in the form of irony, indignation, or the rage with which he drives the money changers from the temple (11:15-19)—is his most characteristic expression of pain. As his story unfolds, Jesus' anger seems to be almost descriptive of who he is.

Re-image God as an indignant power, a power with a sharp edge that cuts into the possibility of accommodation with any relation that is less than

55

just, or right. Jesus' anger feeds his sense of
authority and is fed by his power in relation.

Re-image anger as an alternative to
discouragement--self-doubt, depression, second
thoughts, madness, the sense of impotence that
unhinges one's sense of purpose in the face of mounting obstacles. Rather than withdrawing from, or making false peace with, an increasingly difficult position, Jesus pushes on.

Re-image prophecy as an angry courage:
the impulse to say No when others are saying Yes; the
determination to go that way, when others are going
this way; an insistence that now is the time among
people who are bidding for more time. Re-image Jesus
as a prophet who stood silently when asked to speak
and who died when he could have saved himself had he
had serious misgivings about what he was doing. Re-
image a Jesus who might not have been killed had he
displayed less anger, bearing the relational power of
a sweet, and less bitter, God.

Re-image a lover of humanity as one who
is necessarily angry at injustice in the world. It
may be the only way to keep one's courage.

We cannot re-image Jesus' anger as hav-
ing been directed at God, except perhaps in his final
full realization of the cost of relation, which is
implicit in his cry, "Eloi, Eloi, lama sabachthani?"
(15:34) Jesus' anger was not at God, or "reality," or
"life," or "the world," or "the way things are." The
anger was not diffuse or unfocused. Jesus' anger had
a specific target: non-relation, broken relation,
violated relation, the destruction of God in the world:
injustice, misuse and abuse of humanity by humanity.

Re-image Jesus' passion as an angry
passion, his death as an angry death. Jesus' death
was an evil act, done by humanity to humanity, no
more and no less evil than that which is always done
to persons who are tortured and killed because they
take justice seriously.

56

Death and Resurrection

> And Jesus uttered a loud cry, and
> breathed his last. And the curtain
> of the temple was torn in two, from
> top to bottom. And when the centu-
> rion, who stood facing him, saw that
> he thus breathed his last, he said,
> "Truly, this man was the [or, a] Son
> of God." (15:37-39)[42]

Jesus' death was unwelcomed. His
friends could not understand why he had virtually
given himself up to be crucified. But Jesus could
have been no more surprised by his own violent end
than by the murder of John the Baptist (6:14-29) or of
other prophets who had spoken in judgment of the exis-
tent order. The "Son of Man" prophecies, which Jesus
expounds when he realizes the extent to which opposition against him is mounting, suggest Jesus' sense of
his own fate as in keeping with the apocalyptic prediction that a "Son of Man" will be killed (8:31-33;
9:12; 31-32; 10:33-34; 45; 14:21, 41; also 12:1-19).[43]

Re-image the "Son of Man": child of
humanity, brother of sisters and brothers, lover of
human beings, one who gods, one whose power in relation will not be accommodated into the present social
order, one who will pay with his life for the brokenness of the humanity which he loves:

> For the Son of Man ... came not to be
> served but to serve, and to give his
> life as a ransom for many. (10:45)

Re-image the ransom: Jesus' death re-
leases his friends to live, not because his death is
good, but rather because in his refusal to re-lease or
ransom himself from death, those who have known Jesus
realize the dead-seriousness of what he was doing
among them.

Re-image a Jesus who does not overcome
death. There is nothing unreal or penultimate about
the death of Jesus. His is an unnecessary, violent
death, as are all unjust deaths. It is a final death,
as are all deaths. There is nothing before, during,
or after Jesus' death that removes the sting of its
injustice, making it a blessing or cause for great
thanksgiving.[44] Whatever the resurrection may be

taken to mean, in no way does it justify, much less
nullify, the injustice of Jesus' death on the cross.
Any theology which is promulgated on an assumption
that followers of Jesus, Christians, must welcome pain
and death as a sign of faith is constructed upon a
faulty hermeneutic of what Jesus was doing and of why
he died. This theological masochism is completely
devoid of passion. The notion of welcoming, or sub-
mitting oneself gladly to, injustice flies in the face
of Jesus' own refusal to make concession to unjust
relation.

A "theology of glory," on the other
hand, which ignores or distorts the injustice in human
life and lulls us into illusions of a peace that
passes understanding as more real than our conflict
and brokenness, is superficial and dangerous. For
such a theology is rooted in our capacity for self-
deception, by which we deny the reality of both Jesus'
passion and our own.[45]

The resurrection may have been a
reflection of Jesus' friends' unwillingness to admit
his death. Unable to realize their own capacity to
make God incarnate, these people may have insisted
upon Jesus' "spiritual" presence as their continuing
head, the risen-one without whom they themselves had
no power. If so, the resurrection is a sham.

The resurrection may have been the
miraculous attestation to God to raise the dead. We
cannot dismiss the possibility of physical resurrection without suggesting that we know all there is to
know about the natural world, God, and the mysteries
of living and dying. But Christian faith does not
rest on the fact of Jesus' physical resurrection.
Christian faith is a functional, ethical, way of acting in history, not a metaphysical or speculative system. As such, Christian faith cannot rest upon the
so-called "supernatural." Moreover, Christian faith
does not encourage us to deny the finality of death in
the course of a lifetime. To the contrary, it seems
to me most faithful--empowering--to acknowledge the
death of Jesus as the final act of contempt against
this lover of God and humanity; and to acknowledge the
resurrection as an event not in Jesus' life but rather
in the lives of his friends.

Re-image the resurrection as a seed
planted in the soil of Jesus' decomposition and har-

vested forever in his friends' subsequent refusals to give up the intimacy and immediacy of God. Following Jesus' death, his friends came to life. What began between Jesus and those who loved, and were loved by, him, continues among these lovers of humanity. What was initiated by the passionate investment of one person in relation to others is carried on among these people in relation.

The mustard seed becomes a great shrub (4:30-32).

The small measure is increased (4:24).

The grain ripens and the harvest comes (4:26-29).

The relation becomes the realm of God.[46]

FOOTNOTES: CHAPTER II

[1]Dennis Nineham, "Epilogue," in The Myth of God
Incarnate, ed. John Hick (Philadelphia: Westminster Press, 1977),
pp. 201-02.

[2]Richard Crashaw, Epigrammata Sacra: Aquae in
vinum versae. Reference: Stanley Morrow, S.J., Weston Seminary,
Cambridge, Massachusetts, February 1980. Another translation of
the poem is, "The water looked at its creator and blushed" (John
P. Bradley, Provost of Belmont Abbey College, Belmont, North
Carolina) who attributes it incorrectly to A. E. Housman,
Charlotte [North Carolina] News, July 14, 1978.

[3]Dorothee Soelle, Beyond Mere Obedience: Reflections on A Christian Ethic for the Future (Minneapolis: Augsburg
Publishing House, 1970), p. 10.

[4]See essay by H. Richard Niebuhr in How My Mind
Has Changed, ed. and intro. by Harold E. Fey (Cleveland: World
Publishing Co., 1961), pp. 69-80.

[5]Albert Schweitzer suggests that "there are few
characters of antiquity about whom we possess so much indubitably
historical information." The Quest of the Historical Jesus: A
Critical Study of its Progress from Reimarus to Wrede (New York:
Macmillan, 1961), p. 6. Nonetheless, "we can only get a Life of
Jesus with yawning gaps. How are these gaps to be filled? At
the worst with phrases, at the best with historical imagination"
(Ibid., p. 7). Other critics of the Quest confirm Schweitzer's
insight. "Our information is painfully incomplete. There is
almost no record of him outside our four gospels, and three of
them overlap to such an extent as to reduce their contents by
half .... [Furthermore], an historical person may become obscure
by the growth of unhistorical data about him." Henry J. Cadbury,
The Eclipse of the Historical Jesus (Haverford, Pennsylvania:
Pendle Hill Publications, 1963), p. 8. Schweitzer's most significant contribution to christology was his grasp of the primacy of
Jesus' apocalyptic/eschatological milieu, which in itself,
Schweitzer believed, constituted the absolute inaccessibility of
the "historical Jesus" to subsequent (non-apocalyptic) generations.

Moving beyond Schweitzer, James M. Robinson summa-
rizes the reason for the failure of the Quest: "The nineteenth
century saw the reality of the 'historical facts' as consisting

largely in names, places, dates ..., things which fall far short
of being the actuality of history, if one understands by history
the distinctively human, creative, unique [and] purposeful, which
distinguishes man from nature .... It is this deeper level of
the reality of 'Jesus of Nazareth as he actually was' which was
not reached by 'the reconstruction of his biography by means of
objective historical method.'" A New Quest of the Historical
Jesus (London: SCM Press, 1959), pp. 28-9. Robinson affirmed
the "new quest" by such Bultmannians as Ernst Käsemann and Gün-
ther Bornkamm who have based their scholarship on the distinction
between the Historie and the Geschichte of Jesus, the latter
being a broad and deep enough concept to embrace the kerygma
itself as a legitimate focus for historical investigation (pp.
66f).

[6]Victor Schramm has pointed out to me there are
only a few references to Jesus in the works of secular writers
during the first and early second centuries. For example, Pliny
mentions "Christ" in his letter to the Emperor Trajan concerning
the persecution of Christians (Ep. X. 96; Trajan's reply, X. 97).

[7]Schweitzer, The Quest of the Historical Jesus,
p. 401.

[8]See Hans Werner Bartsch, ed., Kerygma and Myth,
by Rudolf Bultmann and five critics (New York: Harper & Row,
1961), especially Bultmann's "New Testament and Mythology," pp.
1-16; also Bultmann's Jesus Christ and Mythology (New York:
Charles Scribner's Sons, 1958).

[9]Jesus Christ and Mythology, pp. 17f.

[10]Ibid., pp. 60-85.

[11]Ibid., p. 62.

[12]Ibid., p. 81.

[13]Norman Perrin, Rediscovering the Teaching of
Jesus (London: SCM Press, 1967), p. 236, quoted by Dennis
Nineham, "Epilogue," Myth of God Incarnate, p. 196.

[14]John Knox, Criticism and Faith (London: Hodder
and Stoughton, 1953), p. 32.

[15]D. E. Nineham, "Some Reflections on the Present
Position with Regard to the Jesus of History," in Historicity
and Chronology in the New Testament, Theological Collections #6
(London: S.P.C.K., 1965), p. 10.

[16]Ibid., pp. 9-10. English translation of the Greek: "for that which is not assumed is not healed." (Gregory of Nazianzen, Epistle 102, To Cledonius).

[17]I agree with Tom Driver: "Divine transcendence ... is not to be looked for in separation from the world, but rather engagement with it. Transcendence is radical immanence .... The psychological damage done by the myth of a pure (because purely other) God who condescends to humankind in the name of love without getting his essence dirty (immaculate conception, creation without encounter) seems to me horrifying. It breeds either self-contempt or the arrogance of purity. The Church has fabricated a myth of a God who is self-sufficient yet loving. This myth makes the church schizophrenic." Patterns of Grace, pp. 164-5.

[18]See Appendix B for discussion of Chalcedon's significance.

[19]See above, pp. 27f.

[20]According to Reginald H. Fuller, while "the son of God" with its roots in Assyrian royal mythology, "was just coming into use as a Messianic title in pre-Christian Judaism ..., it meant not a metaphysical relationship, but adoption as God's vice-gerent in his kingdom." The Foundations of New Testament Christology (New York: Charles Scribner's Sons, 1965), p. 32. This relational, adoptionist designation, denoting a moral righteousness, became, in Hellenistic Judaism, a designation of super-human qualities and divine appointment; still later, in the Gentile mission, "The Son of God" denoted Jesus' pre-existence (Gal. 4:4f; Rom. 1:3, 8:3; John 3:16). Thus, as time passed and Christian attention shifted from parousia to exaltation, "a full-blown doctrine of incarnation was evolved. The redeemer was a divine being who became incarnate, manifested the Deity in his flesh, and was subsequently exalted to heaven" (Ibid., p. 232). This linkage of the pre-existent Logos, its epiphany, and its revelation-in-incarnation, together denoted by the title "the Son of God," served as a foundation for the patristic christology eventually consummated at Nicea (325) and Chalcedon (451).

Trinitarian orthodoxy was shaped at Nicea, specifically in establishing the co-equality, co-eternality, and consubstantiality (homoousios) of the Son and the Father. Not only was Jesus Christ "The Son of God"; he was, moreover, "God the Son"--eternally divine, "begotten not made," from "the substance of the Father, God from God, light from light, true God from true God ...." Against Arianism, the Nicene creed reflected an effort to secure the monotheistic basis of Christian faith.

The Redeemer was not a creature, but was rather God Himself [sic] in human flesh. See J. N. D. Kelly, Early Christian Doctrines (New York: Harper & Row, 1958), especially pp. 223-79.

These designations--the Son of God and God the Son, together with the title Kyrios (Lord)--misrepresent the human-divine relation in their setting apart Jesus from full and real human experience and thereby shaping and sustaining an experience and concept of divinity as that which is higher-than, better-than, and more-valuable-than humanity. These are patriarchal designations in that the cultures in which they were rooted and shaped were patriarchal cultures in which, for example, the obedient "Son of God" imagery was employed in Hebraic literature in contrast to the willful, disobedient harlot figure (Hosea); and in which Jesus expressed his own relation to God as that of a person to his father. See Appendix C for a feminist critique of Jesus as Lord.

[21]See Appendix C.

[22]cf. Jon Sobrino, Christology at the Crossroads: A Latin American Approach, trans. John Drury (Maryknoll, N.Y.: Orbis Books, 1978), pp. xv-xvii.

[23]Howard C. Kee, Community of the New Age: Studies in Mark's Gospel (Philadelphia: Westminster Press, 1977), pp. 46-7. Kee is borrowing an insight from J. A. Fitzmyer (Ibid., pp. 47; 190, n. 164).

[24]Ibid., p. 49.

[25]Unless otherwise indicated, all quotations from Scripture are from the Revised Standard Edition (Grand Rapids: Zondervan Publishing House), 1952.

[26]Schleiermacher wrote, "The immediate feeling of absolute dependence is presupposed and actually contained in every religious and Christian self-consciousness as the only way in which, in general, our own being and the infinite Being of God can be one in self-consciousness." The Christian Faith, English trans. of second German edition, ed. H. R. Mackintosh and J. S. Stewart (Philadelphia: Fortress Press, 19281 latest impression, 1976), p. 131. This, I believe, describes very well the sense of a young child ("our own being") in relation to a parent ("the infinite being of God"). What it does not describe well is the relation between the maturing child and the parent, in which the "dependence" has been realized by both child and parent as mutual, voluntary, and relative--not absolute.

[27]See Jane Pearce and Saul Newton, The Conditions of Human Growth (New York: The Citadel Press, 1969), pp. 197-216.

For a helpful economic analysis of the cause and effects of the
nuclear family, see Friedrich Engels, The Origin of the Family,
Private Property and the State (New York: International Publishers, 1942), first published, 1884.

[28]See Appendix D on Gustavo Gutiérrez.

[29]See Edward Schillebeeckx, Jesus: An Experiment
in Christology, trans. Hubert Hoskins (New York: Seabury Press,
1979), p. 637.

[30]cf. Dorothee Soelle, Christ the Representative:
An Essay in Theology After the 'Death of God' (Philadelphia:
Fortress Press, 1967). Soelle builds her thesis on the Hegelian
dialectic between the "irreplacability" of the person and the
personal experience of "interchangeability" (or replaceability)
among us all in the post-modern world. Soelle's synthesis is
that human beings are "irreplaceable yet representable." Using
present-tense language, Soelle refers to Christ as the one who
"represents the kingdom of identity and joy and laughter, and
does not establish it as a superior reality" (p. 15). Furthermore, she notes, the concept of representation "can only be used
to describe the work of Jesus if it is firmly rooted in human
relationships in society" (p. 15). This is because the only
"conditions under which representation can appear [are] personality and temporality .... Whenever man is not thought of as a
person existing in time, that is to say, whenever he is thought
of either as timeless and self-sufficient or as non-personal and
therefore replaceable, the necessary conditions of representation
are missing" (pp. 55-6). For Soelle, Christ represents both
humanity to God (Christ represents "provisionally" our identity
to God, pp. 107f; and God to humanity ("Christ represents the
absent God so long as God does not permit us to see himself ....
[Christ] is the representative of the living God, of the God who
like man is irreplaceable yet representable" (pp. 132, 134). See
Appendix E for an assessment of Soelle's Christology.

[31]This re-image bears an obvious resemblance to
the concept of God in Process Theology—specifically, to the
"concrete," "actual," or "consequent" nature of the "dipolar"
God, who has also an "abstract" or "primordial" nature, "strictly
eternal, unchanging, absolute, and infinite." David R. Griffin,
A Process Christology (Philadelphia: Westminster Press, 1973),
p. 182. Griffin is elaborating Charles Hartshorne's doctrine of
God. For Hartshorne, God is "the unique because unsurpassable
individual, ... absolutely cosmic or universal in his capacities,
interacting with all others, relevant to all contexts, and in
this sense absolutely universal—the only strictly universal
individual, or individual reversal" (A Natural Theology for Our
Time (LaSalle, Illinois: Open Court, 1967), p. 136. Hartshorne

defines "individual" as "subject of interaction" (Ibid., p. 134). The question I would put to Process Theology is in what sense the primordial God, "subject of interaction" is "absolute" and "unchanging" when, in actuality, an interacting subject is relative (in relation) and affected (changed)? That God may be transcendent or unable to be confined in history and time (that is, in human experience) does not necessitate a philosophical assessment of God as either "absolute" or "unchanging" in any intelligible sense of these words. John Stuart Mill wrote, "When we mean different things we have no right to call them by the same name, and to apply to them the same predicates, moral and intellectual. Language has no meaning for the words Just, Merciful, Benevolent [I would add, absolute, unchanging, impassible], save that in which we predicate them of our fellow-creatures; and unless that is what we intend to express by them, we have no business to employ the words." "Mr. Mansel on the Limits of Religious Thought," in God and Evil, ed. Nelson Pike (Englewood Cliffs, N.J.: Prentice-Hall, Inc., 1964), pp. 41-2. What does it mean to say that God is "absolute" love or an "unchanging" resource of power if we have no experience of any actual love or power that is absolute or unchanging and no sense of what such love or power would actually be?

It seems to me that if God has a primordial, unchanging, and absolute nature, it is in the same sense that humanity does: we are unchanging, or constant, in our changing; we are absolutely, or constantly, relative to one another and the rest of creation. An attempt to speak generally of what it means to be human (as I am doing in this book) is a philosophical process that leads toward "primordial" conclusions. An attempt to describe the experience of particular people (as I am also doing) is a process (theological, ethical, sociological, psychological, and so forth) that may provide glimpses--images--of ourselves and God as we actually exist in the world. My primary interest is in this actual existence. I believe it is basic to any philosophical discussion of what is human or divine; and, thus, that the "primordial" (so-called in Process Theology) aspect of God is, in actuality, the "consequent" aspect, and vice-versa. In other words, if we are to do philosophy, we will begin with actual human existence (including our experience of the divine) and, from this vantage point, image whatever "universals" or "abstractions" seem most apparent to our logical sensibility.

[32]I am using the word "realm" rather than "kingdom," which is a patriarchal and explicitly sexist designation. See Appendix C.

[33]See Prologue, pp. xviii-xix, and especially p. xxiv, note 13.

65

[34]A similar, but not identical, concern underlay Rudolf Bultmann's attempt to show that the New Testament must be "demythologized" in existential terms in order to be not only helpful, but even comprehensible, for persons today (see above, pp. 27-9).

Bultmann's interest was _similar_ to mine in that _he_, _too_, _believed_ _Scripture_ _must_ _be_ _re-interpreted_ _within_ _a_ _contemporary_ _cultural_ _milieu_--that is, that we today will understand concepts such as "pre-existent" and "Son of God" in ways that may differ radically from an understanding of these concepts in terms of a tiered-universe. But my concern is different from Bultmann's in that _I_ _do_ _not_ _accept_ _Scripture_ _as_ _an_ _absolute_ _norm_--even within a new hermeneutical framework--because the divinization of Jesus begins in Scripture itself, most notably in the Fourth Gospel, although--as my book is meant to demonstrate--also in the synoptics in terms of people's responses to Jesus' authority.

[35]See especially Jon Sobrino's _Christology_ _at_ _the_ _Crossroads_. "From his preaching about God we can deduce certain important things about the figure of Jesus. First, Jesus did not preach about himself. His whole preaching is relational in character. The center of Jesus' person is not in himself but in something distinct from himself. Second, Jesus did not simply preach about 'God' either. He preached about the 'kingdom of God.' The correlate of Jesus' person is not God but the 'reign of God.'" (p. 357) See Appendix E for an assessment of Sobrino's christology.

[36]My struggle here begins with the kind of question posed by Langdon Gilkey: "If events, viewed naturally, [have] an immanent explanation in terms of natural and historical causes, what [does] it _mean_ to say that they are _God's_ _actions_?" (_Naming_ _the_ _Whirlwind_: _The_ _Renewal_ _of_ _God-Language_ [Indianapolis: Bobbs-Merrill, 1969], p. 92. My suggestion is that if we keep our attention on "the natural"--specifically, on _human_ relation and its manifest power--we may discover something miraculous-- that is, surprising, extraordinary--about this power, which is revealed, in _acts_ at once human and divine.

[37]Referring to the so-called "Messianic secret" in Mark, C. F. D. Moule writes, "[W]e have seen Jesus trying to keep his great authority a secret .... He must at all costs fight the idea that victory is by the hand of Messiahship or kingship which the general public want." _The_ _Gospel_ _According_ _to_ _Mark_ (Cambridge: Cambridge University Press, 1965), p. 67. Howard Kee, interpreting the Messianic secret from the perspective of the Markan community rather than from Jesus' perspective (Kee does not see Jesus' attitude as secretive) writes, "The 'secret' for Mark and his community lies in the insight that, contrary to

appearances, there is not a hopeless incongruity between this [Messianic] claim of Jesus made before the seats of religion and political power that are about to put him to death and the death he did shortly experience" (Community of the New Age, p. 173). I am attempting to re-image both Moule's and Kee's images of the Messianic secret. Unlike Moule and Kee, I do not image Jesus as claiming, secretly or otherwise, to be the Messiah--that is, in possessing a power unto himself. Kee does acknowledge, however, that "the secret [a congruity between message and event in the activities of Jesus and his community of disciples] ... points to both Jesus and the community, to the present and the future" (Ibid., p. 174). I think Kee is right here--that is, that Jesus and his friends (later, the church) must undergo a process of claiming messianic power as radically re-defined in terms of relation. See Chapter V, pp. 167-70.

[38]Emil Brunner writes, "Only in the Mediator Jesus Christ do we know ourselves as we really are. (This does not mean that outside of Christ there is no self-knowledge, but it does mean that outside of Christ there is no self-knowledge which goes to the root of the matter)" (The Mediator: A Study of the Central Doctrine of the Christian Faith [Philadelphia: Westminster Press, 1947], p. 600). For Brunner, to be "outside of Christ" is to be without "faith" in Christ. "When I know that it is God who is speaking to me in this event [Christ]--that God is really speaking to me--I believe. Faith means knowing that this fact is God speaking to me in His word" (Ibid., p. 524). Of Christ, Brunner writes, "To be the Mediator means that He stands alone" (Ibid., p. 490). Without faith in Christ as one who stands alone, bridging this gap between God and humanity, "we cannot act ethically. Apart from Christ man tends to judge himself and the world of human beings ... either from a cynical determinist point of view or in an enthusiastic ideological manner" (Ibid., p. 601). Brunner objects to both the determinist (Realist) and the enthusiastic (Idealist) perspectives: "The Realist sees--distorted by this one-sidedness--Original Sin ... The Idealist ... does not see that [humanity's original] freedom ... has been lost. The one sees the present reality [sin] apart from its origin [human freedom], the other sees the origin [freedom] apart from the reality [sin]" (Ibid., p. 602).

Brunner lifts up what I believe to be our fundamental ethical dilemma: namely, how to act responsibly (ethically) in the world neither as cynical "Realists" nor as fantasiful "Idealists." His solution to the dilemma is that we ourselves cannot. Christ "stands alone" as the One who does. I take more than a semantic issue with Brunner (and the mainstream of Christian orthodoxy, out of which he speaks). The question is whether we can act im-mediately (without "faith" in Christ, in Brunner's terms) to love God in the world. It may be that when we do, we are "in Christ" (whether or not we "believe in," or have ever heard of, Christ); but to insist that we are "in Christ," or that, if we love God, we are de facto Christians, seems to me an arrogant, parochial, and unnecessary claim to make.

[39]Lyrics of "Fight Back" by Holly Near, Hereford Music, 1978, on record album Imagine my Surprise!, Redwood Records, 1978.

[40]"Passion" is from Late Latin passio (trans. of Greek pathos, from Latin pati [past participle passus]), meaning "to suffer." "To suffer" is from Middle English suff(e)ren (from Norman French suffrir, from Vulgar Latin sufferire, from Latin sufferre), meaning "to sustain," or "to bear up"; sub--up from under + ferre--to bear.

[41]See the following passages in Mark which Jesus "bears up" the brokenness of relation: 3:5; 6:4-6, 45-52; 7:9-13; 8:14-21, 31-33; 9:17-19; 10:13-14, 17-31, 35-44; 11:27-33; 12:38-40; 14:32-45, 47, 50, 66-72; 15:2-20.

[42]The RSV says, in a note, "or a son." The Jerusalem Bible (Garden City, New York, 1966), reads, "In truth this man was a son of God" (15:39b). In the Greek, "son of God" (υἱὸς θεοῦ) has no definite article, and, as such, is ambivalent (Victor Schramm).

[43]Reginald Fuller writes, "There is a body of evidence which, as plausible interpretation, indicates that the figure of the Son of Man [υἱὸς ἀνθρώπου] as the pre-existent divine agent of judgment and salvation was embedded in the pre-Christian Jewish apocalyptic tradition. This tradition provides the most likely source for the concept of the Son of Man as used by Jesus and the early church" (Foundations of New Testament Christology, p. 42). He continues, agreeing with Bultmann: "There is an inner inconstituency within the Son of Man sayings. There are some in which a clear distinction is drawn between Jesus and the Son of Man (Mark 8:38, Luke 12:8, Q). In the rest of the future sayings the identification of the Son of Man is an open question" (Ibid., p. 121). "Bultmann concludes that only the passages in which the distinction is drawn, or the identification not asserted, are authentic" (Ibid.). Fuller, however, "reached the conclusion that while Jesus distinguished himself from the future Son of Man who was to come in glory (since he was then upon the earth) he nevertheless regarded himself as proleptically performing the functions of the coming Son of Man" (Ibid., p. 122). "The distinction between Jesus and the coming Son of Man corresponds to the distinction between the kingdom as it is breaking through in Jesus and its final consummations" (Ibid., p. 123).

Whether or not Jesus regarded himself as "proleptically performing the functions of the coming Son of Man," the events in his life were linked by the early Church with its understanding of the Son of Man prediction. What seems important to me here is that the Son of Man image provided for the early Church, and provides for us, a connection between the present and future (eschatological) realm of God, and between the vocation of effecting this realm and the high cost of doing so. Even more important is the sense in which "Son of Man," as used by Jesus or attributed to Jesus' usage, denotes a proleptical function: something is going to happen, because something is being done already.

Walter Wink suggests that we might consider "Son of Man" as reference "to an immanent principle of eschatological wholeness in each of us." Wink asks, "Is God transcendent God immanent in the Son of Man" The Bible in Human Transformation: Toward a New Paradigm for Biblical Study (Philadelphia: Fortress Press, 1973), p. 60. Wink is employing the methodological and analytical (Jungian) psychological tools brought together and developed by Elizabeth Boyden Howes, who writes that the "'Son of Man' phrase describes the Self at work in concrete life, a Self lived existentially, not as a hope or a vision .... [I]t is always in terms of vocation, functioning, activity, and inner power." "Son of Man--Expression of the Self," in Intersection and Beyond (San Francisco: Guild for the Psychological Studies, 1971), pp. 171-97; especially 174, 176.

While the Howes-Wink suggestion commends itself in processes of re-imaging as a means of comprehending our existence (I took a course from Elizabeth Howes in 1976), I think it falls short in much the same way most Christian theology does--namely, in encouraging us to analyze Jesus and/or ourselves primarily as individuals whose power, attitudes, actions, and lives can be comprehended as our own individual ("inner," private) possessions or attributes.

[44] The Eucharist, as a liturgical act of thanksgiving, is an act of gross distortion, I believe, if it is a celebration of the death, or "sacrifice," of Jesus. Geoffrey Wainwright concentrates on the eschatological dimension of the eucharist, noting that much theology has "dealt with the relation between the Cross of Christ and the sacrificial nature which classical liturgical tradition has ascribed to the eucharist ... [by] looking back to the past event of the Lord's death much more than as forward to the future event of His coming ...." Eucharist and Eschatology (London: Epworth Press, 1971), p. 1. Unlike Wainwright, I cannot image Jesus' death as a "sacrifice" at all (see Chapter V, pp. 168-9).

I do not believe the eucharist must be understood in sacrificial terms, which are derived from an ontology of

Jesus' Sonship. As an act of remembrance of what Jesus did, the eucharist is, as Wainwright demonstrates, a celebration of the "already" and the "not yet," "the individual in community," "a divine gift and its human appropriation," "the material as well as the spiritual," the "universality" of God's active presence, "progress in the establishment of the kingdom," and "judgment and renewal" (Ibid., pp. 147-9). I believe the eucharist can be "a taste of the kingdom [realm]," "a sign of the realm" (Ibid., pp. 147-54), if we are celebrating the active power of God among us, relationally; if we understand Jesus and ourselves not as persons called by God to "sacrifice" ourselves--give ourselves over to injustice and death--but rather as persons committed to undoing evil--injustice (both in social structures and in the more immediately experienced dimensions of our own lives). The eucharist makes sense to me only if celebrated as a moral (ethical) act--grounded most deeply in the present and future, not in the past; in life, not in death; and in our own life together, not in a "once and for all" notion of Jesus' having lived, and died, for us and, thus, replaced us as human lovers.

[45]In his Heidelberg Theses (1518), Luther wrote, "The one who perceives what is invisible of God, through the perception of what is made (cf. Romans 1:20), is not rightly called a theologian (#19). But rather the one who perceives what is visible of God, God's 'backside' (Ex. 33:23), by beholding the sufferings and the cross (#20). The 'theologian of glory' calls the bad good and the good bad. The 'theologian of the cross' says what a thing is (#21)." Martin Luther: Selections from his Writings, ed. and intro. by John Dillenberger (Garden City, N.Y.: Doubleday & Co., 1961), pp. 502-3. In these theses, Luther was making an implicit attack on Catholicism's sacramental "theology of glory" in which the invisible is made visible by faith in God's natural presence in creation. In dispute with Catholic faith and practice, Luther exhorted Christians "to be zealous to follow Christ, their Head, through penalties, deaths, and hells; and ... thus [to] be more confident of entering heaven through many tribulations rather than through a false assurance of peace" ("Ninety-five Theses [#94, #95], Ibid., p. 500). Although Luther's "theology of the cross" might not have been an exhortation to welcome pain and death, its roots and overgrowth suggest that we must fix our theological vision on the Cross, complete with its pain, blood, and guts, if we are to "follow" Christ. This translates, psychologically, into an experience of ourselves as Christian only insofar as we are in pain. The opposite extreme, that which Luther refers to as "the theology of glory," finds a modern expression in the thought of Teilhard de Chardin: "[B]y the crucifixion and death [of Jesus], Christianity signifies to our thirst for happiness that the term of creation is not to be sought in the temporal zones of our visible world, but that the effort required of our fidelity must be consummated beyond a

total transformation of ourselves and of everything surrounding us." The Divine Milieu (New York: Harper & Row, 1960), p. 103. I shall quote Teilhard more fully, because he is an eloquent spokesperson for a theology of glory, in which pain and suffering lose their bite and are softened by an otherworldly peace: "[T]he Cross means going beyond the frontiers of the sensible world and even, in a sense, breaking with it. The final stages of the ascent to which it calls us compel us to cross a threshold, a critical point, where we lose touch with the zone of the realities of the senses .... The royal road of the Cross is no more nor less than the road of human endeavor supernaturally righted and prolonged. Once we have fully grasped the meaning of the Cross, we are no longer in danger of finding life sad and ugly. We shall simply have become more attentive to its barely comprehensible solemnity .... The Cross is therefore not inhuman but superhuman. We can understand that from the very first, from the very origins of mankind as we know it, the Cross was placed on the crest of the road which leads to the highest peaks of creation. But, in the growing light of Revelation, its arms, which at first were bare, show themselves to have put on Christ: Crux inuncta. At first sight the bleeding body may seem funereal to us. Is it not from the night that it shines forth? But if we go nearer we shall recognise the flaming Seraph of Alvernus whose passion and compassion are incendium mentis. The Christian is not asked to swoon in the shadow, but to climb in the light, of the Cross" (Ibid., pp. 103-04).

The theology of the cross and the theology of glory are equally fastened in a dualism between a higher and a lower order and equally determined to undo human attachment to the material world of body, sensibility, and relation to tangible, concrete, beings. In both cases, neither Jesus' death nor our own is taken seriously as always final, often terrifying, and sometimes unjust. Rather, death is "glorified" (by the theologian of the cross as well as the theologian of glory) and made right--"justified"--thereby allowing us to forget the terror, and often the immorality, of human death and of other experiences of concrete, physical pain--both our own and those of others--which, if we remembered, we might be able to undo or otherwise address.

[46]See Appendix E for brief assessment of some christological positions in relation to my own.

CHAPTER III

THE EXPERIENCE AND QUESTIONS OF ELIE WIESEL:

IMAGE OF NON-RELATION

> Anne Frank's The Diary of a Young Girl
> was termed a forgery by an ambassador
> at the United Nations. We find no
> monument for Jewish victims at Babi
> Yar, as there is none at Buchenwald.
> There were no Jews gassed anywhere,
> claims Sorbonne Professor Robert Fau-
> risson. No Jew was ever burned in
> Auschwitz, says a former S.S. judge
> in a recently published book in Ger-
> many. The chimneys? Bakeries, he
> explains, they were the chimneys of
> bakeries.[1]

Praxis of Evil

The realm of God cannot be taken for
granted. It does not just happen. It does not happen
on its own. The realm of God is in the relation, a
relation chosen by human beings; a relation mutually
effected among us.

Another choice was made, another effect
rendered, some forty years ago in Europe. Between
1933 and 1945, in the name of "God" and on behalf of
"cleanliness," an elaborate and systematic effort was
undertaken to rid the world of "vermin." The result
was the Holocaust--"total destruction, usually by
fire"--of almost six million Jewish people.

Were we to approach the Holocaust, in
the confidence of retrospect, as a unique and monstrous achievement, an event incomparable to any other
in history and unlikely ever to happen again, we might
feel the gnawing of the fangs of anti-Semitism, Christian culpability and technological progress infused by
the poisonous gasses of national and racial zeal. But
while the Holocaust demands an acknowledgement of its

outrageous particularity in history, it is best
approached <u>morally</u> not as a <u>sui generis</u> phenomenon,
but rather as one particularly hideous revelation of
evil in history.

Why the Holocaust in particular? Why
not the evil of American slavery? women's oppression?
genocide in Vietnam? nuclear power unharnessed? systematic poverty and triage? torture, violent crime,
violent punishment, totalitarian domination both left
and right? Is the rape and burning of a Jewish virgin any more evil than the butchering of a Chicano
woman by a quack abortionist? The beating to death of
a Jewish rabbi any more evil than the mutilation of a
Palestinian guerilla? The shooting of a Jewish beadle
any more evil than the burning of French witches with
"faggots"? The moral indifference of a technology
that produced Zyklon B any more evil than that which
produces Hydrogen bubbles in the cores of nuclear
reactors? I think not--which is why the Holocaust
demands attention as a transparently obscene and
enormous display of the evil that is done elsewhere.
I have sought a particular focus in order to begin to
touch upon the meaning of evil in history. Elie
Wiesel is right: "The more I am able to write out of
my Jewishness, the more universally I am able to communicate."[2] I have chosen to write about the Holocaust because I have been terribly shaken by what I
have read and heard. The Holocaust demands particular
attention because it represents so forcefully a universal moral problem.

Since I am not a Jew, I risk overstep-
ping my bounds even to speak of these things. This
would be the case most certainly if my interest here
were simply pedantic: a matter of demonstrating how
seriously I have reflected on the meaning of Jewish
suffering. This would be the case also if my intention were to speak either to, or for, the survivors of
Auschwitz, Treblinka, Buchenwald and Belsen, or to
their Jewish sisters and brothers. I am interested
neither in pedantry nor in presuming to speak to, or
for, the Jews.

I am writing as a Christian who is
appalled and perplexed by the Holocaust. I have heard
Wiesel's indictment, "In Auschwitz all the Jews were
victims, all the killers were Christians."[3] I have
read Pope Pius XII's response to the plea that he
voice strong protest against the extermination of

74

Jews: "Dear friend, do not forget that millions of
Catholics serve in the German armies. Shall I bring
them into conflicts of conscience?"[4] I agree that "as
surely as the victims are a problem for the Jews, the
killers are a problem for Christians."[5] Yes, there
were exceptions--Dietrich Bonhoeffer, Martin Nie-
moeller, Father Bernard Lichtenberg, Cardinal Faul-
haber, many others, Catholic and Protestant. But even
so strong an antagonist to Hitler's policies as Eberhard Bethge admits that

> even in Bonhoeffer's writings a theo-
> logical anti-Judaism is present ....
> [I]t did not occur to Bonhoeffer that
> there are differences between anti-
> Judaism, Christian anti-Semitism,
> anti-Christian Semitism and racial
> anti-Semitism.
>
> We had seen and abhorred Nazi racial
> anti-Semitism. Now what about our
> previously unconscious Christian anti-
> Semitism? The other survivors, the
> Elie Wiesels, look at us even when
> they appear not to be looking.[6]

It is imperative that we who are Chris-
tians purge ourselves of whatever among us it is (and
of whatever theological expression we give it) that
permits the obliteration of humanity, the negation of
human experience. I believe that the same sacred
tenets to which many Christians held fast to justify
the Holocaust--that is, the theological underpinnings
of Bonhoeffer's "anti-Judaism"--are precisely those
which allow, even encourage, many contemporary Christians to trivialize and despise not only Jews but also
women, homosexuals, Blacks, the poor, and human life
itself.

We meet the Holocaust in its contempo-
raneity, for therein lingers its malignancy. The
Holocaust becomes a mirror, in which we may fix our
eyes upon our capacity to reduce one another to ashes.

The Experience and Questions of Elie Wiesel

I know that Treblinka and Auschwitz [7]
cannot be told. And yet I have tried.

A difficulty besetting Wiesel, and any
of us who attempt to speak of the Holocaust, is that
we find no traditional categories within which to
frame the experience. To speak of "murder," for example, even of "mass murder," is to fail to convey an
important distinction between that which is familiar
and that which is alien to human consciousness.

> ... [M]urder is only a limited evil.
> The murderer who kills a man ... still
> moves within the realm of life and
> death familiar to us; both indeed have
> a necessary connection on which the
> dialectic is founded .... The murderer
> leaves a corpse behind and does not
> pretend that his victim has never
> existed; if he wipes out any traces
> they are those of his [victim's]
> identity, and not the memory and grief
> of the persons who loved his victim;
> he destroys a life, but he does not
> destroy a fact of existence itself.[8]

A contributing factor to the destruc-
tion of "the fact of existence itself" was the inability of its victims to make sense of their experience.
The Nazis, on the other hand, were able to comprehend
the Holocaust by replacing human categories with a
subhuman structure of reality, in which Jews became
"vermin." According to Himmler,

> Anti-Semitism is exactly the same as
> delousing. Getting rid of vermin is
> not a question of ideology; it is a
> matter of cleanliness. In just this
> same way, anti-Semitism for us has
> not been a question of ideology but
> a matter of cleanliness.[9]

This may suggest that neither the Jews
nor the Nazis could function within traditional categories, or symbolic constructions of reality. When
the traditional categories, such as "human" and
"relation" interrupted the extermination process, the
characteristic results were madness (an occurrence
among the victims which Wiesel describes and to which
we shall return) or denial, to which Eichmann alluded:

> ... Although I was wearing a leather
> coat which reached almost to my ankles,

76

it was very cold. I watched the last
group of Jews undress, down to their
shifts. They walked the last 100 or
200 yards--they were not driven--then
they jumped into the pit without offering any resistance whatever. Then the
men of the squad banged away into the
pit with their rifles and their machine
pistols.

Why did that scene linger so long
in my memory? Partly because I had
children myself. And there were children in that pit. I saw a woman hold
a child of a year or two into the air,
pleading. At that moment all I wanted
to say was, "Don't shoot, hand over the
child." Then the child was hit. I was
so close that later I found bits of
brain splattered on my long leather coat.
My driver helped me remove them. Then we
returned to Berlin.[10]

Bethge remarks on the inadequacy of the
language employed to denote the slaughter of the Jews.
He prefers the term "Holocaust" to "murder" or "catas-
trophe," noting that "this problem of terminology is
... not a verbal peculiarity; it is an act in an
ongoing fight,"[11] and that "the term 'Holocaust'
(unlike others) carries profound transformational
qualities. The word and its use ... is an action in
itself."[12]

To communicate the experience; to tell
the story; to speak, theologically or otherwise,
necessitates our re-creation of the structures of
reality, our construction of new categories for new
experience, our investment in an "ongoing fight"
against the evil elusively symbolized--and perhaps
protected--by those structures of reality most familiar to us. As Irving Greenberg warns,

Insofar as the Holocaust grows out of
Western civilization, then, at least
for Jews, it is a powerful incentive
to guard against being overimpressed
by this culture's intellectual
assumptions and to seek other philosophical and historical frameworks.[13]

77

By "seeking, by pushing silence," Wiesel "began to discover the perils and the power of the word."[14] This he has done despite the fact that he can find no adequate framework, no meaningful structure of reality, within which to articulate his experience. Thus, Wiesel writes "to understand as much as to be understood"--in order to understand, perhaps even to believe, his own experience.[15]

> There are no parallels to life in the concentration camps. Its horror can never be fully embraced by the imagination for the very reason that it stands outside of life and death. It can never be fully reported for the reason that the survivor returns to the world of the living, which makes it impossible for him to believe fully in his own past experience.[16]

At age fifteen, along with his father, mother and seven year old sister Tzipora, Wiesel was transported from the world of the living to Auschwitz. Immediately upon arrival, his mother and sister disappeared into the night. "I did not know that in that place, at that moment, I was parting from my mother and Tzipora forever."[17] During the year that followed, Wiesel and his father managed to avoid the fateful "selection"[18] and to remain together, both being eventually transferred to Buchenwald. Several months before the camp's liberation by the Allies, Wiesel's father--broken by beating and delirious from disease--died of dysentary. Upon re-entering the world of the living, Wiesel took an oath

> not to speak, not to touch upon the essential for at least ten years. Long enough to see clearly. Long enough to learn to listen to the voices crying inside my own. Long enough to gain possession of my memory. Long enough to unite the language of man with the silence of the dead.[19]

In writings that span twenty years, Wiesel wrestles with questions of good and evil, humanity and God, nihilism and affirmation. Nothing is resolved. Throughout, "everything is question."[20] "Why do I write? Perhaps in order not to go mad. Or,

on the contrary, to touch the bottom of madness."[21]
"I knew the story had to be told. Not to transmit an
experience is to betray it."[22] Yet, "What if I were
wrong? Perhaps I should not have heeded my own advice
... (perhaps I should have) stayed in my own world
with the dead."[23]

Anguished, and angry at humanity and
God, Wiesel offers no systems, no categories, no
formal hypotheses. He tells stories and asks questions. His words pierce open our theological categories. We begin to perceive that such words as
"love," "relation," "justice" and "redemption" may
have been built upon sand and, as such, are in immi-
nent danger of being washed away. Unwilling to drift
whimpering into absurdity, we are faced at once with
the task of radical perception--that is, of probing
beneath old presuppositions for new meanings of human
experience.

Wiesel's Experience of Humanity

Nothing is of more fundamental value
for Wiesel than relation. His Hasidic heritage is
itself "a protest against solitude."[24] That which is
meaningful is relational, bound essentially to some
other. "There is more of eternity in the instant
which unites two people than in the memory of God."[25]
The faithful person does not tolerate loneliness; she
seeks instead friendship and justice, the moral act
of love.[26]

To flee to a sort of Nirvana--
whether through a considered indifference or through a sick apathy--
is to oppose humanity in the most
absurd, useless, and comfortable
manner possible ... It's harder to
remain human than to try to leap
beyond humanity ... They'll probably tell you that it's all only a
play, that the actors are in dis-
guise. So what? Jump onto the
stage, mingle with the actors, and
perform ... Get out of the nest,
but never try to reach the heights
by flying away from thirsty children
and mothers with milkless breasts.
The real heights are like real

depths: you find them at your own
level, in simple and honest conversation, in glances heavy with
existence.[27]

From within a world of relational expectation that
human experience will be meaningful exactly to the
extent that humanity values close friendship, Wiesel
is plunged into its negation.[28]

Auschwitz and Buchenwald are experi-
enced by Wiesel not simply as the antithesis to relation, out of which might be drawn some reasonable
synthesis, such as an acceptance of ambiguity or of
imperfection in human relation. The Holocaust is
experienced as the negation--obliteration, total
destruction--of relation. To the degree that relation
is that which is, for Wiesel, radically good, the
Holocaust is the experience of radical evil: the
extinction of the meaning and the value of human
experience; the nullification of human existence; that
which is utterly without relation.

As early as 1933, Germany under Hitler
had begun to calculate and implement steps necessary
for the construction of a cultural climate in which
Jews could be deprived of their experience of themselves as human beings. Segregation was legislated;
economic boycotts were instigated; political, educational, and cultural participation with Aryans, for-
bidden. In 1935, the Nuremberg Laws were passed, pro-
scribing intermarriage between Jews and non-Jews and
providing the legal definition of a Jew.[29] These laws
set the stage for the creation of residential ghettoes
and for the rapidly ensuing removal of Jews from any
visible role in German society.

[In 1936], a German movie company
claimed that it had the right to fire
a Jewish stage manager with whom it
had a long-term contract because of a
clause terminating employment in case
of "sickness, death, or similar causes
rendering the stage manager's work
impossible." The court [Germany's
highest, Reichsgericht] held that the
clause was applicable without qualifi-
cation on the ground that "the racial
characteristics" of the plaintiff
amounted to sickness and death. In

80

the thinking of Germany's highest
judges, the Jews had already ceased
to be living organisms.[30]

The outbreak of World War II in 1939
allowed the Germans to dress their anti-Semitic compulsion in the guise of domestic policy--thus, they
believed (rightly), a step-removed from international
concern. Finally, between 1941 and 1945, the Nazis
succeeded, to an extraordinary degree, in the carrying
out of the Endlösung--Final Solution--"the transformation of human nature itself"[31] from the experience of
relationality among the living to the unprecedented,
hence unbelievable, state of limbo between life and
death, in which the Jews were

treated as if they no longer existed,
as if what happened to them were no
longer of any interest to anybody, as
if they were already dead ...[32]

The device upon which the Final Solution hinged completely was the methodological dis-integration of
human experience itself, among both victims and execu-
tioners. It is with the former that we are concerned
at this point. We turn to the victim:

As one number among the living-dead--
specifically, Number A-7713 in Auschwitz--Wiesel's
experience ceased, by his own relational definition,
to be "experience," just as both Jews and Aryans
ceased to be "humanity."[33] It seems appropriate,
therefore, to attempt here not an assessment of Wiesel's "experience of humanity," for these categories
are too familiar, too intrinsically relational, but
rather of "what happened to A-7713" between the
seventh day of Passover, 5705 (1944), and April 11,
1945.[34]

The Story of A-7713

"For what purpose, may I ask, do
the gas chambers exist?"

"For what purpose were you born?"[35]

What happened first was disbelief and
denial. "Who knows? Perhaps we are being deported
for our own good?"[36] Madame Schächter has gone mad.

From the train she screams, "Fire! I can see a fire!
I can see a fire! ... Jews, listen to me! ... There
are huge flames! It is a furnace!"[37] The "madness"
induced by clarity of vision, or the madness resulting
from denial: these are the first options for A-7713.
He chooses the latter.

To the extent that, in the other world,
A-7713 had valued humanity, his capacity for denial
impedes his construction of the present world in which
numbered-characters like himself are fed to furnaces.
To begin to face reality--Auschwitz--A-7713 must begin
to realize that he is vermin, born for the purpose of
extermination. To begin to define himself as a louse
is to begin to go mad--not like Madame Schächter,
whose "madness" is rooted in her prophetic dunamis--
but rather to be transformed into the ideal victim of
domination: a creature incapable of relation, an
insect moving by instinct alone from event to event,
capable only of minimal resistance to the Final Solution. "I had become a completely different person ...
A dark flame had entered my soul and devoured it."[38]

Crawling deeper into madness, A-7713
observes:

> Not far from us, flames were leaping up
> from a ditch, gigantic flames. They
> were burning something ... little chil-
> dren. Babies! Yes, I saw it ... those
> children in the flames.[39]

In madness, he flits between horror and denial. "None
of this could be true. It was a nightmare ...."[40] In
madness, he creeps between the love for his father and
the realization that "here, there are no fathers, no
brothers, no friends. Everyone lives and dies for
himself."[41] It is a world unimagined, a macabre place
between life and death. In it there is no meaning, no
value, perhaps least of all in the absurdity of memo-
ries ... of friends and family.

> [P]ieces of bread were being dropped
> [to us] .... I decided that I would
> not move .... I knew that I would
> never have the strength to fight with
> a dozen savage men! Not far away I
> noticed an old man dragging himself
> on all fours .... His eyes gleamed;
> a smile, like a grimace, lit up his

dead face. A shadow had just loomed
up near him. The shadow threw itself
upon him. Felled to the ground,
stunned with blows, the old man cried:

"Meir. Meir, my boy! Don't you
recognize me? I'm your father ...
you're hurting me ... you're killing
me .... I've got some bread ... for
you ... for you too ...."

He collapsed .... His son
searched him, took the bread, and began
to devour it .... Two men hurled themselves upon him. Others joined in.
When they withdrew, next to me were two
corpses, side by side, the father and
the son.[42]

Madness pivots his feelings toward inappropriate
objects. "Any anger I felt ... was ... directed
against my father."[43] Madness strips his feelings,
allowing him a capacity to cope with that which cannot
be comprehended within bounds of sanity. "Sons aban-
doned their fathers' remains without a tear."[44]

Bela Katz--son of a big tradesman from
our town--had arrived at Birkenau
[reception center for Auschwitz] with
the first transport, a week before us.
When he heard of our arrival, he managed
to get word to us that, having been chosen for his strength, he had himself put
his father's body into the crematory
oven.[45]

Madness is survival among the living-
dead. A-7713's only, last, and bare vestige of relation is with his father. Herein is his sole glimmer
of meaning. Even this is an ephemeral relation which
necessitates cnstant re-creation so that son and
father might believe, again each day, that the other
has escaped the furnaces. The madness of Auschwitz
and Buchenwald fostered for its victims only one category of experience, extended suffering, and only one
means by which to cope with it--denial, totally passive resignation to the process of lingering beyond
the realm of human experience, including eventually
the experience of suffering itself. Upon his father's

death, A-7713 "did not weep."[46] "Nothing could touch me anymore."[47]

At first, madness had presented to A-7713 the illusion of choice, bestowing credibility upon deception: "To the crematory. Work or to the crematory. The choice is in your hands."[48] The "choice," he slowly realized, was between a prolonged stay among the living-dead and an immediate release by blows, disease, gas, or fire. It was a matter only of timing, of choosing when to die on the basis of his choice to endure or end present suffering.

Madness served his decision by dulling his senses. A-7713 was less and less moved by the "selection," by betrayals and brutality done by Jew to Jew, by the Kapos' dilemma.[49] "The idea of dying, of no longer being," had begun to fascinate him.[50] But while madness enabled him to yearn for death, it enabled him also to crave survival. Madness enlarged his sense of body, as in opposition to his sense of mind. Madness split him. "I could feel myself as two entities--my body and me."[51] "I was a body. Perhaps less than that even: a starved stomach."[52] Madness was titillated by starvation, the process designed to reduce further still the human being to the level of animal instinct. A-7713 was a starving body with a lost soul. "It seemed to me that we were damned souls wandering in the half world."[53] Madness was consummated in A-7713's preoccupation with his body as an isolated entity, unrelated to other bodies--that is, incapable of transcendence.

Elie Wiesel's transformation into A-7713 was complete. He had become vermin, incapable of relation and, hence, of experiencing the meaning of either "good" or "evil." Lines between victim and executioner, submission and domination, innocence and guilt had blurred into meaninglessness.

Starved, absorbed in body-instincts, mad, A-7713 was removed from Buchenwald by the Americans. He ate food. He felt no anger, no grief, but rather only shame and guilt--for what had happened to him? for what he had seen? done? not done? for what he was. Having been transported back to the world of the living, A-7713 remained in the world of the living-dead.

> One day I was able to get up,
> after gathering all of my strength.
> I wanted to see myself in the mirror ....
>
> From the depths of the mirror, a
> corpse gazed back at me.
>
> The look in his eyes, as they
> stared into mine, has never left me.[54]

The "Other Side" of the Story

What A-7713 did not know, Elie Wiesel
was to find out: (1) that what had happened to A-7713
had happened also to numbers up to six million; (2)
that what had happened to the six million had been the
culmination of a carefully-constructed design to rid
the world not only of Jews but also of any memory of
Jews simply because they were Jews; (3) that although
the Western world had known of the exterminations,
indeed of the Final Solution as the master-plan--from
at least as early as 1942--it had remained silent.

> Hitler had declared that
>
> Nature is cruel; therefore we too may
> be cruel. If I don't mind sending the
> pick of the German people into the hell
> of war without regret for the shedding
> of valuable German blood, then I have
> naturally the right to destroy millions
> of inferior races who increase like
> vermin.[55]

In 1933 he had addressed leaders of Germany's Catholic
Church, noting that Christians have always despised
and ghettoized Jews and that his policy would be
merely an extension of the same.[56] Testimony during
the Nuremberg trials bears witness to the fulfillment
of Hitler's promise to continue "merely" what the
Church had begun:

> Witness: ... women, carrying children,
> were always sent with them to the cre-
> matorium. (Children were of no labor
> value so they were killed. The mothers
> were sent along too, because separation
> might lead to panic, hysteria, which
> might slow up the destruction process,

and this could not be afforded. It was
simpler to condemn the mothers too and
keep things quiet and smooth.) The
children were then torn from their parents outside the crematorium and sent to
the gas chambers separately. (At that
point, crowding more people into the gas
chambers became the most urgent consideration. Separating meant that more children
could be packed in separately, or they
could be thrown in over the heads of the
adults once the chamber was packed.) When
the extermination of the Jews in the gas
chambers was at its height, orders were
issued that children were to be thrown
straight into the crematorium furnaces,
or into a pit near the crematorium,
without being gassed first.

Smirnov [Russian prosecutor]: How am I
to understand this? Did they throw them
into the fire alive, or did they kill
them first?

Witness: They threw them in alive.
Their screams could be heard at the
camp. It is difficult to say how many
children were destroyed in this way.

Smirnov: Why did they do this?

Witness: It's very difficult to say.
We don't know whether they wanted to
economize on gas, or if it was because
there was not enough room in the gas
chambers.[57]

Reports of these atrocities in the press were "remarkably clear and prompt" in Europe and in the United
States.[58] Newspapers published pictures and editori-
alized on "extermination" and "the chronicle of the
massacre ... (as) wholly in keeping with Hitler's many
times avowed policy."[59]

        To these reports neither the Church nor
the Allies made significant response. Governments
were hesitant to call attention to the Jewish situation in particular, fearing that "(such specific) reference might be equivalent to an implicit recognition
of racial theories which we all reject."[60] Similarly,

"the Vatican could not protest particular atrocities and had to condemn moral action in general."[61] Furthermore, while the Allies were preoccupied with the War and with victory "in general," and were thereby able to look upon the Final Solution of the "Jewish problem" as a less immediate and urgent concern, the churches within Germany, both Catholic and Protestant, were less afraid of National Socialism (which voiced theistic claims) than of atheistic Communism; and "after all, it was the Nazis, not the Bolsheviks, who were destroying [Jews]."[62] Robert McAfee Brown has suggested that Protestants, in particular, made no major collective move against Hitler because he had come to power legally.[63] Nora Levin concurs:

> Most German Protestants had been deeply
> conditioned not only by Martin Luther's
> vehement and often coarse anti-Semitism,
> but (also) by his insistence on absolute
> obedience to political authority.[64]

Whether there would have been any survivors had they known at the time what they do know now must remain a question. Wiesel terms it "fortunate" that the survivors found out "only after the Liberation."[65] He emphasizes with Rabbi Leonard Beerman that

> it is difficult to say which has been
> the more pernicious ...: the intoler-
> ance which committed the wrongs or the
> indifference which beheld them undis-
> turbed.[66]

The implementation of the Final Solution, encouraged by the indifferent silence of Western civilization, invites an analysis of the ingredients of the structures of domination. What goes into the construction of a system in which people so fully dominate others that the latter are deprived even of their capacity to experience themselves as human? In structures of domination, traditional categories of "relation," "love," and "human experience" fall away as points of reference for the dominant persons as well as for the submissive.

Does it follow that we need to consider "what happened to Gestapo Officer No. 401"? Must we permit the S.S. the irresponsibility of denial and madness that A-7713 demands? No. For despite the

denial that allowed loving Christian parents to throw
Jewish parents and children into the crematories;
despite the madness that permitted Hitler, Himmler and
Mengele to concoct a lice-extermination system and to
believe that they were ridding the world of vermin for
the sake of God and cleanliness; despite the infinite
depths of denial and madness which engulfed both Jews
and Nazis in the Holocaust, there is a significant
difference between A-7713 and the Gestapo officer:
the former had no choice; the latter did. Unlike the
effects of submission to domination--effects, such as
madness and denial, which are extended to the victims
by the dominant persons--the ingredients of domination
are fixed fast within the parameters of domination
itself. These ingredients do not extend to the victims. It is in the nature of domination that certain
rights be reserved for itself. The most basic of
these rights is the power to choose: the voluntary
power, or the freedom of will.

Wiesel suggests that, in an evil situation, there are six options from among which people
with voluntary power can choose: (1) to be a victim,
(2) to be executioner, (3) to commit suicide, (4) to
go mad, (5) to be spectator, (6) to involve oneself
and participate in the resistance of non-relation.

Wiesel details these options in his
first four books.⁶⁷ From the outset (in Night),
Wiesel implies that the victim also has options within
the world of the living-dead: she can kill others;
she can kill herself; she can go mad; she can simply
observe; she can participate, involving herself with
others, resisting evil's capacity to destroy relationship. The one option that she does not have is that
of not being victim. This marks the moral distinction
between the victim of domination and the persons who
dominate.

Conversely, the power to choose not to
be victim is the basic ingredient of total domination.
In the Holocaust, this voluntary option is the common
link between the Nazis, the Allies and the Church.
Opting not to be victim, they were able to choose from
among other options. The Nazis chose the role of executioner; Allies and Church, the role of spectator.
In effect, the ingredients of choice, destruction, and
silence were blended together--voluntarily--in the
crematories, producing ashes of Jewish humanity.

88

The Holocaust was implemented on the assumption that Jews were non-relational, inhuman, "vermin." The destruction of Jews was, in effect, chosen by Aryan German leaders, the Church, and the Allies. This evil was the result of a voluntary denial of power in relation, a negation of relation itself: Jewish friends, lovers, spouses, workers, children were experienced as lice and therefore were exterminated with cool, dispassionate efficiency. The more systematic the structures of domination in a society, the more radical the evil in the society-- that is to say, the less relational and more destructive to human beings.

The Holocaust was the evil effect of a domination-submission motif constructed socially in the theological likeness of a dominating deity who overcomes, and negates, human relation and human choice. This strong christological theme in orthodox Christianity represents historically a socio-political reality, an evil, an unjust structure which is concretely present in acts of rape, war, the on-going possibility of nuclear genocide, and the ever-present possibility of another Holocaust/death by fire/death by torture/death by hunger/death by indifference of any given category of "vermin": Jews, Palestinians, gays, women, black people, red people, poor people, boat people . . .

Wiesel's Interrogation of God

Wiesel begins with a tale of humanity. His work peaks in an interrogation of God--God of the universe? God of mercy? God of justice? For the Hasidic Jew, God is a friend. "God is not indifferent and man is not His enemy."[68] There is relation between God and humanity. God is present everywhere the same, though humanity is not.[69]

The evil of Auschwitz drove Wiesel into an "endless quarrel with God."[70] Brown has remarked that, by any definition, "madness is a judgment upon God."[71] A-7713 brought judgment upon God. Wiesel's struggles with God are steeped in "dialectical moves and understandings ... that stretch our capacity to the limit and torment us with their irresolvable tensions."[72] His insistence upon a dialectic of ambiguity distinguishes him from other contemporary Jewish

89

philosophers who, in the wake of the Holocaust, have been driven into reaffirmation of theism (Fackenheim) or atheism (Rubenstein).

We have seen that Wiesel's reflections on humanity lead toward an understanding of evil, rooted in social structures of domination, as the destruction of the relational basis of human existence itself; the destruction of that which is good in the world.

The Jewish (and Christian) God has been conceived traditionally as all powerful--that is, omnipotent. Closely related to God's omnipotence has been the assumption that God is good. When, as in the case of the Holocaust, power seems evil, we cannot easily avoid the questions: Is God evil--unwilling to effect good? Or is God powerless--unable to effect good? Within this philosophical framework (theodicy), Jewish and Christian theologians have labored to "justify" an omnipotent and wholly good God who is believed to be present everywhere as friend and advocate of those who believe.

Wiesel, however, makes no attempt to justify God. He is antagonistic to theodicy. Wiesel rages against God, turns away from God, curses and yet prays "to that God in which I no longer believed."[73]

> Ani maamin [I believe], Abraham
> Despite Treblinka.
> Ani maamin, Isaac
> Because of Belsen.
> Ani maamin, Jacob
> Because and spite of Majdanek.
>
> Dead in vain
> Dead for naught
> Ani maamin.
> Pray, men.
> Pray to God,
> Against God,
> For God.
> Ani maamin.[74]

But what God is this? What does it mean--to pray against God? If God needs our help, worse yet, if God is destructive to us, what--in the name of humanity--is God? What does it mean, to believe in God? What theological affirmation is possible "in the presence of burning children"?[75]

For Wiesel, only the most dialectical affirmations are possible, those in which "I (am) the accuser, God the accused."[76] He tells a tale of Rebbe Pinhas of Koretz (1728-1791). Rebbe Pinhas once asked God,

> "Why do you leave Your people in exile?
> Why is it to last so long? Only
> because we did not--and do not--observe
> Your law? But tell me, tell me, who
> compelled You to give it to us? Did we
> ask for it? Did we want it?"[77]

In The Town Beyond the Wall (1964), the novel in which Wiesel pushes madly through the pathos and nihilism locked within the story of A-7713, Michael, a survivor, speaks of his efforts not to pray:

> I want to blaspheme, and I can't quite
> manage it. I go up against Him, I shake
> my fist, I froth with rage, but it's
> still a way of telling Him that He is
> there, that He exists, that He's never
> the same twice, that denial itself is
> an offering to His grandeur. The shout
> becomes a prayer in spite of me.[78]

The dialectical dynamic of Wiesel's relation to God is nowhere better expressed than in Michael, when at last he breaks from the stranglehold of the past which has prevented him from touching, or being touched, by friendship, love, humanity itself:

> [W]ho says that the essential question has an answer? The essence of man
> is to be a question, and the essence of the question is to be without an answer.
>
> But to say, "What is God? What is
> the world? What is my friend?" is to
> say that I have someone to talk to,
> someone to ask a question of. The
> depth, the meaning, the very salt of
> man is his constant desire to ask the
> question ever deeper within himself,
> to feel ever more intimately the
> existence of an unknowable answer.[79]

91

To question is to affirm. More basically yet, to invest oneself in humanity--to question humanity, to make demands on humanity, to insist upon friends--is to affirm God, for "It's in humanity itself that we find both our question and the strength to keep it within limits--or on the contrary, to make it universal."[80] Questions about God, questions to God, abound from one's investment in humanity. Theological affirmation is, first and most importantly, anthropological affirmation.

To deny humanity is to blaspheme.

To be indifferent--for whatever reason--
is to deny not only the validity of
existence but also its beauty. Betray,
and you are a man; torture your neighbor, you're still a man. Evil is human,
weakness is human; indifference is not.[81]

Indifference, the silence of the soul, the turning away from humanity--that which was implemented by German Aryans, encouraged by Church and Allies, and ingested finally by Jews among the living dead--is the only certain negation of God, just as it is the only negation of humanity. The alternative is friendship or love, the fundamental act of relation between humanity and humanity, humanity and God.

For Wiesel, friendship with humanity and God pushes the limits of faith and reason. Phantasy (Soelle)--imaging--enables some affirmation and probably plays a part in his decision to express reality--truth--often in the form of novels--"fiction."

Employing the metaphor of relation as a literary device because his experiences of God are meaningful only inasmuch as they are experiences of relation, God is able to be for Wiesel a friend, to whom in relation the same dynamics are present and heightened as in the relations between human friends and lovers.

Taking seriously the bonds of human friendship, the friendship between God and Israel, and his own friendship to God, Wiesel asks the same devastating questions of God that he asks of humanity. And it is with greater anguish that he puts them to God, given his lingering, albeit questionable, expectation of God's friendship with humanity as that which

encompasses the power and the goodness to transform
the quality of human relation in the world.

For Wiesel, there was no transformation
from evil to good in the Holocaust. Therefore, he
demands: <u>Where was God? Where is God?</u> Is God victim? Is God executioner? Does God kill Himself
[sic]? Does God go mad? Is God a spectator? Does
God participate, involving Himself [sic] in the
resistance to the evil of non-relation? Does God too
have options? Which does God choose?

Is God a victim? Wiesel tells the
story of the hanging of a little boy in Auschwitz.
"He had the face of a sad angel."[82] He was to be
hanged with two adults.

The three victims mounted together
onto the chairs.

The three necks were placed at the
same moment within the nooses.

"Long live liberty!" cried the two
adults. But the child was silent.

"Where is God? Where is He?" someone behind me asked. At a sign from the
head of the camp the three chairs tipped
over ....

The two adults were no longer alive
.... But the third rope was still moving;
being so light, the child was still alive
.... For more than half an hour, he
stayed there, struggling between life and
death, dying in slow agony ....

I heard the same man behind me, asking "Where is God now?"

And I heard a voice within me answer
him: "Where is He? Here He is--He is
hanging there on the gallows."[83]

Is God hanging on the gallows? Perse-
cuted "as a stranger in His own creation?"[84] Must God
and humanity struggle together against melancholy? Is
God without power? Or is God's victimization a deceptive concealment of God's power? If God has no power,

in what sense can humanity put its faith in God? Is
this not faith in humanity's own destruction? If God
is deceptive, in what sense can humanity trust God's
promises?

> Never shall I forget those moments which
> murdered my God and my soul and turned
> my dreams to dust.[85]

> Never shall I forget these things, even
> if I am condemned to live as long as God
> Himself. Never.[86]

God has not died on the gallows. Unlike that of the
six million, the death of God is always pretense--a
concealment.

What is dead is Wiesel's faith in God's
goodness. "I did not deny God's existence but I
doubted his absolute justice."[87] Recalling the rape
of young girls in the camps, Wiesel interrogates God.
He accuses God of liking "to sleep with twelve-year-
old girls."[88]

> God ... tortures twelve-year-old children
> .... Whoever sees God must die. It is
> written in the Bible. I had never under-
> stood that .... Now, everything became
> clear. God was ashamed .... He doesn't
> want us to know. Whoever sees it or
> guesses it must die so as not to divulge
> God's secret. Death is the only guard
> who protects God, the doorkeeper of the
> immense brothel that we call the universe.[89]

This is an indictment of God the executioner, who "had
thousands of children burned in the pits."[90] If God
has power and uses it to gas Jews then "darkness
replaces light and truth is swallowed up by emptiness."[91] Is not such a God evil, and not worth the
death of a single human being? Nihilism. Nausea.
Never such a God! Wiesel considers and reconsiders
the option that God has to destroy humanity. He
wrestles it fiercely and pushes beyond it, always to
return.

Yet, is nihilism not too weak a
response to the burning children? Does it not grant
Hitler a "post-humous victory"[92] and remove from
humanity the necessity of the "dialectical torment of

living with the Holocaust"?[93] Is the dialectic not
vital for human life? Was not the Holocaust itself
the direct result of an attempt to destroy the dialec-
tic--tension, irresolvability--of human experience?
Was not the Holocaust the product of an unwillingness
to deal with ambiguity, and instead a desire for sim-
plistic, and final, solutions? May not atheism as
well as theism, nihilistic despair as well as non-
dialectical affirmation, indeed, "every solution that
is totally at ease with a dominant option"[94] drive us
into "idolatry and prepare the legitimization of
another Holocaust?"[95] Only question. "Everything is
question."

　　　　　　　Is God mad? For the Hasidic Jew there
are no coincidences.[96] It is no coincidence that in
the works in which Wiesel reflects most explicitly on
the theme of madness,[97] his protagonists emerge, like
Madame Schächter, as people whose "madness" is a prophetic inversion of the values of the world.

　　　　　　　Moché the Beadle is recurrent in Wiesel's works: "Poor fellow, he's gone mad."[98] Moché,
a foreigner, had been one of the first Jews taken from
Sighet. He had "miraculously" managed to escape the
slaughter that was to follow and had returned to Sigh
Sighet to warn his friends. No one believed him, "and
as for Moché, he wept."[99] Like his Hasidic forebear,
the Holy Seer of Lublin (1745-1815) who had "seen"
what was to come for Jews and had "felt lonelier ...
more heartbroken than ever,"[100] Moché "had changed.
There was no longer any joy in his eyes. He no longer
sang. He no longer talked to me of God."[101] The one
who is "mad" is heartbroken because no one listens.
No one believes.

　　　　　　　Has madness been God's experience too?
Is God neither dead nor indifferent? Is God in some
sense dependent upon humanity's will and capacity to
listen and believe? Does human tragedy and God's as
well lie in "man's inability to desire"?[102] In the
superficiality of humanity's investment in either
itself or God? In humanity's apathy toward friendship? Must God struggle against melancholy?

　　　　　　　Does God, remembering the past--the
covenant, the promise, humanity's broken words and
perhaps God's own--consider suicide--that is, deicide?
Does God choose to rid humanity of all meaning, all
value, all friendship by casting Godself into the

furnaces? Did this happen long ago, and in Auschwitz, and still today? Does it happen all the time? Does God stretch God's own capacity for friendship beyond the boundaries of God's own faith in humanity and in Godself?

> "Grandma, tell me, does God die too?"
>
> "No, God is immortal."
>
> Her answer came as a blow. I felt like crying. God was buried alive! I would have preferred to reverse the roles, to think that God is mortal, and man not. To think that when man acts as if he were dying it is God who is covered with earth.[103]

"Never shall I forget those flames which consumed my faith forever."[104] Never.

> Angel: God knows,
>   that is enough.
>
> Abraham: No, it is not enough![105]

The Silence of God

> We are entering a period of silence in theology--a silence about God that cor-responds to His silence.[106]

> Victim, executioner, madness, deicide? Wiesel wrestles with God, again and again, struggling to wring from God's heart some confession, some com-mununication. What has God chosen to do with, for, or against the Jews? There is no response, not a word. God is silent.

> Amen, death. Amen, night. The killers kill, the killers laugh. And God is silent--God is silent still. Amen. Men stumble, mothers falter. Amen. Amen, divine silence .... And the silence of God is God.[107]

Having come to believe that even to question is to affirm the existence, if not the justice, of God, Wiesel is slapped in the face by divine silence. How is it possible to avert the perception that God has chosen the role of spectator? Nothing could be more diametrically at odds with Jewish faith than deism. Friendship and indifference are contradictions. Thus, for Wiesel, God's silence poses the strongest possible challenge to humanity's desire for friendship with God. Hasidism itself is, after all, a protest against the indifference that promotes human solitude.

> The spectator is entirely beyond us. He sees without being seen. He is there but unnoticed .... He never applauds nor hisses; his presence is evasive, and commits him less than his absence might. He says neither yes nor no, and not even maybe. He says nothing. He is there, but he acts as if he were not. Worse: He acts as if the rest of us were not.[108]

In The Town Beyond The Wall, Michael returns after many years to his hometown, from which he and his family were removed by train into the night. He is unclear on why he has felt compelled to go back. Walking the streets of the town, attempting to remember, he recalls suddenly a face in a window, a face that watched the Jews be rounded up, packed into box cars, and deported. "Finally! Everything was clear .... This was the thing I had wanted to understand .... Nothing else."[109] Michael gravitates toward the house with the window and the face. He opens the door and enters .... "There he was."[110]

> "Let's talk," I said.
>
> "About what?"
>
> "A Saturday in spring. Nineteen forty-four. On one side, the Jews; on the other, you. Only the window—that window—between."
>
> "I remember."
>
> "With shame?"

97

"No."

"With remorse?"

"No ...."

"What did you feel then?"

"Nothing .... I had a shocked feeling that I was a spectator at some sort
of game--a game I didn't understand: a
game you had all been playing, you on one
side, the Germans and the police on the
other. I had nothing to do with it."[111]

Is it possible, can it be, that the
face in the window is not only that of an indifferent
Hungarian man, but also the face of God? For Wiesel,
this is the most ravaging question, in part because it
is the most unavoidable. If God has the power to
effect right relation and can choose not do die and
not to kill, but rather to do nothing at all in history, this must surely be divine madness at its most
perverse, malice at its cruelest. The face speaks:

"You hate me, don't you? ...."

"No," I said, "I don't hate you ....
I feel contempt for you .... You don't
feel contempt for the executioner; you
hate him, and you want him dead. You
feel contempt only for cowards ....
Hatred implies humanity ... but contempt
has only one implication: decadence."[112]

Michael continues:

"Your duty was clear: you had
to choose. To fight us or to help.
In the first case I would have hated
you; in the second, loved. You never
left your window: I have only contempt
for you."[113]

The interrogation of God climaxes in
Wiesel's effort to maintain a dialectical faith in the
face of decadence, the apparent decadence of both
humanity and God. If God was the face in the cosmic
window, humanity's response to this God can be only
agonizing contempt, that which drives humanity further

into mad clarity of vision, permitting neither absolute theism nor atheism, but rather passionate investment in humanity--for its own sake, regardless of God.
If indeed "God and man ... are two strangers who try
to become friends,"[114] it is incumbent upon humanity
to rail against God's silence and to allow neither
love nor hatred of God to distract us in our efforts
to break through divine indifference. In relation,
we cannot tolerate the silence of indifference. We
demand God's friendship on our terms.

Wiesel's contempt for God pushes him
beyond any concern for God in God's aseity. To
imagine God in God's self-sufficiency is, in fact, to
imagine an evil God, non-relational in and of Godself.
Wiesel will not permit this possibility. What difference in the world does it make who God is "in Godself"
or "for God's sake"? Philosophical speculations?
Never! Theological affirmations? Impossible! The
only statement that counts, theological or otherwise,
is that "which would be credible in the presence of
the burning children."[115] The only statement that
counts is right relation in human life. As Greenberg
insists,

> To talk of love and of a God who cares
> in the presence of the burning children
> is obscene and incredible; to leap in
> and pull a child out of a pit, to clean
> its face and heal its body, is to make
> the most powerful statement--the only
> statement that counts.[116]

Wiesel tells of three-year-old Yaakov-Yitzhak, who ran
into the forest:

> [His] father wanted to know: "Why are
> you wasting your time in the forest?
> Why do you go there?" -- "I am looking
> for God," said the three-year-old boy.
> -- "Isn't God everywhere?" asked the
> father. "And isn't He everywhere the
> same?" -- "He is--but I am not,"
> replied the child.[117]

Wiesel's plea to religious persons and
theologians is sharp and urgent. Theological specula-
tion--such as theodicy, the philosophical effort to
justify God--provides dangerous deflection from the

immediate moral business of taking humanity seriously
on its own terms in order to effect justice in the
world. God may, or may not, be the same everywhere.
The more compelling question for us is what we,
humanity, will choose to do and be anywhere.

FOOTNOTES: CHAPTER III

[1]Elie Wiesel, A Jew Today, translated from the French by Marion Wiesel (New York: Random House, 1978), p. 44.

[2]Quoted by Robert McAfee Brown, in class, Union Theological Seminary, New York, February 15, 1978.

[3]Elie Wiesel, A Jew Today, p. 11.

[4]Nora Levin, The Holocaust: The Destruction of European Jewry, 1933-1945 (New York: Schocken Books, 1973), p. 691.

[5]Wiesel, A Jew Today, p. 12.

[6]Eberhard Bethge, "The Holocaust and Christian Anti-Semitism: Perspectives of a Christian Survivor," Union Seminary Quarterly Review, XXXII:3 & 4 (Spring & Summer, 1977), p. 13.

[7]Wiesel, "Why I Write," Confronting the Holocaust: The Impact of Elie Wiesel, eds. Alvin H. Rosenfeld and Irving Greenberg (Bloomington: Indiana University Press, 1978), p. 204.

[8]Hannah Arendt, "Radical Evil: Total Domination," Guilt: Man and Society, ed. Roger W. Smith (New York: Doubleday & Co., 1971), pp. 224-5.

[9]Levin, p. 314.

[10]Ibid., pp. 291-2.

[11]Bethge, p. 153.

[12]Ibid.

[13]Irving Greenberg, "Cloud of Smoke, Pillar of Fire: Judaism, Christianity and Modernity After the Holocaust," Auschwitz: Beginning of a New Era? Reflections on the Holocaust, ed. Eva Fleischner (New York: KTAV Publishing House, Cathedral Church of St. John the Divine, and Anti-Defamation League of B'nai B'rith, 1977), p. 30.

[14]Wiesel, "Why I Write," p. 200.

[15] Ibid., p. 202.

[16] Arendt, p. 227.

[17] Wiesel, *Night* (New York: Avon, 1969), p. 39.

[18] A reference to the procedure developed by Dr. Josef Mengele by which those deemed least able-bodied, hence least capable of manual labor, were exterminated.

[19] Wiesel, *A Jew Today*, p. 15.

[20] Wiesel, *A Beggar in Jerusalem* (New York: Avon, 1970), p. 254.

[21] Wiesel, "Why I Write," p. 200.

[22] Ibid.

[23] Ibid., p. 204.

[24] Wiesel, *Four Hasidic Masters and Their Struggle Against Melancholy* (Notre Dame: University of Notre Dame Press, 1978), p. 122.

[25] Wiesel, *The Gates of the Forest* (New York: Avon, 1966), p. 212.

[26] Wiesel portrays the faithless pathos of loneliness and solitude in *Four Hasidic Masters* especially.

[27] Wiesel, *The Town Beyond the Wall* (New York: Avon, 1964), p. 188.

[28] cf. *Four Hasidic Masters*, p. 22.

[29] "The Jew is ... someone who is descended from at least three Jewish grandparents, or from two if: (a) he belonged to the Jewish religious community on September 15, 1935, or later; (b) he was married to a Jew as of that date, or later; (c) he was the offspring of a marriage contracted with a three-quarter or full-Jew after September 15, 1935." Levin, p. 70.

[30] Levin, p. 72.

[31] Arendt, p. 251.

[32] Ibid., pp. 229-30.

[33]"I became A-7713. After that I had no other name." _Night_, p. 53.

[34]The dates of the Wiesel family's removal from its hometown (Sighet, Hungary) and the liberation of Buchenwald by the Allies, respectively.

[35]Arendt, p. 233.

[36]Wiesel, _Night_, p. 31.

[37]Ibid., pp. 34-35.

[38]Ibid., p. 47.

[39]Ibid., p. 42.

[40]Wiesel, _Night_, p. 42.

[41]Ibid., p. 122.

[42]Ibid., p. 113.

[43]Ibid., p. 66.

[44]Wiesel, _Night_, p. 104.

[45]Ibid., p. 45.

[46]Ibid., p. 124.

[47]Ibid., p. 125.

[48]Wiesel, _Night_, p. 49.

[49]Kapos were Jews who were forced by the S. S. to guard, discipline, and often kill other Jews. The Kapos knew that if they refused to do their duty all the Jews under their guard would be killed. Like A-7713, they often did their duty under the illusion that they were protecting Jewish life.

[50]Wiesel, _Night_, p. 98.

[51]Ibid., p. 97.

[52]Ibid., p. 79.

[53]Ibid., p. 46.

[54] Wiesel, _Night_, p. 127.

[55] Levin, p. 297.

[56] Ibid., p. 502.

[57] Greenberg, "Cloud of Smoke ...," pp. 9-10.

[58] Greenberg, Levin, Wiesel and Bethge point this out.

[59] See Levin, p. 673. The quotation from the London _Daily Telegraph_, June 27, 1942, was followed in July by a report of "a new poison gas (Zyklon B) discovered by the Nazis following experiments on Jews and political prisoners."

[60] Levin, p. 669.

[61] Ibid., p. 687.

[62] Ibid., p. 693.

[63] In class, Union Theological Seminary, New York, February 15, 1978.

[64] Levin, p. 505.

[65] Wiesel, _A Jew Today_, p. 190.

[66] See Leo Baeck, _Judaism and Christianity_, translated with an introduction by Walter Kaufmann (Philadelphia: The Jewish Publication Society of America, 1958 - 5719), p. 275; quoted in Robert McAfee Brown, "The Holocaust: The Crisis of Indifference," _Union Seminary Quarterly Review_, XXXII:3 & 4 (Spring & Summer, 1977), p. 134.

[67] _Night_ (1958); _Dawn_ (1960); _The Accident_ (1961); _The Town Beyond the Wall_ (1964).

[68] Wiesel, _Four Hasidic Masters_, p. 15.

[69] Ibid., p. 73.

[70] Wiesel, _A Jew Today_, p. 163.

[71] In class, Union Theological Seminary, New York, March 15, 1978.

[72] Greenberg, "Clouds of Smoke ...," p. 22.

[73] Wiesel, *Night*, p. 104.

[74] Wiesel, *Ani Maamin*, p. 105.

[75] Greenberg, "Clouds of Smoke ...," p. 23.

[76] Wiesel, *Night*, p. 79.

[77] Wiesel, *Four Hasidic Masters*, p. 21.

[78] Wiesel, *The Town Beyond The Wall*, p. 123.

[79] Ibid., p. 187.

[80] Ibid., p. 188.

[81] Ibid.

[82] Wiesel, *Night*, p. 75.

[83] Ibid., p. 76.

[84] Wiesel, *Four Hasidic Masters*, p. 44.

[85] Wiesel, *Night*, p. 44.

[86] Ibid.

[87] Ibid., p. 56.

[88] Wiesel, *The Accident* (New York: Avon, 1961), p. 98.

[89] Ibid., pp. 97-8.

[90] Wiesel, *Night*, p. 78.

[91] Thomas A. Idinopulos, "Christianity and the Holocaust," *Cross Currents*, XXVIII:3 (Fall, 1978), p. 265.

[92] Emil Fackenheim's point, cf. Brown, "Crisis of Indifference," p. 113.

[93] Greenberg, "Clouds of Smoke ...," p. 50.

[94] Ibid., p. 50.

[95] Ibid., p. 40.

[96] Wiesel, *Four Hasidic Masters*, p. 101.

[97]Wiesel, The Town Beyond The Wall (1964) and Zalmen, or The Madness of God (1974).

[98]Wiesel, Night, p. 16.

[99]Ibid.

[100]Wiesel, Four Hasidic Masters, p. 94.

[101]Wiesel, Night, p. 16.

[102]Wiesel, Four Hasidic Masters, p. 119.

[103]Wiesel, The Accident, pp. 34-5.

[104]Wiesel, Night, p. 44.

[105]Wiesel, Ani Maamin, p. 71.

[106]Greenberg, "Clouds of Smoke ...," p. 41.

[107]Wiesel, Ani Maamin, p. 85, 87.

[108]Wiesel, The Town Beyond The Wall, pp. 161-2.

[109]Wiesel, The Town Beyond The Wall, pp. 158-9.

[110]Ibid., p. 164.

[111]Ibid., p. 167.

[112]Wiesel, The Town Beyond The Wall, p. 170.

[113]Ibid., p. 171.

[114]Wiesel, Four Hasidic Masters, p. 45.

[115]Ibid., p. 23.

[116]Greenberg, "Clouds of Smoke ...," pp. 41-2.

[117]Wiesel, Four Hasidic Masters, p. 73.

CHAPTER IV

JUSTIFICATION OF GOD: ANOTHER TIME, ANOTHER PLACE

> Alleluia! Alleluia! Alleluia!
> The strife is o'er, the battle done,
> The victory of life is won;
> The song of triumph has begun.
> Alleluia![1]

> . . .

> He is risen, he is risen!
> Tell it out with joyful voice;
> He has burst his three days' prison;
> Let the whole wide earth rejoice:
> Death is conquer'd, man is free,
> Christ has won the victory.[2]

> . . .

> You speak of Christ. Christians love to
> speak of him. The passion of Christ, the
> agony of Christ, the death of Christ. In
> your religion, that is all you speak of.
> Well, I want you to know that ten years
> ago, ... I knew Jewish children every one
> of whom suffered a thousand times more,
> six million times more, than Christ on
> the cross. And we don't speak about them.
> Can you understand that ....? We don't
> speak about them. (Elie Wiesel)[3]

Two Directions

Heralding the victory of Jesus Christ over sin and death, the loudest Christian voices have spoken historically of God's justice as characteristic of another time (the eschaton) and/or another place (heaven). If violence and injustice characterize fifth century Rome, sixteenth century England, twentieth century Germany, and humanity's life in the world in general, then surely faithful persons will know peace and justice someday and can find it, perhaps

107

even now, somewhere else. Christian theology's justification of God—theodicy—has been to direct our
attention beyond the here and now in one or both of
two directions.[4] One direction begins in the thought
of Irenaeus, second century bishop of Lyons (Gaul);
the other, with Augustine, early fifth century bishop
of Hippo.[5] The two directions are taken on the basis
of several common assumptions: that God is omnipotent
and wholly good; that nature (including human nature)
is not in itself evil; that evil is the result of
human disobedience—hence, that humanity is responsible for evil in history; and that Jesus Christ has
effected the resolution of the problem of evil. These
assumptions constitute the theological basis of Christian theodicy.

        The divergence from common assumptions
into two directions is, in final effect, more a matter
of theological emphasis (Irenaeus on creation as good;
Augustine on ths sin of fallen humanity) than of a
basic theological disparity, so strong are the shared
assumptions on which they begin, and into which they
converge, in Christian praxis. To examine the thought
of Irenaeus and Augustine in their distinctiveness
from each other is to explore a single reality—human
experience—from two different angles. Relative to
each other, Irenaean theodicy is optimistic; Augustinian is pessimistic. Irenaeus plants seeds for a cul-
tivation of a theology of humanity, while Augustine
bids us focus our attention and passion on God.

                    Another Time: Irenaeus

        Now it was necessary that man should in
        the first instance be created; and hav-
        ing been created, should receive growth;
        and having received growth, should be
        strengthened; and having been strength-
        ened, should abound; and having abounded,
        should recover [from the disease of sin];
        and having recovered, should be glorified;
        and being glorified, should see his Lord.[6]

                    Irenaeus wrote in the last quarter of
the second century, following his elevation to the
episcopacy of Lyons in the far western regions of the
Roman Empire and of the church. A native of Asia
Minor about whose early life we know little, Irenaeus
was a missionary to new outposts of the church. He

                              108

probably assumed the see of Lyons as the immediate
result of his predecessor, Pothinus', martyrdom in c.
177 A.D. As bishop and writer, Irenaeus was embroiled
in conflicts between state and church and between
heretical and orthodox Christians. His theology was
not motivated by speculative interest or academic sys-
tematization, although his Against Heresies is the
first "systematic theology" of the church. His interest was pragmatic and urgent: the need to strengthen
Christianity from within so that a unified church
might survive the threats of both heresy within and
Roman persecution from without.[7]

       In Against Heresies, Irenaeus elabora-
ted differences between orthodox and Gnostic Christianity. Gnosticism was a metaphysical system of salvation by which the pneuma (spirit) could be released
through reception of gnosis (knowledge) and return to
God, thereby departing from human flesh, the world,
and the dominion of the Demiurge (creator, Yahweh).
Refuting Gnosticism, Irenaeus attempted to set forth
the tenets of orthodoxy not as a metaphysical, but
rather as a moral, religion of salvation dependent
entirely upon the goodness of both creator and creature. For Irenaeus, neither creator nor creature is,
by nature, evil.

       Yet, "Gnosis ... has in common with
[orthodox] Christianity its experience of man and the
world and a longing for freedom from death, fate and
sorrow, in short for redemption."[8] For Irenaeus, as
for the Gnostics, the human experience of evil in the
world provided motivation for the shaping of redemp-
tive doctrine. Gnosticism is widely held to have
been, first, an attempt to explain the existence of
evil.[9] Hence, a burden of proof lay on Irenaeus to
show in what adequate way orthodox Christianity might
account for the existence of evil in the world. This
he attempted with insight and apparent enthusiasm.
According to Cullman,

              There has scarcely been another theolo-
              gian who has recognized so clearly as
              did Irenaeus that the Christian procla-
              mation stands or falls with ... redemp-
              tive history.[10]

       The key to Irenaean theology is the
oneness, or unity, of God as over and against the
Gnostic dualism which separated the all-knowing (good)

109

First Father (God beyond Yahweh) from the ignorant
(evil) dominion of the Demiurge (Yahweh, creator of
the world). The unity of God embraces the wholeness
of God's enigmatic presence in history. God's immediate and constant business in the world is creativity.
There is no "divine world" set apart from the world
that humanity occupies. Irenaeus insists upon the
unity of God as the "interchanging, interspersing,
unsubordinated persons" of the Trinity in relation to
the world.[11] Richard A. Norris elaborates:

> What happens if you don't like the
> God-world dualism? (1) You can put gods
> back into the world as cosmic powers;
> (2) You can lose God altogether from the
> world; (3) You can lose the world alto-
> gether; or (4) You can do something dif-
> ferent, like Irenaeus.

> Suppose you're a character in a
> play. It dawns on you that somebody's
> running the show. You figure it must be
> one of the characters. Within the frame-
> work of the play, you decide it's "that
> one" who's running it. Later you decide,
> no, there's another play--a model play--
> that's running this play. The one thing
> you don't think of, if you're Hamlet, is
> that Shakespeare is running the play.[12]

So it is with Irenaeus' God, who like
Shakespeare is "running the play." God is completely
inaccessible to human categories of reason, faith, or
imagination--except through Christ's "recapitulation"
(summing up) of the meaning of both God and humanity
in history. Each has its own reality; each is incapable of being either identified with or contrasted to
the other.[13] The relation between God and humanity is
so completely pervasive in human experience, a bond of
such ongoing immediacy, that no distinction can be
drawn adequately between the two--until the Incarnation, in which humanity is able for the first time to
see both itself and God. Only in the eternal Christ,
as Mediator, do God, world, evil, and redemption make
sense, for only in Christ are God and humanity
revealed to each other as "perfect," a designation
both of God and of humanity's original potentiality
and eschatological actuality. It is through Christ
that humanity knows itself as "only at the beginning

of a process of growth and development in God's continuing providence, which is to culminate in the finite 'likeness' of God ...."[14]

In Christ, humanity sees itself as made "after the image and likeness of God."[15] Irenaeus distinguishes between "image" and "likeness." To the former, he ascribes the ontological character of perfection. We are created in the image of a perfect God. This is who we are. Yet, the created cannot be perfect, for the perfect is uncreated (God). Hence, our "likeness" to God is our function as created beings. We are to act "like" God. In such a way do we move towards our perfection, the development of our perfect image. In Christ, we see the coincidence of perfection in image and likeness--an ontological and functional merger.

Irenaeus employs the imagery of childhood to describe humanity. We are infantile, immature, in our imperfection. The soteriological journey is a process of maturation, of growing into perfection.

> For the Uncreated is perfect, that is, God. Now it was necessary that man should in the first instance be created; and having been created, should receive growth; and having received growth, should be strengthened; and having been strengthened, should abound; and having abounded, should recover [from the disease of sin]; and having recovered, should be glorified; and being glorified, should see his Lord. Irrational, therefore, in every respect, are they who await not the time of increase, but ascribe to God the infirmity of their nature.[16]

In this passage, Irenaeus suggestively sums up the meaning of human life: development, growth. Moreover, he remarks upon the "irrationality" of those who are impatient with themselves and who even blame God for their own weakness by suggesting that God is imperfect. Irenaeus presupposed a strong-willed and patient humanity. He reflected a positive, even optimistic, view of human nature. And evil?

111

> Man has received the knowledge of good
> and evil. It is good to obey God, and
> to believe in Him ... and this ... is
> life; ... Not to obey God is evil, and
> this is death.17

Whereas for Gnostics, evil is the metaphysical principle of ignorance, the opposite of good
(knowledge), for Irenaeus evil is the human act of
disobedience.

> God made man a free agent from the
> beginning, possessing his own power,
> even as he does his own soul, to obey
> the behests of God voluntarily, and
> not by compulsion of God. For there
> is no coercion with God but a good will
> [towards us] is present with Him con-
> tinually.18

Human freedom reflects God's willingness to allow
humanity to disobey. God does not force us to do anything. It is, in fact, precisely by trial and error
that we are educated in the ways of God and develop
into God's "likeness." Thus, for Irenaeus, the mystery of not only evil, but also good, is rooted in the
voluntary function--freedom of will--God has given
humanity. A person can choose to obey, or not to
obey, God.

> All ... are of the same nature, able
> both to hold fast and to do what is
> good; and, on the other hand, having
> also the power to cast it from them
> and not do it.19

Although human imperfection is
necessary (since that which is created is necessarily
imperfect), the fall into sin was not. For Irenaeus,
the act of disobedience is both sinful and evil. Sin
is evil. Thus, evil--which is generated by, but not
necessary to, imperfection--is unnecessary in God's
plan for humanity and the world. Human beings can and
should rise above evil. According to Irenaeus, that
is specifically what humanity is here to do: to
choose to obey God.

Irenaeus believes that there is a
devil, Satan, a created being (angel):20 Satan is "the
'god of the world'; ... who was designated God to

those who believe not."[21] Satan has been appointed by God as "Father" to disobedient daughters and sons, not as their "natural" parent, who is God, but as a surrogate parent:

> For as, among men, those sons who disobey their fathers, being disinherited, are still their sons in the course of nature, but by law are disinherited, for they do not become the heirs of their natural parents .... [so too with the children of Satan].[22]

While Irenaeus attributes to Satan responsibility for the Fall, he tends to present him as a mythological figure, in significant contrast to his concept of God as a historical reality. For Irenaeus, evil is also a historical reality. Consequently, he does not literally place the responsibility for evil outside the parameters of human freedom in history. Nor does he place the responsibility for good outside of history. Irenaean theology, including theodicy, emphasizes moral choice and human responsibility in relation to a God who is present in history. Irenaeus blames neither God nor Satan for human disobedience. He does not solve the philosophical problem of God's ultimate responsibility for evil--that is, of why God gave humanity free will.

Irenaean soteriology, with its emphasis on moral choice, has no place for the Gnostic concept of gnosis as a means of salvation.

> It is ... better and more profitable to belong to the simple and unlettered class, and by means of love to attain nearness to God, than, by imagining ourselves learned and skillful, to be found blasphemous .... Some ... fall away from the love of God, and imagine that they themselves are perfect.[23]

Robert F. Brown cites the incompatibility of what he perceives in Irenaeus to be two different eschatological salvation-schemes: (1) a restoration scheme, by which humanity is restored to its original state, prior to the Fall; and (2) an elevation scheme, by which humanity is elevated to perfection.[24] Brown elucidates Irenaeus' inconsistency but concludes that the contradiction between the two cannot be resolved and that we have no way of knowing what Irenaeus meant. This may be so. But since the restoration scheme denotes a perfect creation (which Irenaeus rejects as impossible), the elevation scheme which admits to the necessary imperfection of creation seems to me the more "Irenaean."

In summary, humanity is portrayed by Irenaeus as naturally childlike. There is an almost whimsical quality about who we are. Happily, we learn from our mistakes. Gradually, we grow into the maturity which is our imperfection, our eschatological status which is revealed in Christ. We make progress and ascend toward perfection which, in history, "approximates the uncreated One."[25] Evil is a problem, but not so large that we cannot come to terms with it. We can obey. We can outgrow our own disobedient inclinations. Death, which results from evil, remains with us, because we continue to fall short of the perfect likeness of God. In Christ, however, death is no longer experienced as universal punishment for the Fall, but rather, like evil itself, as an almost-natural--if imperfect--aspect of an individual's life in the world. Irenaeus views "our world of mingled good and evil" as the arena in which God's creative providence is lifting humanity, through our own mistakes and lessons, towards perfection.[26] Within the arena of human experience, evil is part of a whole, a means by which we "learn ... what is the source of [our] deliverance."[27] As for God's justice, God shall at the eschaton

> judge those who, enjoying His equally distributed kindness, have led lives not corresponding to the dignity of his beauty ....[28]

Hick refers to Irenaean theodicy as "the eschatological approach to the problem of evil," designated so presumably by the future-movement of our maturation process.[29] Creation moves towards an end in which will be the final consummation of a perfected humanity. Whereas Irenaean theodicy reappears in the teachings of such Eastern orthodox theologians as Clement of Alexandria (d.c. 220 A.D.) and Gregory of Nazianzus (c. 329-c. 389 A.D.), it does not re-emerge with vigor in modern or pre-modern theology, and not in any significant way in the Western tradition, until the early nineteenth century work of Friedrich Schleiermacher.[30]

114

For Schleiermacher, humanity is being lifted upward. The capacity for elevation is humanity's "original perfection"--that is, "The totality of finite existence, as it influences us ... works together in such a way as to make possible the continuity of the religious self-consciousness."[31] "Original" refers to that which is continuous, immediate, fundamental, and constitutive of created nature. As such, "original perfection" does not denote a beginning in time, but rather an ever-present capacity for God-consciousness. "With Irenaeus, Schleiermacher locates perfection in a latent power or potentiality of human nature."[32]

"Original sin" is part of "original perfection."[33] It is both an immediate element of human nature and an element of continuity. Humanity is created both perfect and sinful. This is the natural human condition: to be potentially capable of union with God--in history (through consciousness) as well as beyond history (eschatologically). Humanity grows up. This is its nature and its purpose. For Schleiermacher, the process of creation--world history --continues without a "fall" that is, in any sense, a cosmic or universal event. Adam (Eve) is one person. Each of us is he, or she. The sin that we do--that is, "the failure to take command of ourselves," the "lack of awakening to God-consciousness"[34]--is our fault, always a "misuse of free will."[35] But our sin is within the schema of universal perfection, which is itself "under the universal system of absolute dependence."[36] The Divine Causality (God) is the source of our free will and our choices and, in its providence, foreknows our sin.

Evil is that which "hinders human life."[37] For Schleiermacher, all "natural" (physical) evil and "social" (moral) evil derives from sin. Social evil is the punishment for sin, but only within a social context--that is, not necessarily related to the sin of the individual.[38] Schleiermacher admits that natural evil cannot be linked intelligibly to sin,[39] but rather must be attributed to the wisdom of God. Like sin, evil is allowed by God only in the context of redemption, without which there would be no sin and without which neither sin nor evil will disappear.[40]

Irenaean theodicy--given modern voice by Schleiermacher and developed further in modern

115

"liberal" theology--depends upon humanity's _posse_ _non_
peccare (capacity not to sin) and God's capacity to
bring good out of all evil--perhaps even to permit or
ordain evil so that good may be experienced, by contrast, in human life.[41]

> The faculty of seeing would not appear
> to be so desirable unless we had known
> what a loss it were to be devoid of
> sight; and health, too, is rendered
> all the more estimable by an acquaint-
> ance with disease; light, also, by
> contrasting it with darkness; and life
> with death.[42]

          In this theology, evil is not "damnable
... but a calling forth of God's compassion on account
of [humanity's] weakness and vulnerability."[43]   In
such a way, "man is being taught by his contrasting
experience of good and evil to value the one for himself and to shun the other."[44]

          God's justification lies implicitly in
humanity's _faith_ that all evil remains mysteriously
under the subjection of God's providential creativity
and foreknowledge, and is functionally vital to
humanity's moral growth. In the wisdom of goodness
of the Divine Causality (Schleiermacher), evil is, by
contrast, rather insignificant--both within and beyond
history. Such a theodicy is almost light-hearted. It
soars, beckoning us to cheerfulness, to faith in both
God and ourselves.

                Another Place: Augustine

> For God, the creator of nature, not
> of vices, created man upright; but
> man, being of his own will corrupted
> and justly condemned, begot corrupted
> and condemned children. For we all
> were in that one man, who fell into
> sin by the woman who was made from
> him before the sin.[45]

          Augustinian theology, more than
Irenaean, has shaped the predominant Catholic and
Protestant doctrines of sin and evil, in which empha-
sis is on the Fall as a disruption of creativity, and

on the "privative" (or unnatural) status of evil
rather than on the creative process itself as "needing" sin and employing evil for good ends.

Whereas Irenaeus laid emphasis on the
purposefulness of creation in its natural imperfection
(so "natural" that Schleiermacher called it "perfect"!) and on creation's tendency to move towards
perfection, the Bishop of Hippo viewed the same naturally good creation as having been severely and universally disrupted--broken--by humanity's misuse of
free will. For Augustine, humanity is not evolving or
growing towards perfection, but rather has literally
fallen from its posse non peccare. We are stuck in
our sin--that is, in a state of unnatural (evil)
alienation from God, in which we are bound to sin.
This evil condition serves no good or necessary purpose whatsoever. To the contrary, it is the universal
obstacle to right-relationship between God and humanity.

We know more about Augustine's theological development than about Irenaeus'. As a privileged member of society, Augustine appears to have had
greater exposure to, and interest in, philosophy than
did Irenaeus. Augustine is more speculative, more
introspective. We know from his Confessions that he
was a "person of the world," a person of intensity,
and that in his sojourning he spent nine years under
the influence of the radically dualistic Manicheans.

> My soul did not dare to find fault with
> my God, and therefore it would not admit
> that what it found distasteful had been
> created by you. This was why it went
> astray and accepted the theory of the
> two substances [good and evil].[46]

Ostensibly, Augustine's attraction to
the Manicheans was a result both of his inability to
hold God responsible for evil and of his inability to
perceive God as spiritual (as opposed to material)
substance. "I thought of you, O Life of my life, as a
great being with dimensions extending every-where,
throughout infinite space ...."[47] More importantly,
perhaps, Augustine's attraction to the Manicheans may
have been a consequence of his evasion of responsibility for sin--that is, of his unwillingness to acknowledge his own voluntary function in relation to God, or
the freedom of his own will (in contrast to the Mani-

chean theory of the self's being held in bondage by
evil substance). Under Manichean influence, Augustine
was unwilling to admit that, in deciding whether to
serve God, it was he himself who was responsible. "It
was I and I alone. But I neither willed to do it, nor
refused to do it with my full will. So I was at odds
with myself."[48] Here we catch a glimpse of Augustine's emphasis on the will as the voluntary function
of self which unites the rational and irrational soul
(reason and feelings) and which is central to his doctrines of humanity, evil, freedom, and grace; a
glimpse, moreover, into Augustine's belief that to
know God (as good, immutable, eternal), one must know
oneself (as deficient, mutuable, temporal, and dependent upon God for whatever good may occur in human
life).

        Augustine attributes his spiritual
growth to the influence of the Platonists (Neoplato-
nists). In particular, he found in Neoplatonism a
solution to the Manichean problem of dualism between
good and evil substances. "I awoke in you and saw
that you were infinite, but not in the way I had sup-
posed."[49] C. N. Cochrane heralds this insight as
Augustine's realization of a new arché, or starting
point, in theology, which he had inherited from
Athanasius and which was opened up for him by the
writings of Plotinus: namely, the spiritual or
incorporeal realm.[50] "By reading ... the Platonists,
I had been prompted to look for truth as something
incorporeal, and I caught sight of your invisible
nature, as it is known through your creatures ....
You are infinite, though without extent in terms of
space."[51]

        For Augustine, this breakthrough was
thoroughgoing. It enabled him to begin to reformulate
his ideas of God and humanity on the basis of that
which he "preferred"--the spiritual, the Platonic
ideal of an eternal principle underlying all reality.
He was able to postulate the value of God as the immutable, omnipresent source of all being, goodness, and
truth. God, he realized, had been present to him all
along, but "unacknowledged" as a result of his failure
to perceive God as spiritual.

        Indebted to the Platonist suggestion of
the immutability and invisibility of the Eternal One,
Augustine nonetheless departed from Platonism in an
original and independent way.[52] He did not share

Platonism's contempt for the mutuable--that is, for
the visible material world. More accurately, it seems
to me, he did not want to share this contempt, since
he believed that the Creator was incapable of creating
anything other than that which is good. But, as Cochrane maintains, a real difficulty beset Augustine in
that "as materialism had failed to do justice to the
problem of mind, so idealism failed to do justice to
the problem of matter, which it sought to define as
the 'all-but-nothing.'"53

Augustine's solution to this problem
was, on the one hand, to draw a strong line of demar-
cation between spirit and flesh, similar to (though
not identical with) the Platonic distinction between
the ideal and the real; and, on the other hand, to
break with Platonism in his affirmation of both the
otherness of spirit and flesh (that is, their sepa-
rateness) and the relation between them. Spirit and
flesh are not incapable of relation. The spirit moves
towards and into the flesh. The flesh responds by its
receptivity and, in so doing, is transformed by the
spirit. For the Platonists, "change was more shocking
than permanence."54 For Augustine this was not so.
Rather, change is natural, an essential part of harmony and order. The process of reconciliation between
creator and creature, spirit and flesh, is that of
"ordered harmony," foreordained by God, in which the
human being whose flesh is purified by spirit is able
to move into unity with God.

Here, on the theme of God's providence
in an ordered harmony, is where Augustine and Irenaeus
seem to be saying the same thing about God's capacity
to bring good out of evil. Certainly an ordered harmony might be, or involve, a developmental process.
Augustine and Irenaeus share an affirmation of the
ultimacy of God's goodness in relation to the world.
What they do not share is a common view of where God's
goodness is located in relation to the world. This
difference in "location" provides a clue to the two
significantly different approaches to the problem of
theodicy.

For Augustine, God is "above" the
world--that is, higher in value than the world and
essentially beyond human time and human space. God is
pure spirit, which is contrasted with flesh, all that
is changeable. Such a God can be known only in opposition to evil. For Irenaeus, as we have seen, God is

not experienced as "above," or even higher in value than, the world. God is "in" the world, "mingled with" humanity, and is in creative tension with-- rather than opposition to--evil. Whereas Augustine's preference is for the spiritual, Irenaeus' first interest seems to be in the world and humanity.

The God-world dualism in Augustine is not absolute, in that there is the possibility of reconciliation between them. But Augustine is biased towards the "otherworldly,"[55] similarly to his Platonic predecessors. While he maintains that neither the world itself nor humanity is naturally evil ("Let no one ... look for an efficient cause of the evil will; for it is not efficient, but deficient"),[56] his marked emphasis on the helplessness of the human will to do good on its own leaves no question about Augustine's difficulty in actually affirming human nature or creation itself. Praise of God is condemnation of the self. It was, after all, Augustine's own insight that "the reality of the spiritual is apprehended because, and when, the spiritual is preferred to the material."[57] The only appropriate, faithful, position of humanity in relation to God is one of confession, "realized or completed knowledge of God,"[58] which is at the same time "an accusation of the human condition." The word confessio summed up his attitude to humanity.[59]

This is so despite Augustine's belief that the natural condition of humanity is good. Regarding creation, he writes, "If we ask, 'who made it?' the answer is 'God.' If we ask, 'how?' the answer is that 'God said, 'Let it be, and it was done.' If we ask, 'why?' the answer is, 'Because it is good.'"[60] Indeed, "all natures ... are simply good because they exist ... and each has its own measure of being, its own beauty, even, in a way, its own place."[61] A good God would not have created anything other than that which is good. Since Augustine, following the Platonists, equates being (essence) with goodness, all that is good is all that is: all that naturally exists or is created. This is true of the soul, the body, and all organic and inorganic creation. On the other hand, "his sense of the reality of moral evil caused him to relapse into Manicheanism with his doctrine of original sin, in which the Not-Being, the Nothing out of which man was created, is transformed into a Something with fatal power."[62] The spirit-flesh distinction becomes increasingly a

dualism as "spirit" becomes synonymous with the unify-
ing aspect of the trinitarian Godhead and "flesh" is
equated with fallen (corrupted) creation. The doctrine of a natural (good) creation fades into the
background as the doctrine of the Fall mounts in pro-
portion.

It is interesting to note that Augustine's early works, such as the Confessions, were
written primarily to underscore the goodness of God,
in opposition to the Manicheans, whereas his later
works, culminating in The City of God, were produced
in the context of pagan and Pelagian emphases on the
autonomy and capacity of humanity to get along without
interference from Yahweh. The City of God, in particular, was written in the years after the fall of Rome
in 410 A.D. In it, Augustine stresses humanity's complete dependence upon God's grace, and the world's
subjection under the historical providence of God's
ordered harmony. Possibly, Augustine's movement
towards a radical dualism between spirit and flesh
reflects his transition from the Manichean struggle to
the political turmoil in Rome and the Pelagian challenge. It may also reveal, as Burnaby suggests,
Augustine's heightened preoccupation with his own
diminishing confidence to "persevere" in the spirit.[63]

Whereas for Irenaeus, Jesus Christ
recapitulates the entire purpose of and possibility
for creation, Augustine's Christ is he who draws our
attention to the corruption of our own voluntary capacity in contrast to the grace of God. For Augustine,
we are non posse non peccare (not able not to sin)
without spiritual help, or grace, given to us by God
in Jesus Christ.

> For there was need to prove to man
> how corruptly weak he was, so that
> against his iniquity, the holy law
> brought him no help towards good,
> but rather increased than diminished
> his iniquity; seeing that the law
> entered, that the offense might
> abound; that being thus convicted,
> he might see not only that he needed
> a physician ... and, in this way,
> where sin abounded grace might much
> more abound--not through the merit
> of the sinner, but by the interven-
> tion of his Helper.

121

> Accordingly, the apostle [Paul]
> shows that the same medicine was mys-
> tically set forth in the passion and
> resurrection of Christ.64

Augustine's Christ is not simply the
Irenaean-Schleiermacherian archetype of a perfected
humanity, in whose person God and humanity are mingled
in the unity of creative purpose and will. Augustine's Christ is "Helper" in that he is Judgment upon
our unnatural unwillingness to submit ourselves to
God's will. Whereas free will is, for Irenaeus,
always a valuable and potent dimension of human experience, it is, for Augustine, a corrupted device by
which humanity is bound to sin and evil.

For both Irenaeus and Augustine, grace
is God's free gift to humanity, given (Augustine) or
revealed (Irenaeus) in Christ. The distinction here
is important. For Irenaeus, grace has been present
and active in the world from the beginning, via the
creative and revelatory Logos. What has been true all
along in history comes to light in the person of Jesus
Christ. Grace is not new. What is new in Christ is
humanity's realization of grace; this is not simply,
for Irenaeus, a psychological awareness of the good,
but rather is a wholly transforming appropriation of
the reality of both humanity's and God's purposeful
creativity.

For Augustine, the grace given by God
in Jesus Christ is new, set directly in opposition to
the "old" assumption that humanity could achieve anything good on its own--for example, by adhering to
God's commandments. Prior to Jesus Christ, humanity
was in bondage to its own sin: after the Fall, there
was no revelation of grace at all; grace was "con-
cealed," "hid under a veil" from the Jews. Thus, the
Christ event is, for Augustine, more than recapitulation; it is revolution.

For Irenaeus, Christ's earthly life is
in continuity with human history. For Augustine,
Christ appears in drastic discontinuity with human
history. Augustine's Christ is not simply a high-
point in human history; he is the reversal of human
history. In Christ, we are turned from death to life.
For Augustine, free will is not held up by Christ as
that which can be perfected, but rather is put down as
the seat of evil in the world and, hence, as that

which must be overcome completely by the infusion of
grace at God's initiative.

Augustine develops an elaborate dualism
in his major work, in which the spirit-flesh dualism
characterizes the citizenry of the "two cities." The
"City of God" is the society in which humanity becomes
spiritual, even in the flesh; the "City of Men [sic]"
is the society in which people become fleshly, even in
the soul.[65] The two cities co-exist on earth throughout history and are separated only at the Last Judgment, at which point the residents of the City of God
will be ushered into perfect peace with God, and the
residents of the other city cast into eternal damna-
tion. World history has moved on its linear course
from its naturally good created state, through the
Fall and condemnation of all humanity, through the
gracious Incarnation of Absolute Spirit in flesh and
the offering of redemption to the elect, to the present (whether in 413 or 1980), in which the entire universe is divided between two cities, and in which the
redeemed experience themselves as "resident aliens" of
this world.

The Platonic ideal of the spiritual led
Augustine into a dualism only slightly less gripping
than the cosmic divisions in the Manichean system.
Augustine believed that this world, and humanity, must
be naturalized (spiritualized) in order to really be
at all.[66] We encounter a split in Augustine himself--
between the "humanist" who affirms creation as essentially good and even now under the power of redemption, and the "ascetic" who longs to escape the world
and the flesh, writing, "Any peace we have on earth
... is more like a solace for unhappiness than the joy
of beatitude."[67]

Augustine's mature theodicy is best
able to be lifted out of his anti-Pelagian thought,
which culminates in The City of God. Pelagianism represented to Augustine what, for us, might be envisioned fairly as the Irenaean position drawn out to an
extreme fixation on humanity's posse, or possibilitas.
I imagine that Irenaeus, like Augustine, would have
been disturbed by Pelagius' non-developmental and completely individualistic concept of free will in the
context of a disconnected and unrelated series of
human acts. Pelagius set forth no concept of human
growth or movement, and no doctrine of humanity as a
corporate body. The Pelagian human being is the

individual possessor of free will.[68]   But Irenaeus,
despite striking differences from Pelagius on the
basis of radically different doctrines of both God and
humanity, also plants seeds for a theology of humanity
--that is, a theology founded upon positive anthropo-
logical and social assessments.

        In the Irenaean schema, God's relation
to evil is presented in Christ as God's purposeful and
developmental creation, which involves evil so that,
by contrast, humanity may know, appreciate, and choose
good.   In Augustinian theodicy, God's relation to evil
is conceptualized as that of pure goodness (God) which,
attempting to overcome spiritually its own deficiency
or privation (evil), is thwarted by humanity's
refusal to cooperate--until, in Christ, evil is van-
quished at last, once and for all, as a significant
theoretical problem.   For all practical purposes,
evil, suffering, and death may provide occasions for
humanity's spiritualization--or rising above present
distress.[69]

        At base-line, Augustine's theodicy is a
matter of aesthetics.   Why did a wholly good God with
foreknowledge of human disobedience create humanity
with free will?   Why does an omnipotent God allow
human freedom, and with it evil, to go unchecked in
the world?   "As oppositions of contraries lend beauty
to the language, so the beauty of the course of this
world is achieved by the opposition of contraries
...."[70]   "The universe is beautified even by sinners,
though, considered by themselves, their deformity is a
sad blemish."[71]

              For God would never have created any,
              I do not say angel, but even man, whose
              future wickedness he foreknew, unless
              He had equally known to what uses in
              behalf of the good He could turn him,
              thus embellishing the course of the
              ages, as it were an exquisite poem set
              off with antithesis ....[72]

        Madden and Hare contend that, unlike
Augustine, Karl Barth evades the theodicy problem, in
declaring that faith alone is justification enough of
God.[73]   I think, however, that Barth not only stands
in continuity with the Augustinian tradition, but also
clarifies it.   He does this by his insistence upon
fides sola gratia as the way--the only way--to an

                            124

appreciation of God's complete goodness and omnipotence in relation to creation, humanity, and evil:

> "I believe" is consummated in a meeting
> with One who is not man, but God, the
> Father, Son, and Holy Spirit, and by my
> believing I see myself completely filled
> and determined by this object of my
> faith. And what interests me is not
> myself with my faith, but He in whom I
> believe. And then I learn that by
> thinking of Him and looking to Him, my
> interests are also best provided for.
> I believe in, credo in, means that I am
> not alone. In our glory and in our misery we men are not alone ....[74]

Like Augustine, Barth believes that God is in relation to humanity ("I am not alone"); and like Augustine, Barth also believes that the divine-human relation is a spiritual relation, of higher value than human relation on the earth. "Creation is not to be undone or to perish. It belongs to its Creator and to no one else"[75]--although from a materialist perspective creation may appear to be undone by evil acts. The Augustinian-Barthian response to evil in history is that material distress is not spiritually calamitous for persons of faith. In the transcendent company of the triune God, there is eternal peace and justice.[76]

In summary, for both Irenaeus and Augustine, God is justified by faith in a process, an order, a harmony, in which evil is employed for good purpose. For Irenaeus, evil provides moral contrast, strengthening humanity's capacity--will power--to do what is good. For Augustine, it enables aesthetic contrast, enhancing the beauty of the universe. In neither case do the theologians pose the question of why contrast in the world is good. Is such a world really better than a world devoid of contrast and full of life and pleasure? There is no answer forthcoming. Leibniz echoes these early Christian writers in his famous assertion that God has created the best possible world. How do we know this? Because what else would a wholly good and omnipotent God do?

We return to Auschwitz, where it makes no moral sense to speak of evil as childlike and immature; or as an ultimately unreal experience in a tran-

sitory "city." It makes no sense to imagine a City of
God in which eternal happiness is given to believers
and a city of humanity in which non-believers are cast
into the hell-fires of furnaces. Such a statement is
incredible "in the presence of the burning children"
(Greenberg).

As Barth reveals, these Christian theodicies lead us full circle back to the faith which
claims invulnerability to reason. In the praxis of
evil, an easy affirmation of God's position, without
concommitant assessment of humanity's position, stands
on faith and topples on good sense. Neither heavenly
nor eschatological promises of perfection speak adequately to the questions of why humanity suffers evil
here and now, and of what we might reasonably do about
it.

A Response to Irenaean and Augustinian Assumptions

I must have justice or I will destroy
myself. And not justice in some
remote infinite time and space, but
here on earth, and that I could see
myself. I have believed in it. I
want to see it, and if I am dead by
then, let me rise again, for if it all
happens without me, it will be too
unfair. Surely I haven't suffered
simply that I, my crimes and my suffering, may manure the soil of the
future harmony for somebody else.77

Human Irresponsibility

Irenaeus made a case for humanity's
imperfection, or immaturity. We are made in the image
and aspire to the likeness of God. Moral evil is
functionally indispensable to our growth toward perfection. Evil is as vital to human life as imperfection is to our perfectability. What is most problematic in Irenaean (and Schleiermacherian) theodicy is
the lack of human responsibility for evil in history.
God is, after all, responsible for humanity's original
imperfection, which is the root of moral evil. Only
the Uncreated (God) is perfect; the created (humanity)
is naturally imperfect and therefore bound to sin on
the basis of trial and error in the world. While

126

there may be some valuable instruction in terms of our acceptance of the <u>fact</u> of our imperfection, there is also quick relief <u>from</u> the evil that we do: all things (including evil things) work together for good.

Irenaean theology, refined in modern liberalism, is a theology of humanity, in which we are attaining the likeness of God--that is, the power, knowledge, and goodness which we ascribe to God. Thus, Irenaean theology does not postulate the ultimacy, or radicality, of a divine-human dualism. In order, however, to support the thesis of humanity's divinization, and to take seriously humanity's <u>posse</u>, we must ignore, or rationalize, the ruinous dimensions of moral evil in history. For as long as we can place evil under the rubric of humanity's movement toward perfection via trial and error, we can imagine that evil is something we are learning our way out of rather than as a given in human experience; as something we outgrow, rather than as something for which we are <u>immediately</u> responsible.

The question of how we move from present imperfection to future perfection is not as significant in Irenaean thought as our faith in the movement itself, an eschatological faith. Our attention is averted from present responsibility for evil in the world to an anticipation of future perfection, which is being effected by God--irrespective, ultimately, of what we do or do not do. In effect, we are being subsumed by divine process.

Our voluntary faith in this process is more important than our voluntary participation in it. Religion supercedes ethics. A natural process of perfection transcends our choices to proceed or not. A sense of monistic unity with God, a single stream flowing toward the future, is stronger than our experience of relation to God which we choose to accept or reject. The determinism of a happy ending seems more real to us than the possibility of effecting justice in the present world and of thereby creating the happy ending.

In short, we do not need <u>relation</u> to God. We are <u>in</u> God (panentheism). And whereas we are growing, becoming perfect "like" God, God has been perfect all along--impassive, unchanging--and hence is completely unaffected by our choices and acts. The Irenaean God transcends human experiences and, transforms human error, human evil, into eschatological good.

Unlike Irenaeus, Augustine placed the responsibility for evil directly on humanity's dis- obedience of divine command. As we have seen, Augus- tine—and with him most of Western Christendom—empha- sizes sin and evil in the world and contrasts this fallen human condition with God's goodness, which is essentially and eternally above the world. Augus- tinian theology effectively discourages us from taking too seriously our _posse_ to know and do what is _good_ in the world.

While _Irenaeus_ can be faulted for his failure to acknowledge our immediate responsibility to come to terms with our own _evil_ effects, _Augustine_ can be cited as having failed to acknowledge emphatically our immediate responsibility to know and do what is _good_ in the world. Here are flip sides of the coin. Both theologies are set in a gap between the human experience of what is real (present, immediate, worldly) and what is ideal (not yet present, in need of mediation, to be enjoyed in an other-worldly arena of human experience). Irenaeus and Augustine charted theological responses to the same dilemma: how to live in the gap between loneliness and relationality, injustice and right relation. But the Irenaean and Augustinian solutions fall short of helping us under- stand ourselves as _agents of both moral good_ (justice) and _moral evil_ (injustice) _in the world_.

If, as Irenaeus understood, God cannot be contrasted with humanity; if the ideal, or ultimate meaning of all creation, is not resident in a city above human experience; if God is, rather, active in human relation, then _Augustine's_ anti-Pelagian assault on human _posse_ signals the inadequacy of his doctrine of creation. Grasping the reality of human evil with- out grasping also the reality of human good, Augus- tinian theology becomes a bedrock of our senses of self as universally, unavoidably, and irresponsibly corrupt. However compelling the light we may have seen before, beyond, and among us, we are immediately and tragically bound to be "children of darkness" (Reinhold Niebuhr).

If, as Augustine realized, humanity is in an evil condition, then _Irenaeus'_ anti-Gnostic denial of the radicality of evil in the world signals the inadequacy of his doctrines of free will, sin, and evil. Believing that humanity can attain the likeness of God without acknowledging that this does not happen without human choice to do good and not to do evil here and now, Irenaean theology can legitimate too readily the notion of humanity's elevation to a perfection that transcends morality. However terrifying our experiences of brokenness, alienation, and injustice, we "children of light" rise upward through the dark into full union with God.

In the Augustinian schema, the divine-human relation is misperceived. God and humanity relate to each other like the protagonist in a cosmic play. An "original" over-and-againstness characterizes the relation. The drama unfolds around a struggle between higher and lower, stronger and weaker, better and worse characters. There is no room for the possibility of voluntary and mutual relation between God and humanity.

The Irenaean schema is subtler and more interesting to me. Here too I believe that the divine-human relation is misconceived. But for Irenaeus, and later for Schleiermacher, the problem is not that God is personalized as a divine actor with whom we are locked in struggle. The dualism is less strident. Irenaeus may be read as coming rather close to a perception of God as the power in relation, or of humanity's creative power. The Irenaean God is not a heavenly "person" who may or may not choose to intervene in human affairs. Human affairs are in God. The dualism in the Irenaean-Schleiermacherian schema is one of time--an experiential gap between present and future, "yet" and "not yet," immediacy and eschatology, lower and higher (elevated) condition, or between immediate human experience and its ultimate meaning, which may be a subtler dualism between humanity and God.

There may be no way to experience present reality in the world--our pain and divisions, wars and hunger, confusions and fears--without hoping for a distinction between what is happening here and now and what will happen someday. But this existential distinction too readily becomes a gap--a dualism--at the active juncture of moral imperative: what do we do in the creation of the future? If we cannot imagine that we ourselves participate in shaping the future, we will imagine either that the future is already created (predestined by God), or perhaps even that "the power of the future" creates the present.[78] In either case, humanity is relieved from ultimate responsibility for what happens in history.

Eschatology

Our participation in creating the future presupposes our knowledge of good and evil. But traditional Christian teachings advise us that we ought <u>not</u> to know good and evil. The image of the Fall (Genesis 2:15-24) reflects human error, specifically the error of seeking moral knowledge, the act which unleashes evil in history. Humanity impales itself on the moralism that we ought to give up the pretense of knowing good and evil and accept gladly an infinitely wide gap between divine omniscience and human ignorance. We are not, and ought not to experience ourselves to be, like God in the present world at the present time. To the extent that we are unwilling to abdicate responsibility for knowing and doing good, we are bound to do evil. Our search for the knowledge of good and evil is an evil quest, since, as seekers, we proudly challenge the moral dualism between divinity and humanity. In orthodox Christianity there is no greater sin than pride.

Early Christian attacks on the salvific benefits of <u>gnosis</u> may provide some indication of the fervor with which anti-Gnostic Christians denounced the human effort to <u>know</u> good and evil. To be a faithful and orthodox Christian is to be innocent of this knowledge. It is to let God be God and to accept the lot of humanity as one of ignorance, hence ineffectiveness, as proactive agents of good in the world.

The problems with the relation between an omniscient and perfect God and an ignorant and imperfect humanity are serious. First, there is the problem of humanity's moral passivity, our resignation to evil, in the world. It is ultimately more important--more effective--to pray to God than to work together to create a just world. Rather than seeking to know, and thereby to effect, what is happening here and now, we are tempted to wonder at God's mysterious ways, and to believe that we cannot know or effect seriously the dynamics of our life together on earth.

130

Second, it presupposes the existence and activity of either (a) a transcendent and wholly other deity, essentially extrinsic to human life (Augustine), or (b) a deity moving in human life, ultimately irrespective of human choice (Irenaeus). In either case, we may assume that God does or will finally determine humanity's course, and, with or without our chosen participation, will effect the redemption of humanity and the world itself.

Third, if we take seriously the problem of evil in history—such as in the Holocaust—we come to the question of when, how, and under what conditions, God will save the people. Six million Jews are exterminated; countless millions of people in history are starved, tortured, put to death unjustly. Are we to understand the redemption of humanity only as an eschatological (future) event, effected by God? As God's final salvific benefit to be enjoyed in some other time and place than the present world, in some future arena of human and divine life?

This understanding of redemption presupposes the ultimacy of an essentially ahistorical deity and the penultimacy of human life in the world. It presumes a scale of higher and lower values: God is more valuable than humanity; heaven, more valuable than earth; the future realm of God, more valuable than present relation. To understand redemption eschatologically is to attribute penultimate value to ourselves and to what we experience as real in the present world. There is always something more, something better, than our life together on earth. Even such a moral outrage as the Holocaust cannot be taken with ultimate seriousness, for, in the end, God will redeem the world, including perhaps the Jews and other (non-Christian) victims of humanity's injustice to humanity.

The alternative to an eschatological interpretation of redemption is not a protological one, in which we long for a return to a primordial state of innocence. In either case, our focus is distracted from the present and drawn to the mistaken value of human ignorance (or false innocence).[79] In terms of moral effect, there is little difference between eschatology and protology.

How then are we to understand redemption? Elie Wiesel pushes us beyond eschatology toward

131

an understanding of redemption, first and most importantly, as the liberation of human beings from unjust
relation in the present world. The responsible
alternative to eschatological and protological schemes
of redemption is that of immediate redemption. We
seek to make right relation between and among ourselves here and now. Our power in relation compels us
to take and eat the fruit of the tree of the knowledge
of good and evil, and to thereby know that the power
in relation is good--redemptive--in and for the present world. Our redemption is our justice, between and
among persons whose relation to neighbor as self is
our fundamental, constitutive and overwhelming prior-
ity in the world. There is no greater a commandment,
no more effective an act.

The Politics of Dispassion

Justice is love, the relational act,
the actualization of constant possibility. The immediate and intimate power in relation is ever present--
here and now--to be affirmed, made incarnate, in the
world. To love passionately, to "have a passion" for
justice, is to be willing to bear up (suffer) the
pain, pleasure, ambiguity, tension, and "becoming"
aspects of relation.

To love passionately, to touch and be
touched, transformed and transforming, is to live on
earth "as it is in heaven"; to know ourselves in rela-
tion--not monistic oneness (Spinoza), but rather as
voluntarily co-operative, expressing a relation so
constitutive of who we are as to be "the original"
(Schleiermacher) experience of what it means to be
human: to be able to love, to act relationally, to
know what we are doing, and to believe that it is good.

. . .

Perhaps the most thoroughgoing experi-
ence shared by contemporary feminists is that the personal is political. There is relation between world
and home, society and self.

We realized that while each woman's
life follows a distinctive course,
there is a general pattern that
unites us all. We realized that

132

women inhabit a different culture
from that inhabited by men. We
realized that our relationships
with men, no matter how intimate,
were governed by certain unequal
distribution of power--educational,
economic, social, political, and
physical .... The feminist experience has ... enabled us to penetrate
the superficial differences [among
women] to see the systemic and psy-
chic links between the various forms
of injustice.[80]

Challenging Reinhold Niebuhr's "Christian realism," in which a personal ethic is held to
bear no necessary relation to a social ethic, Sheila
Collins and other North American feminist theologians,
such as Beverly Wildung Harrison, Delores Williams,
Rosemary Radford Ruether and Judith Plaskow, affirm
that personal (private) and political (public) acts
are bound up in a single ethic; and moreover that
theological ethics are expressions of human actions
which are at once of private and public value.

Lesbian feminist artist Holly Near
echoes this theme:

Linger on the detail
the part that reflects the change
there lies revolution
our everyday lives
the changes inside
become our political selves[81]

Decisions which we tend to regard as
"our business"--such as whether to marry, eat meat,
have children, go to church--have public meaning and
value. Each of us is one weaver among many of a relational tapestry, the social order. If we choose to
pull out a particular thread and put another in its
place, the social fabric may or may not be weakened
(depending upon from whose perspective), but it is
changed in any case. New patterns begin to emerge:
social change.

The burgeoning issue of sexuality pro-
vides an example of the systemic linkage between private and public interest.[82] As John Stuart Mill,
Friedrich Engels, and contemporary scientists such as

John Money and Jean Baker Miller have demonstrated, sex roles are not private parts played out between individuals whose acts remain peculiarly irrelevant to the larger social order. An unmarried woman's decision to keep her baby and a married woman's decision to keep her name are not simply personal matters. They are matters of public interest and record. Such decisions contribute to the shaping of public policy and social values.

To make a "private" matter public--such as in "coming out" as a gay man or lesbian or in acknowledging that one has had an abortion--is to unveil the political dimensions of what is commonly and naively held to be strictly personal. To speak publicly at all of one's sexuality is to lend recognition to what has been for generations an important economic and political issue among shapers of social value and policy. Sexuality has never been a private matter. It has always been an issue of pressing public interest--largely negative and proscriptive. Hence, to "come out," "go public," is to name social reality, and to participate in its re-imaging. It is to lift up for re-assessment a piece of covert public policy which needs overt public attention.

The basic issue is relational responsibility. We do not grow in incubators. We are not alone in the world. We are in relation. Nothing that I do is simply "my business." To pretend that it is is to boast that I am stuffed into myself, untouched and non-suffering; relishing primarily my body, my property, my psyche, my needs, my work, my spouse, my friend, my ideas, my creativity, my sexuality, my self, my "God." It is to be puffed up with constant desire to be singled-out and non-co-operative. It is to be alienated and hollow, having "Shape without form, shade without colour/Paralyzed force, gesture without motion" (T. S. Eliot). As the poet images,

This is the way the world ends
Not with a bang but a whimper.[83]

. . .

But in the beginning is the relation, and in the relation is the realm of God. Similarly, in the personal decision is the political value; in the private act is the public good or ill.

This is not to suggest that any one human relationship is, in itself, an agency of social change. For there is no relation "in itself." Every relationship--whether between a person and her friend or between groups of people, nations, religions--is in relation to something else. There is always a "third" something.[84] It may be another person, a group of persons, a topic of interest, a common value, or an otherwise elusive link. The point is that no relation happens in isolation from its social milieu. Thus, no relation is asocial and no act is politically neutral (irrelevant to the dynamics of power in social relations).

Still, social justice cannot be reduced to the sum of an infinite number of good relationships between friends. Right, or mutual, relation helps effect the justice of socio-political structures, but social good and evil (justice and injustice) may transcend the effects of relational power between any two, or twenty, or two thousand persons. It is foolish to imagine that even huge numbers of persons could put an end to all wars, all hunger, all crime, all injustice --forever. If everyone in the United States were to purge her/himself of racism, there would still be South Africa. And if there were no South Africa, there would still be "apartheid"--in Africa, or North America, or Europe--on the basis of psychiatric disease categories, eye color, sexual preference, or on some other basis of fear and antipathy.

The constancy of fear--of whatever we cannot control (dominate); of dunamis, relational power itself--insures the constancy of injustice.[85] Injustice is not, finally, the result of too many good people doing nothing, but rather of too many frightened people doing something so thoroughly, systematically, and often thoughtlessly, that even these same people--good people trying to live in right relation to one another--cannot un-do the systemic evil simply by living good lives from day to day.

Historically, the solution has been revolution--collective action, shaped by social analysis, and implemented on behalf of the possibility of mutual relation in society. But the revolution is never fully won. In time, it is followed by another and then another because social justice is never fully achieved. In the relation is the realm of God, but so also is the fear of God that can break the relation. In every instance, human beings choose to succumb to

fear or to suffer the fear--bear it up (which is our
courage)--in working for right relation in our friendships and homes, our classrooms and offices, our par-
ishes and cities and prisons and governments.

. . .

Justice is the fruit of human passion,
deep love that is willing to bear up fear and tension
and uncertainty in relation to persons, issues, and
possibilities known and unknown. Our passion enables
us to act together rather than separately; co-opera-
tively rather than competitively; on the basis of an
original bonding rather than on the assumption of a
dualistic gap between us, and between our experiences
of what is real and what is ideal (how things once
were, will someday be, and never are).

Passion inspires voluntary bonding.
There is no passion in domination and submission, in
one character's control over another, whether between
God and humanity, you and me, or us and them. To
affirm our relation, to acknowledge the dynamic
between us of reaching and groping and touching and
tension, is to choose to take you as seriously as I do
myself and myself as seriously as I do you. It is to
say Yes to the possibility of giving and receiving in
relation to you; of needing you and being needed by
you; of acting with you in the world; of re-presenting
you in history; of joining with you to do something in
the world, for the world. Passion makes love in the
world. This is exactly what was <u>not</u> made in Auschwitz. Wiesel tells a story of non-relation, a tale of
dispassion so thoroughgoing as to permit the elimina-
tion of human "vermin" in the name of "God."

Dispassion is inculcated by a faulty
Christian hermeneutic which has theological roots in
Irenaean and Augustinian thought. A word of acknowledgement and warning. Patristics provides vital and
constructive information for contemporary Christian
praxis and theology: historical data and helpful perspective on theological development. We cannot legit-
imately hold persons such as Irenaeus and Augustine
responsible for <u>their</u> failures to speak meaningfully
to <u>our</u> social situations and theological praxis. But
we <u>can</u> cite problems in human life that are legitimated still today by the church's conservative impulse
to reify patristic propositions which <u>may</u> have been

constructive in the second or fifth centuries but
which are proving themselves destructive to people
today.[86] Such is the case, I believe, with the
patristic church's dis-passionate emphases on eschatology and spiritualization, given classic expression
by Irenaeus and Augustine, respectively.

To be dis-passionate is to experience
human brokenness, division, isolation, and alienation
as basic to human life; as the "original" or constitutive human experience. In the beginning is not the
relation, but rather the separation of persons from
persons, humanity from God. Dispassionately, we may
envision an ideal of togetherness and communion. We
may project this ideal into "outer space" rather than
choosing to pursue its discovery in this world, this
time, this place. We may lure ourselves and one
another toward some other time and place in which we
can, and will, live together in the realm of God.
Dispassion may move us toward heaven and the future as
escapes from present opportunity to know and love our
neighbors as ourselves.

Irenaean and Augustinian theodicies are
chiseled in a gap between human pain and its removal;
human experience in the present world and our hope for
another world. These theodicies reflect an overwhelming tension between what is real for us in the world
and what is real for us above the world (Augustine);
tension between what we experience now and what we
will experience at the end (Irenaeus). Augustine
emphasizes the radical disjuncture between human life
in the world and the City of God above the world. The
depth of alienation between God (the Good) and fallen
humanity eliminates the possibility of human choice to
do good in the world. As we have seen, the tension,
even incongruity, for Irenaeus is between now and
later, an imperfect humanity and its eschatological
perfection, a maturation process that may transcend
our moral choice.

In either case we are dissuaded from
our effort to establish the realm of God--immediately,
on earth. We are convinced that there is, or will be,
something of greater ultimacy than human passion in
relation, human justice in the world. We have learned
to believe that this "something" is "God," whose ultimate (most important) home is above the world and/or
beyond history. Raising "God" up, we put ourselves

down. The value of the earth, history, and humanity
pales under heaven. And the fate of humanity and of
God-with-us is sealed by our indifference to ourselves.

FOOTNOTES: CHAPTER IV

[1] Latin, pub. Cologne, 1695; translated, Francis Pott, 1861.

[2] Cecil Frances Alexander, 1846.

[3] Elie Wiesel, A Jew Today, p. 18.

[4] I use the word "theodicy" advisedly here, realizing that the philosophical effort to justify God has seldom been granted its serious due in the history of Christian thought. Because an unqualified theism cannot be reconciled logically or rationally with the human experience of suffering and death, theodicy has been dismissed by Christian theology most often under the rubric of "faith." See Edward H. Madden and Peter H. Hare, Evil and the Concept of God (Springfield, Ill.: Charles C. Thomas, 1968), for a philosophical assessment of Christian theology's difficulties with theodicy. The dismissal of theodicy has been most often an implicit one of omission rather than the explicit denunciation of theodicy per se. Irenaeus and Augustine may come as close to any Christian theologians to an articulation of explicit theodicy. Why? Perhaps because Irenaeus was struggling with a theological adversary that offered a "heretical" alternative to the concept of worship of a wholly good God--specifically, the creator Demiurge of Gnosticism; and because Augustine was attempting to refute, first, the notion of good and evil "substances" (Manicheism) and, later, the Pelagian insistence upon humanity's posse non peccare (capacity not to sin). Both Irenaeus and Augustine were responding directly to theological challenges which drew them into the arena of theodicy, or the attempt to "save God's reputation" (Beverly W. Harrison, in conversation, Union Theological Seminary, March 20, 1979). Nonetheless, theodicy can be gleaned only implicitly in their thought since neither Irenaeus nor Augustine makes allowance for the basic questions to which theodicy leads: is God omnipotent? is God wholly good? Unable in faith to pose these questions, Irenaeus and Augustine proceed, on the assumption of God's omnipotence and goodness, to explicate the relation of God to humanity and to evil. This theological process, founded on the assumption of a wholly good and omnipotent God, is Christian theodicy. It is, I believe, less honest than the theodicy of the rationalists (for example, Hume); but perhaps it is fair to say that Irenaeus and Augustine present God's relation to evil as honestly and as thoroughly as any major Christian theologian.

[5]My primary resources here are John Hick, _Evil and the God of Love_ (Glasgow, Scotland: William Collins Sons & Co., Ltd., 1968); and Michael Galligan, _God and Evil_ (New York: Paulist Press, 1976).

[6]Irenaeus, _Against Heresies_, in _The Ante-Nicene Fathers_, Vol. I, pp. 307-567, edited by the Rev. Alexander Roberts and James Donaldson (Grand Rapids: William B. Eerdmans Publishing Co., 1975), Bk. IV:38, p. 522.

[7]In his "Introductory Note" to _Against Heresies_ in _ANF_, Vol. I, A. Cleveland Coxe emphasizes the anti-Gnostic impetus of Irenaeus' writings. "The task of Irenaeus was twofold: (1) to render it impossible for any one to confound Gnosticism with Christianity, and (2) to make it impossible for such a monstrous system to survive, or ever to rise again." Still, Coxe notes, that Irenaeus was killed, "like a true shepherd, with thousands of his flock, in the massacre (202 A.D.) stimulated by the wolfish Emperor Severus" (p. 310).

[8]Aloys Grillmeier, _Christ in Christian Tradition_ (London: Mowbray, 1965), p. 100.

[9]Coxe, "Introductory Note" to _Against Heresies_, p. 311.

[10]Oscar Cullmann, _Christ and Time_ (London: SCM Press, 1962), pp. 56-7.

[11]Richard A. Norris, in lecture at Union Theological Seminary, New York, May 1, 1978. Norris points out that for Irenaeus, the Father, Son and Holy Spirit are "equally creating and revealing persons, doing one and the same thing." Why then the Trinity? "Tradition."

[12]Ibid.

[13]Richard A. Norris, lecture, May 1, 1978.

[14]Hick, _Evil and the God of Love_, p. 218.

[15]Irenaeus, _Against Heresies_, IV:38:4, p. 522.

[16]Irenaeus, _Against Heresies_, 38:4, p. 522.

[17]Ibid., 39:1, p. 522.

[18]Irenaeus, _Against Heresies_, 27:1, p. 518.

[19]Ibid., IV:37:2, p. 519.

[20]Irenaeus, 41, pp. 524f.

[21]Fragments from the Lost Writings of Irenaeus (from the Catena on St. Paul's Epistles to the Corinthians), Ante-Nicene Fathers, p. 575.

[22]Irenaeus, Against Heresies, IV:41:3, p. 525.

[23]Irenaeus, Against Heresies, II:26:1, p. 397.

[24]Robert F. Brown, "Irenaeus' Two Schemata of Salvation," unpublished M.A. thesis, Union Theological Seminary/ Columbia University, New York, 1967.

[25]Irenaeus, Against Heresies, IV:38, p. 522.

[26]Hick, Evil and the God of Love, p. 221.

[27]Irenaeus, Against Heresies, IV:37, p. 520.

[28]Ibid., III:25, p. 459.

[29]Hick, Evil and the God of Love, p. 225.

[30]Hick, Evil and the God of Love, pp. 221-224, cf. Clement's Stromata, vi:11, 12; and Protrepticus, 11; and Gregory's Oration, 45, 47, 48: "[T]he Irenaean or eschatological approach to the problem of evil lay virtually dormant within Christendom ... until it awoke again in the mind of Schleier-macher," p. 225.

[31]Friedrich Schleiermacher, The Christian Faith, ed. by H. R. Mackintosh and J. S. Stewart, Eng. trans. of second German ed. (Philadelphia: Fortress Press, 1928; rep., 1976), p. 233.

[32]R. R. Niebuhr, Schleiermacher on Christ and Religion (New York: Charles Scribner's Sons, 1964), p. 206.

[33]Schleiermacher, The Christian Faith, pp. 281f.

[34]Ibid., pp. 271f.

[35]Ibid., p. 293.

[36]Ibid., p. 190.

[37]Ibid., p. 315.

[38] Ibid., p. 322.

[39] Ibid., p. 321.

[40] Ibid., p. 270.

[41] For example, Henri Bergson, H. N. Wieman, Edgar Brightman, Alfred North Whitehead, Teilhard de Chardin, Charles Hartshorne, Josiah Royce, Norman Pittenger, and John A. T. Robinson. See Madden and Hare for an assessment of the "quasi-theism" of Brightman, Whitehead, Hartshorne, and Royce, pp. 104-132.

[42] Irenaeus, Against Heresies, IV:37, p. 520.

[43] Hick, Evil and the God of Love, p. 218.

[44] Ibid., p. 220.

[45] Augustine, The City of God, Great Books of the Western World, Vol. 18 (Chicago: Encyclopedia Britannica, Inc., 1952), Bk. XIII:14, p. 366.

[46] Augustine, Confessions, translated by R. S. Pine-Coffin (New York: Penguin Press, 1961), Bk. VII:14, p. 149.

[47] Ibid., VII:1, p. 134.

[48] Augustine, Confessions, VII:10, p. 173.

[49] Ibid., VII:14, p. 150.

[50] C. N. Cochrane, Christianity and Classical Culture (London: Oxford University Press, 1940), pp. 363, 376.

[51] Augustine, Confessions, VII:20, p. 154.

[52] Peter Brown, Augustine of Hippo (Berkeley: University of California Press, 1967), p. 95.

[53] Cochrane, Christianity and Classical Culture, p. 425.

[54] Brown, Augustine of Hippo, p. 316.

[55] Ibid., p. 93.

[56] Augustine, The City of God, ed. by Vernon J. Bourke (Garden City, N.Y.: Image Books, 1958), Bk. VII, p. 346.

[57]John Burnaby, _Amor Dei_: _A Study of the Religion of St. Augustine_ (London: Hodder and Stoughton, 1938), p. 35.

[58]R. E. Cushman, "Faith and Reason," pp. 287-314 in _A Companion to the Study of St. Augustine_, ed. by Roy W. Battenhouse (New York: Oxford University Press, 1955), p. 310.

[59]Brown, _Augustine of Hippo_, p. 175.

[60]_The City of God_ (Bourke), XI, p. 228.

[61]Ibid., XII, p. 250.

[62]Burnaby, _Amor Dei_, p. 37.

[63]Ibid., pp. 214-16.

[64]Augustine, "On the Spirit and the Letter," in _The Nicene and Post-Nicene Fathers_, First Series, Vol. V—St. Augustine: _Writings Against the Pelagians_, pp. 79-114 (Grand Rapids: William B. Eerdmans, 1971), p. 86.

[65]E. R. Hardy, Jr., "The City of God," in Battenhouse (pp. 257-283), pp. 267f.

[66]S. R. Hopper, "The Anti-Manichean Writings," in Battenhouse (pp. 148-174), p. 169.

[67]_The City of God_ (Bourke), XIX, p. 480.

[68]B. B. Warfield, "Introductory Essay on Augustine and the Pelagian Controversy," in _The Nicene and Post-Nicene Fathers_, pp. xiii-lxxi.

[69]In the thirteenth century, Thomas Aquinas reiterated Augustine's view of evil as privative; and to the _utrum_, "Whether the highest good, God, is the cause of evil,?" Aquinas responded that "it is manifest that the form which God chiefly intends in created things is the good order of the universe. Now, the order of the universe requires, ..., that there should be some things that can, and sometimes do, fail. And thus God, by causing in some things the good of the order of the universe, consequently and, as it were by accident, causes the corruption of things ... God does not will death for its own sake. Nevertheless, the order of justice belongs to the order of the universe; and this requires that penalty should be dealt out to sinners. And so God is the author of the evil which is penalty, but not of the evil which is fault ...." (_The Summa Theologica_, I.Q.49.Art. 3, in _Introduction to St. Thomas Aquinas_, ed. with

Introduction by Anton C. Pegis, New York: Modern Library, 1948, pp. 276-9). In other words, God is not the cause of evil. An event or act that appears to be evil is, in fact, good to the extent that it is not "for its own sake" but rather for the sake of a higher good that God would permit or cause it to happen. Aquinas made no basic theological alteration in the Platonic Augustinian notion of the spiritual as the highest good, which overcomes evil, and which is itself in no way responsible for evil in the world. In Aquinas as in Augustine, we meet two different worlds--spiritual and material--ordered cosmologically and ontologically in hierarchical relation. God is in the higher; humanity and evil, in the lower. This same ontology leads into the Reformation theologies of Luther and Calvin and, later, to their apologist par excellence, Karl Barth (see note 76).

[70]Augustine, The City of God, Great Books, XI:18, p. 332.

[71]Ibid., XI:23, p. 335.

[72]Ibid., XI:18, p. 331.

[73]Madden and Hare, Evil and the Concept of God, pp. 20-36.

[74]Karl Barth, Dogmatics in Outline (New York: Harper and Row, 1959), p. 16.

[75]Barth, Church Dogmatics (Edinburgh: T. & T. Clark, 1961), III.2, p. 148.

[76]Barth, Church Dogmatics, IV.1, pp. 246-8. Barth sees the resolution to the problem of evil in the passion, crucifixion, and resurrection of Christ. For Barth, God the Son suffers evil and God the Father overcomes it. "The problem posed is not that of a theodicy: How can God will this or permit this in the world ...? It is a matter of the humiliation and dishonouring of God Himself, of the question which makes any question of a theodicy a complete anticlimax; the question whether in willing to let this happen to Him He has not renounced and lost himself as God ..., whether He can really die and be dead. And it is a matter of the answer to this question; that in this humiliation God is supremely alive, that in this death He is supremely alive, that He has maintained and revealed His deity in the passion of this man as His eternal son." Jürgen Moltmann echoes this same theme--of an event between God and God--in The Crucified God (New York: Harper and Row, 1974). More than any modern theologian, Bonhoeffer reflects a shift from this same theme (in Christ the Center, lectures given in 1933), to a focus

on human responsibility for un-doing evil (in Letters and Papers, written in 1943-1945).

[77]Ivan to Alyosha in Fyodor Dostoyevsky's The Brothers Karamazov, The Great Books of the Western World, Vol. 52, translated by Constance Garnett (Chicago: Encyclopedia Britannica, Inc., 1952), p. 126.

[78]Pannenberg refers to God as "the power of the future." See Theology and the Kingdom of God, ed. Richard John Neuhaus (Philadelphia: Westminster Press, 1969, fifth printing, 1977). "God is in himself the power of the future. The reason for this is that the very idea of God demands that there be no future beyond himself. He is the ultimate future" (p. 63). Pannenberg is attempting to emphasize God's freedom in contrast to "the empirical condition of human life" (p. 121). Pannenberg's theology of "postdestination" (my term) is meant to avoid the liabilities of Christian liberalism (in which God's realm is built by human endeavor) and the social irresponsibility of Christian conservatism. His ethical interest is primarily in the individual--hence, his paramount focus on the concept of "freedom." He is critical of "revolutionary movements" which identify their own power structures with the highest good (God). And he reminds Christian activists "of the preliminary state of every possible organization of our world in contrast with the fullness of God's future" (p. 114). Pannenberg suggests that we can do our "best"--that is, live as responsibly as possible in relation to neighbor and world; that whatever "happens" (whatever we do, or don't do) is being done (or not) by a power/God whose eschatological reality and fullness is eternally creative; and that retro-spective vision is, in fact, the true vision, good vision, God's vision. The trouble is that retro-spective vision is impotent as long as it is retro-spective. Pannenberg combines in a fascinating way the Irenaean eschatological focus (what really matters if future) and the Augustinian spiritualization scheme (what really matters is God), to the effect--I believe--of disempowering humanity, stripping us of our sense of power to make a difference and our choice to effect the realm of God.

[79]In discussing the "innocence" of Billy Budd in the Herman Melville novella, Rollo May describes what I refer to as "the mistaken value of human ignorance (or false innocence)": "It consists of a childhood that is never outgrown, a kind of fixation on the past .... When we face questions too big and too horrendous to contemplate, such as the dropping of the atomic bomb, we tend to shrink into this kind of innocence and make a virtue of powerlessness, weakness, and helplessness. This pseudoinnocence leads to utopianism; we do not then need to see the real dangers. With unconscious purpose we close our eyes to reality and persuade ourselves that we have escaped it." Power

and Innocence: A Search for the Sources of Violence (New York:
Dell Publishing Co., 1972), p. 49. May continues, "[This inno-
cence] wilts before our complicity with evil. It is this innocence that cannot come to terms with the destructiveness in one's
self or others; and hence, ... it actually becomes self-destruc-
tive. Innocence that cannot include the daimonic becomes evil
.... [This innocence] is the common defense against admitting or
confronting one's own power" (Ibid., pp. 49-50).

[80]Sheila D. Collins, A Different Heaven and Earth
(Valley Forge, Pa.: Judson Press, 1974), pp. 160-1.

[81]Lyrics from "You Bet!" by Holly Near, Hereford
Music, 1978; on record album, Imagine My Surprise!, Redwood
Cliffs, 1978. True to history, much of what is truly prophetic
is being given expression by artists, such as Adrienne Rich,
Ntozake Shange, Olga Broumas, and Ernesto Cardenal, persons who
see through the sham of personal/political, private/public, and
sacred/profane dualisms and are able to express artistically the
relational character of human life.

[82]See Appendix F for further discussion of
sexuality.

[83]T. S. Eliot, "The Hollow Men," Collected Poems,
1909-1962 (New York: Harcourt, Brace, and World, 1970), pp.
79-82.

[84]Tom F. Driver speaks of this "third" something
in relation. He has been my primary resource here. I realize
the significance of this theme for a doctrine of the Trinity and
appreciate the work Driver is doing in a development of this
theme along trinitarian lines.

[85]See Chapter II, pp. 40-44, and Chapter V, p.153f.

[86]The ecclesiastical condemnation of all sexual
activity outside of marriage bears shrill witness to the church's
"conservative impulse" to legitimate relational attitudes and
behavior marked by fear and dispassion. Taking a defensive posture, church leaders bestow absolute authority on "tradition"
(scripture as interpreted during the patristic period) and set
this authority over and against contemporary relational experience. In this way, the churches (Protestant, Orthodox, Roman)
speak a "language" that is barely intelligible to large numbers
of Christian persons throughout the world. John Paul II is
speaking the language of Cyprian (on centrality of episcopacy),
Augustine (on sexuality), even Vincent of Lérins (on ecclesiastical authority: "quod ubique, quod semper, quod ab omnibus
creditum est"), whereas most people in the world are speaking

146

about food and hunger, love and loneliness, war and peace. Many
have responded enthusiastically to the current pope, I believe,
not because they "hear" or accept what he is saying, but rather
because, in him, they are met by a charismatic and compelling
contradiction between the physicality, sexuality, and relational
warmth of a populist-at-heart and the arrogant "spirituality"
and rigid ecclesiology of a Holy Father. It is the former side
of the split--his dunamis--that draws many people close, and it
will be the latter--his exousia--that "protects" not only John
Paul II from his own dunamis but also many "good Catholics" from
theirs--that is, the church from its own power in relation.

CHAPTER V

PASSION OF HUMANITY: REDEMPTION OF GOD

> We know now we have always been in danger
> down in our separateness
> and now up here together   but till now
> we had not touched our strength.[1]

My anger burns for justice. And it is time. We are ready to learn by doing what we are afraid to think about, because we know already that to touch is to mend brokenness, and that our tender rage may raise the dead.

> Live, by God!
> live by sisters
> and brothers
> pick up your beds
> and walk
>
> yes run
> yes fly
> yes look down
> and back
>
> you will not turn
> into pillars of salt
>
> that was a lie
>
> you will see the world
> you will know humanity
> you will remember yourselves
> as prophets
>
> and you will rage
> and you will be tender
> and you will touch
> and be well

Falling into Co-creation

Look back.

Auschwitz, 1944-1945.[2] Elie Wiesel
could have lived and died without food. He could have
lived and died without his mother, his little sister,
his father. He could have lived and died by beatings,
starvation, cremation. He could have endured these
things, wept and struggled and lived and died madly,
with passion. But at last A-7713 could neither live
nor die with passion--a sense of power in relation.
Because A-7713 had no name.[3] And to have no name is
to have no identity, and to have no identity is to be
without relation, and to be without relation is to be
without humanity. And if one is not human, but rather
only a ghostly apparition of humanity, even to oneself, what is one to do or be except nothing?

If we are nothing; if, by systemic
metamorphosis, we are converted to numbers, robbed of
our names, broken down into pieces of an illusory
whole, stripped of our wills to reach and touch, mea-
sured by cash-flow and security-risk, computed according to sex, gender, color, religion, expediency; if,
in fact, there is increasingly no such thing as humanity, we will neither live nor die with passion. For
there will be nothing to say, nothing to feel, nothing
to do, but be wound up by an insidious invisible key
and slipped with precision from apparition to apparition. Auschwitz offers a radical alternative to human
passion in the world.[4]

So look down
know humanity

Once upon a time the earth creature
had alternatives.[5] "Do not eat." And it did. It
chose to eat. It chose to defy its cryptic God's command (Genesis 2:15-3:7).

And why not? Why should we not eat--
especially of the fruit of the tree of knowledge of
good and evil? Why should we not choose to fill ourselves with a capacity to value ourselves and the
world?

Is something left out of this story?
Something we are not told? Is it possible that human
authors were protecting themselves and us from a

secret too terrible to bear? The secret of humanity itself? Namely, that to be human is to know good and evil and to realize one's power to effect either?

The terror of the secret lies in the terror of relation: in a person's willingness to bear passion; her ability to sustain a sense of her power to make a difference in the world; her agreement to pay the cost of an insistence upon friends.

Might less protective authors have suggested to us that the earth creature's defiance of command was, in fact, its first liberating act from the bondage of a passivity-mistaken-for-innocence which rendered it subject, rather than friend, of God?[6] Might such authors have done well to tell us about human empowerment, in which to become "like God" (Genesis 3:22) is to claim the power to effect good and to contend with evil?

To become "like God" is to become human. So it is that we "fall" into creation.[7] Falling creatively, we ask what God is this God of Genesis/God of Beginnings who desires no friends and needs no help? This God for whom human innocence and human irresponsibility in the world are indistinguishable? This God whose will it is that the earth creature might neither live nor die with passion, any sense of its power to effect the world?

Human authors present here an old story about a puzzled earth creature in defiance of an odd deity. The deity becomes the imaginative construct of humanity's abdication of power to effect; our rejection of responsibility for doing good and un-doing evil in the world. The moral of the story is that it is easier to be ignorant, harder to know; easier to be passive, harder to be aggressive; easier to comply with external authority, harder to claim one's power; easier to be created, harder to create. It is much easier to be established in the garden we have learned to call Paradise than to pick up our beds and walk into the world.

But walk
yes, run
into the world
seek humanity
find God

151

We begin where we are. In time, in the world, as it is in the beginning now and forever. Time is the extension of now. Our time, the only time we have had, the only time we will have, is now, always now. The present. And the reason this matters is that we are now in the world. Wherever Paradise, wherever heaven, we are now in the world. And time-past and time-future have no power, but rather are stretched behind and beyond us by the power of our present necessity to remember, to learn, to hope, and to continue.[8]

And we continue. We go on. History is our movement in the world, our continuation, our collective push, our bodyselves experiencing, we-living, we-dying, day to day, nation to nation, religion to religion, revolution to revolution, century to century. In history, we begin. It can be kairos.[9] There is no time that is not our time, the time, the only time that matters for humanity: now.

. . .

Beginning now, we create: bring into being, make, originate, initiate, act in such a way that by our power in relation something new is effected. A creator is one with the power to effect.

If we fall into the likeness of God, into the possibility of on-going voluntary friendship, into our co-creative capacity; if a creator is one who knows her creativity in relation; if this power is known only in relation--in the intimate and immediate power between self and other--then we are co-creators who reach and are reached, touch and are touched, in the world. To touch is to signify relation. It is the outward and visible sign of co-creation. It is our first co-creative act.

Beginning now, we touch. And it is a struggle. We, you and I, you and we, are born now and always struggling for power to effect in relation to mother, father, friend, stranger, the world itself, into which we come by relation and in which we do not survive except in relation--intimate and immediate bonding. Our ability to survive in the world is fixed in our ability to act effectively in securing what we need: food, shelter, warmth, love--our active reali-zation that we are not alone, and that this is good for others as well as for us. Realizing ourselves as

152

relationally effective, we are co-subjects touching, being touched. Touching is the beginning of creation, the initiation of something new on the basis of common power. To touch is to know ourselves in relation and to signify our desire to do something together that we cannot do alone, simply because we are not alone. To touch is to acknowledge the human condition. And our common condition is a terrible good.[10]

Violation of Relation

        We are afraid
        to see
        the world
        We are afraid
        to know humanity

        The world is created by us, we who are friends of God, we who make God in-carnate. We are afraid to bring God to life.

        Co-creation is our effort to live and die together, a mutual effort, enabled by common choice, effecting common benefit. We are afraid to be common. We are afraid to live and die . . .

        Co-creators, we god in love, a common awareness that no one of us is alone, and that in the relation between subject and subject, there is power. We are afraid to be alone, we are afraid to be together, we are afraid of power.

        Our power is effective. We are afraid to be effective.

        Our power is good. We are afraid to be good.

        We god toward justice, moved by and moving the God given voice by the prophets, the God moving transpersonally in history, by us, through us. We are afraid of justice, we are afraid of the prophets, we are afraid of history.

        So it is in the beginning. We are afraid to re-member ourselves.

153

> But look down
> know humanity
> you will remember

In spite of God, in spite of our relational yearning, six million Jews were fed to furnaces, and blacks were hanged on trees, and wise women were tied to stakes and burned with faggots, and children are beaten to death every day as the earth is raped, and the seas are littered with bodies of refugees, and the deserts are cultivated with atomic particles valued for their capacity to fry humanity, and the cellars of palaces are piled high with members of mutilated men and women whose names are computed away by people who dispose of people with less bother than New York dogwalkers dispose of shit.

Evil is the violation of relation in human life. Radical evil, such as that of the Holocaust, is the violation or breaking apart of relation whereby the power in relation is transgressed so thoroughly as to be ineffective, dead, in human life. Evil is the result of our un-willingness to bear passion--that is, to suffer an active sense of power in relation. Evil is, first, neither God's problem nor the problem of other people than ourselves. Evil is our problem. We can choose, again and again, to claim the power to effect good, or to deny it, and in so doing to effect evil in the world.

Evil is fastened in our fear. We are afraid of power--and of powerlessness. Our fear has become the socially normative, religiously sanctioned, preference to our passion. The destruction of humanity frightens us less than the co-creation of the world. We remember our fear of relation, of power, of touching, of making justice/making love, of sexuality.

. . .

The superintendent of the girls' reformatory instructed us to enforce the rules, the most serious of which was that which proscribed "friendship" between the girls.[11] "There is to be no touching," she emphasized. "Any touching, hand-holding, or embracing should be reported to the cottage supervisors."

154

As she spoke, Trudy, a fifteen year old from the streets of North Philadelphia, lay in the hospital in nearby West Chester. We were later to discover that Trudy had been locked in the "Meditation Unit" (solitary confinement) as punishment for having been caught in bed with another girl. Medically diagnosed as claustrophobic, Trudy had attempted to attract attention and release from the solitary cell by setting her trash can on fire and yelling for help. By the time the guards were able to open the swollen metal door, Trudy had been burned in the third degree over most of her body. A week later she died.

The administration's response to Trudy's death was to further restrict the smoking privileges of all girls and to further lecture the staff on the danger of touching.

. . .

On the one hand we fear our powerlessness. We fear having no control, no say, no vote. Death. On the other hand we fear our power. We fear knowing and choosing God's power as our own in the world. We fear the choices, options, ambiguity in relation. Life.

Fear is incurred in relation. We resist our own possibilities, each other, God. Fearing our power in relation, we deny God. Fleeing God, we break the human bond and subvert God's power in the world. Evil is grounded in our fear of both power and powerlessness; of having no choice (our destiny) and of having options (our freedom) [Tillich]. Moral evil festers in our fearful resistance to ambiguity.12 Seeking to polarize our experiences of reality; seeking to categorize our perceptions of what is what; seeking life without death, freedom without options, truth without change, maturity without growth, God without humanity, humanity without ambiguity, we concoct "final solutions" to situations that may not be problems at all, but rather mysteries that might surprise us with some new sense in our relation, for example, to Jews, to others, to ourselves.

But in our fear we do evil. Seeking solutions to mystery; attempting to control growth and change; trying to impose order upon spontaneity, pluralism, choices, and differences, we are willing to destroy relationality in its enigmatic wonder. We are

155

willing to negate the creative basis of human experience. We are willing to kill humanity in order to
protect humanity from itself. We are willing to put
God to death in order to cling to a deity whom we create in the image of our violent malaise.

It is in the nature of our idol to be
intolerant of ambiguity. His first and only love is
Himself. He is an impassive unflappable character who
represents the headship of a universal family in which
men are best and women least. He is the keeper of an
ethical scorecard on which "reason" gets good marks
and "relation" fails. He is a master plan-maker who
maps out and, by remote-control, directs our journeys
before we have learned to walk. His narcissism is
unquenchable. He demands that he be loved. This cold
deity is the legitimating construct of the patriarchal desire to dominate and control the world. He
is the eternal King, the Chairman of the board, the
President of the institution, the Guru of the youth,
the Husband of the wife, the General of the army, the
Judge of the court, the Master of the universe, the
Father of the church. He resides above us all. He is
our superior, never our friend. He is a rapist, never
a lover, of women and of anyone else beneath Him. He
is the first and final icon of evil in history.

The following poem is meant to articulate my own experience of the patriarchal idol who
legitimates evil in history as the human violation of
voluntary and mutual relation. The characters in the
poem are the dominating male and the victimized female.
These characters could be transposed by another poet--
perhaps into the dominating Christian and the victimized Jew, the dominating "Christ" and the questing
person, or the dominating deity (any dominating deity)
and a submissive humanity, which is, in fact, what my
poem is about: the violation of voluntary and mutual
relation.

> Hold on, daughter,
> do not think
> that your father
> is unaware of you
> do not imagine
> that he is ignorant
> of what you are doing
> do not say, daughter,
> do not say it again

do not tell us again
that you are afraid
of him
and angered by his desire
for you

    Hold on, daughter,
    cling to your innocence
    if you must
    and you must
    remember
    who he is
    and what he does
    for you

        Hold on, daughter,
        to the guardian of your innocence
        to the memory of your delight
        to the memory of his desire
        and your pleasure

            Secure yourself
            hold fast
            for his desire is your life

And lest you doubt us, daughter,
we will remind you of his promise
that he who did not hesitate
to kill
the firstborn of many parents
to save
his son
will not hesitate
to kill
his daughter
to save
his reputation.

        Hold on, daughter
        for your own good
        hold him
        love him
        or at least
        let him believe
        that you do
        for your own good.

Do not think again
of your bruised soul
do not feel again
your battered womb
your bleeding is good
for you
and for him
let him suck your soul
let him pry open your defenses
let him handle your womb
let him touch you, daughter
let him titillate your soul
let him into your womb
because he needs
his sons

Or shall we admit
that we need
your soul
your womb
your blood
because we need
our sons
our brothers
our fathers
our men of God
our Father God

to cope with
the likes of you?

This deity is our promise that in the
beginning is not the relation, but rather "God"; not
touching, but rather nothing but "God"; not human, but
only divine, "creativity"; and not creativity at all,
but rather the negation-by-submission of all that
breathes and grows and changes, humanity itself, and
all creation.

Losing touch, beside ourselves, we
create this deity in the image of our fearful dispassion and bless Him for having created us in His image.
We put ourselves down and raise Him up as the beginning of all that we value in humanity: nothing. He
is the eternal source of all that is above us, unlike
us, not us. Out of our fear of death and fear of life
and fear of the passion that enables us to experience
either life or death, we weave a myth of divine-human
alienation. Alienated from our own possibilitas, from
each other, and from God our friend and lover, out of

158

touch and in the name of the deity we have created, we imagine that we live and die separately "under God." I am on my own, and so are you. I seek comfort from my Master, the deity who assures me that my loneliness is my condition and that my faith in my Master is my only release from this condition, from this time, from this place, and from you.

. . .

> But my anger tenders, burning
> blazing, roaring,
> splintering loneliness--
> No!

There may be nothing more difficult than for us to realize and claim our power to effect good, our capacity to make a positive difference in the world, our co-creative ability to sustain relational passion. It is hard because in relation we are immersed in ambiguity, tension, shifting foci: between self and self, present and past and future, memory and hope, gain and loss, freedom and destiny, what we know and what we dream, what we welcome and what we fear.

To my knowledge, there is no Christian theologian who has held unequivocally that, just as evil is the result of humanity's wrong choices, so too good is the result of humanity's right choices. Christian theologians have tended to berate humanity for evil and praise God for good. This is a serious error, I believe, because humanity cannot un-do evil without doing good, which is a single human act and our common vocation.

Neither good nor evil can be laid on the shoulders of an anthropomorphized deity, for God is "no one" but is rather a transpersonal spirit, power in relation, which depends upon humanity for making good/making justice/making love/making God incarnate in the world. To do so is to un-do evil. The doing of good and un-doing of evil is a human act, a human responsibility. God is our power to do this. We choose this power which is constantly available to us, and it is good. God is a power which we can and do love--that is, actively realize as present and creative in our lives. To love God is to un-do evil. It is a moral imperative, not a sweet feeling, a private personal relation, or a charitable gesture.

159

Because our power frightens us so, from
the beginning we walk the boundary between good and
evil. Evil does not enter history at "the Fall."
There is no person tempting person to take and eat of
a knowledge that subsequently unleashes a reign of
terror on earth. To the contrary, we fall into a
realization of our power to effect good and equally
into the realization of our hesitancy to do so, the
hesitancy with which the earth creature approached the
tree of the knowledge of good and evil. The alternative to the earth creature's decision to eat was its
continuation in passive bondage to the will of some
wholly other, a denial of its power to voluntarily
know and do what is good in the world.

Falling creatively into the knowledge
of good and evil, we are hesitant to claim for ourselves the power that enables us to create the world.
We are tempted to imagine a "God" who assures us, in
our hesitancy, that whatever and wherever is the power
to create in history, it is most certainly not ours,
not here, not now. We are always tempted to rest,
assured that some other(s) will create the world and
set the terms for our minimal service in this on-going
creative process. In so doing, we deny our power to
 ffect good, which is our power to un-do the very evil
that begins to take root in our hesitancy to believe
in ourselves as co-creators.

Our evil is transpersonal, crossing
from persons to persons, nation to nation, generation
to generation.13 In society, good and evil are, at
best, effected on the basis of our decisions as to how
that which is good might be maximized and that which
is evil minimized. Human institutions--religious,
economic, social--rest morally on the foundations of
humanity's knowledge of good and evil and our choices
to effect good rather than evil. The moral fabric of
social institutions such as marriage and family, government, medical and religious establishments, manifests historically a complex and highly ambiguous
interweaving of good and evil intention and effect.

I may intend to do good in relation to
you, and we, in relation to others. But we do not
live in a moral vacuum apart from the structures that
are the constant arenas of our perhaps careful, but
imperfect, learning to know and choose what it means
to love. There is no simply, or purely, good intention or effect between or among us. No one of us, nor

all of us together, can choose to effect good without also experiencing, and maybe choosing to participate in, evil--destruction of the good, the breaking apart of the relation, the co-creation, the power to touch and be touched that we so value here and now. We who co-create must acknowledge our own evil effects.

In order to live creatively, with an active sense of our power to effect good, we must help one another learn to walk more confidently along the boundaries of good and evil. It is a matter of learning to tolerate ambiguity without allowing ourselves to be duped into either the passivity of apathy and indifference, or the panic which seeks final solutions.

Confused and frightened by ambiguity, we find it terribly hard both to confess our sin--that is, our denial of our power in relation--and to realize our deepest yearnings to touch and be touched.[14] It is awkward and difficult simultaneously to acknowledge our on-going participation in the systemic destruction of humanity and to commit ourselves to the healing of a broken humanity. Gestalt psychology reminds us that we do not often see at once both ground and figure; the good and the evil in a single act here and now. In order to see one or the other, in order to acknowledge either, we shift focus, intention, and only then see whatever we are looking for. Our co-creative task is to see at once both ground and figure; to see more fully what we are doing in the world.[15] To see not only what we are looking for, but also what is, in fact, happening. And what is happening is dynamic. There is no stasis. Nothing simply good, nothing simply evil, in human experience, but rather immediate movement between and among us, pushing us toward a realization of our sin, driving us into confession of our participation in evil, moving us sharply into the experience of guilt, which can be immediately the experience of repentance, an act of love, an act of justice, an act effecting good in the world. Our passion drives us into our confession which is always our first just act.

Although we know we participate in evil, we do not welcome evil; we acknowledge it. We acknowledge that we are afraid to take seriously power in relation, but we do not tolerate--accept willingly --this injustice in our own lives or elsewhere in the world. We acknowledge both ground and figure, both good and evil, in our lives and choices, and we are

161

driven again and again by our power in relation to push with tender insistence through our sin into the celebration of ourselves in relation.

At whatever level of human life (individual or communal, race, sex, class, nation), in whatever institution (friendship, family, government, church, business), for whatever reason (greed, selfishness, competition, reputation, war), evil is that which is done by person to person.

Evil breaks apart the power of the relation that binds us together and thereby rips and shatters its victims' realizations of themselves in relation. Evil destroys humanity's sense of power to create in relation to others. Victims of evil (injustice) are rendered subordinate, submissive, dependent upon the will and judgment of masters who have broken the mutuality, the possibility of friendship. Victims of evil are ineffective--unable to effect good--until they are able to reclaim their power, which they can do only in relation. When this happens, when friends revolt against their own oppression, against the evil that is done to them, revolution becomes the act of the people toward mutual relation. Revolution is the effort to establish an order that will be of common benefit to persons equally able to give and receive in relation.[16]

. . .

With you, I begin to realize that the sun can rise again, the rivers can flow again, the fires can burn again.

With you, I begin to see that the hungry can eat again, the children can play again, the women can rage and stand again.

It is not a matter of what "ought" to be.[17] It is a power that drives toward justice and makes it. Makes the sun blaze, the rivers roar, the fires rage. And the revolution is won again. And you and I are pushed by a power both terrifying and comforting.

And "I love you" means, let the revolution begin!

. . .

162

Our alternative is resignation to dispassion, in which we condemn God to death. Persons
who have no passion, no sense of power to effect good
in relation, are incapable here and now of making God
incarnate. And wherever there is no incarnation,
there is no God.

The Redemption of God

and you will be tender
and you will reach out
and touch
and be well

Who will help us god in the world? Who
will help us know good and evil? Who will push us
tenderly but with insistence beyond our hesitation to
claim our power?

A messiah meets us where we are,
between the "yet" and the "not yet," to impress upon
us not who the messiah is, but rather who we are.
Messianism is our incessant longing for an active
realization of our power in the world. Messianism is
as constant a dimension of human experience as the
hesitation with which we tend to approach the "not
yet."[18] Our messianic expectation is functional. We
seek someone to do something, to help us. We seek
someone to encourage us--impart courage to us--and
thereby help us claim our power in relation, the
active realization of what it means to make God
in-carnate.

But whom do we seek? And are we able
to seek? Or must we, in our passive hesitation, be
sought by someone who is not hesitant, here and now,
to reach out to us? Our hesitation suggests our need
for an advocate, an encourager, someone who will take
more seriously our possibility for relation than we
ourselves can, at this time, in this place.

And so we stand confused and reluctant
in the abyss between what we have experienced as fact
and what we have envisioned as possible, unable either
to linger forever in whimpering passivity in bondage
to idols in which we no longer believe or to leap
through our fear in the passion that threatens to
transform us. We wait. We hope. We seek change.
And because we are hesitant, we are bound to assume

163

that the change will be brought to us, rather than by
us. Hesitant, we assume the position of reactive
rather than proactive agency in the realization of
what it means to love. Thus, the possibilities of our
co-creativity are dependent upon our messiah(s)' willingness and capacity to encourage rather than control
us, to love rather than possess us, to enable our ini-
tially reactive instincts to be transformed by us into
proactive power in relation. Messiahs must be friends,
not deities, of humanity.[19]

Fortunately, there are always persons
who are friends of humanity, persons through whom
transpersonal dunamis is represented personally in
the world; persons who will neither manipulate us nor
leave us comfortless if they find us still vulnerable
to relation. It is through and with such persons that
we realize that, here and now, for us and by us, and
with us, God is sister, God is black, God is struggling for survival in the world.

God's incarnations are as many and
varied as the persons who are driven by the power in
relation to touch and be touched by sisters and brothers. To focus messianically on any one person, to
try to locate and establish God in any single figure,
to insist that relational tension and ambiguity be
broken and that the definition of "God" be handed to
us as a package in the person of a lone messiah, is to
deny the movement of power in relation through many
incarnations in history. To worship a messianic figure is to lose touch with our power in relation. It
is to distance ourselves from God.

. . .

Our problem, in the hesitation to know
and do what is good in the world, is not simply that
of our own "internal" fear, something "inside" the
individual psyche. It is rather that we are suspended,
quite literally in the passive sense, by a complex and
often chaotic interplay of forces both internal and
external to our senses.

If in the beginning is the relation,
then we are never without the input and influence of
others in our lives. We may feel alone, but we are
not. As surely as this fundamental relationality provides the basis of our creativity in the world, it
feeds also our fearful hesitation to claim our power

to create. For we have only to look around us and see
the cost of creative relation--such as in the story of
Jesus--to be intimidated by the realization of what
may happen to us if we choose to take seriously our
power in relation.

We need encouragement that will simultaneously compel us beyond this fearful impasse, and
comfort us, enabling us to be patient with ourselves--
to pace ourselves with whatever measure of reason and
caution we must in order not to be swallowed-up in the
confusing chaos of relational movement in which we are
compelled to participate. Messiahs must be careful in
relation to hesitant people.

It is rare in the course of a hesitant
lifetime to be found by friends who both compel and
comfort us in this way; people whose passion for is
also passion with us--compassion, a sense of relation
characterized by empathy, in which a messianic friend
is able to receive from us as much as she gives. Such
a friend is able both to push us and to assure us that
we ourselves are the only ones who can and will determine when and how to claim our power.

Such a friend--the true counselor,
teacher, lover, sister, brother--realizes her own on-
going neediness to be pushed and comforted and, hence,
that any creative relation is mutually-messianic. She
who encourages us is encouraged by us. She who pushes
us is pushed by her own hesitation to take herself as
seriously as she takes us--for the messianic impulse
is directed toward others. She who comforts us in the
slow, grinding, motions of our own coming to courage
is comforted by us in her own fearful temptation to
renounce the painstaking value of what she is doing in
relation.

Our social order does not encourage
mutuality. The possibility of friendship, mutual
relation, God's incarnations between us, gives way
historically to the perpetuation of an order in which
relationships are structured on the basis of greed-
for-more-rather-than-equal, and on the fear which
feeds the greed. Institutional structures--from
multinational corporations to the psychosocial structures of the individual--are sealed fast by a deep and
common fear of friendship and love; fear of chaos,
anarchy, pain, and loss; fear of power in relation and

165

of what may happen to our "gain" if we take one
another more seriously as prospective friends than as
potential competitors.

The social order spills over with human
pain and fear, human waiting and yearning for something more than nervous breakdowns; relationships
bonded by contempt; crime and punishment; the moral
vacuity of education and religion; sexist, racist,
classist, and warmongering denials of friendship; and
the "lies, secrets, and silence" with which we paste
together our flimsy constructions of the world.[20]

In this situation, we find little
encouragement to act our way into thinking mutually.
Mutuality is not encouraged between adults, classes,
sexes, races, or nations. Hence, even the idea of
mutual-messianism poses a contradiction to what we
experience as real: a lack of belief in mutuality
that continues to thwart most of the rare possibilities for cultivating the mutuality that we have.
Receiving and giving little encouragement for mutuality, we are hard pushed to know, even imagine, what it
would be like to be encouraged to take seriously our
power in mutual relation. We do not know how to
"expect" a messiah in whom we do not believe. We have
learned to expect that our redemption will be handed
down to us from on high. We wait for a messiah whom
we can imagine only as divine--that is, as better than
human. We expect the messiah to be our God, not our
friend, because we are as yet unable to value ultimately the mutuality of friendship. We expect a
divine savior, because we are unable to realize that
we ourselves are the saviors of God.[21] In such a
world, the possibility of mutual-messianism evokes
both exhilaration, for what we have seen through a
glass darkly, and sadness, for what is so uncommon
and improbable in human life.

We are blessed if we have friends who
are lovers of humanity. Still, however, we live with
these lovers always in the ambiguous stop-gaps
between waiting for justice and its fulfillment.
Mutually, we may push one another beyond present hesitation; mutually, we may comfort one another; mutually, we may be blessed by one another. If so, it is
very good. But fear and injustice are ours to be
reckoned with, and our common passion does not permit
an amnesia to evil in the world, beginning in our own
lives.

166

The most gracious messianic friend will
be one who reminds us that we live, now as always, in
the stop-gap between waiting and fulfillment. Yes,
the realm of God is at hand--and we are still afraid,
even in our capacities to encourage and be encouraged
by each other. Still in pain, because together we
have envisioned and are drawn by the vision of a better world which continues to elude us.

Hesitant and confused, yearning and
fearfully beginning to encourage one another, we realize that to move together beyond our hesitation is
never a small step, but rather a revolutionary leap
toward future possibility on the basis only of a present vision which we may not fully trust. It is enough
to land us at the edge of madness, because whatever is
to be will be created by us; and, in the here and now,
we cannot imagine our co-creative power. We tremble
in the terrifying abyss of possibility.

. . .

We need a perspective on our experience
that will enable us to examine ourselves in relation
to others who have experienced passion and fear. We
need to be able to assess the value and cost of what
we are doing, or of what we want to do, on the basis
of what others have done in the world--experiences
which the passage of time may have helped clarify in
terms of value and cost.

History gives us the stories of per-
sons. Jesus is one. We may find his story helpful
only if it encourages us, pushes and comforts us, in
the realization of our power in relation.

Christians have manipulated the figure
of Jesus, maintaining that he, the Messiah, sits high
above humanity at the right hand of the Father, and
that he is a divine "person" without need of mutual
relation.[22] This Christolatry is devastating to power
in human relation because it symbolizes something more
important than God incarnate, more important than the
power in human relation. The Jesus who is caricatured
as the Eternal Christ has been constructed by Christian men who have missed the point of the Jesus who
knew no higher value than God's in-carnation--active
presence in the world.[23] We are not encouraged by
Scripture or subsequent tradition to take seriously

167

either (1) Jesus' own mutually messianic presence or (2) our responsibility to "follow him" by participation in a mutual messianism that was neither begun nor completed in the life of Jesus, but rather was revealed in his relation to others as the only way to incarnate God.[24]

If Jesus was God (God the Son) or if he was the Christ, our Lord and only Savior (a demi-god unlike you and me), his story encourages me in no way. I can read it only as an attempt to highlight humanity's unwillingness to love and our need for a super-human Mediator between what is human and what is divine. Such a story is perverse in that it reinforces our hesitation to claim our power, and it legitimates a theology constructed upon assumptions that are "turned completely around"--from immediacy to the need for mediation; from intimacy to distance in relation; from concrete acts of justice to an intangible peace that passes understanding; from the power of human relation to the omnipotence of a deity above human relation; and from human passion to the worship of "God" and the condescending pity of a humanity created in "God's" lonely image.[25]

If, however, Jesus was human, a person like you and me, it is a remarkably different story. For we have here an image of a Jesus who needed friends, a Jesus who lived into the immediate and intimate dimensions of relation. This image can reflect our own possibility. The image of a Jesus who "felt the power go out from him" when he was touched, a Jesus who berated his friends for their failures to take him or themselves seriously, can push us toward re-imaging how seriously we are empowered in relation to create the world. The image of a Jesus who tried repeatedly, with patient if indignant forebearance, to show others what was happening in the world, can remind us that we are neither the first nor the last persons in history who have been afraid to know and love God. The image of a Jesus who contravened unjust relation, who suffered pain rather than compromise this ethic, who hated rather than welcomed unjust death, including his own, can push us beyond our temptations to make easy peace with injustice in the world, including that which is planted in the soil of our own hesitation.

The image of a Jesus who, in the prophetic tradition of Israel, despised the blasphemous

168

notion of a deity who likes sacrifice, especially
human sacrifice, can assure us that we are not here to
give ourselves up willingly to be crucified for anyone's sake, but rather to struggle together against
the injustice of all human sacrifice, including our
own.[26] There is, I believe, a difference between sacrificial death, which is steeped in a sense of impotence and characterized by the zeal with which martyrs
seek it, and passionate death, which is borne unwelcomed, simply because lovers of humanity are willing
to die rather than compromise the terrifying possibilities of relation in the world.

This image of Jesus is an image of a
friend; a companion who received as well as gave; a
lover who was encouraged by those who loved him; a
teacher who knew the cost of--yet valued ultimately--
his power in relation, a brother who was killed for
this reason; a man whose friends began to claim their
own power; a person whom they remembered.

This image may mirror our own power
only if we are already open to it and are looking at
Jesus for clarification of what godding may involve
and cost. Otherwise, the image thrown back upon us is
one of magic, pain, and death. Unless we have already
some sense, however hesitant, of the power in relation;
unless we know already something of what Jesus knew,
the image of Jesus will deflect our vision from God
in-carnate. If, however, we realize already that the
passion of Jesus was uncommon but not unique; and if
we recognize already in the lives of other men and
women the ultimate value of passion, the image of
Jesus may clarify for us the high value and high cost
of our own relational lives in the world.

The image of Jesus may shed light upon
us only if we are willing to de-ecclesiologize and
re-liturgize Jesus in order to celebrate mutual passion, and co-creative power among ourselves rather
than continue to denigrate these values in the name of
a lofty, dispassionate, and omnipotent Christ of the
Church.

If we are not encouraged by the image
of Jesus, there is no need to belabor it.[27] The image
of Jesus intimates that we will find and keep our
courage in relation to those persons or stories which
touch us most immediately. But if we are encouraged
by this image, there is no good reason in the world

not to probe it; no reason not to encourage it to show
us more about what it means to incarnate God; no reason not to ponder it as a story of the redemption of
Jesus Christ from "God," and of God from human dispassion.

. . .

No
again, no
I refuse
to get lost
in "God"
again

I will live
without "God"

I will suffer
without "God"

I will rejoice
without "God"

I refuse
to be snuffed out
by His possessive
dispassion

And my refusal is enabled by your
friendship, you who love me. You do not accept my
isolation or my "God," and this is your blessing of
me, you who re-member the intimacy of our relation,
you who are infused by the immediacy of who we are,
you who have not forgotten that we are not alone.

But you fear death, do you not? Or are
you in touch with something that I am not: in touch,
that is, with me and the constancy of who we are
together? Is this why you rage--for me? O tender
sisters, you remember our power to effect, simply by
touching; our power to create, simply in relation.[28]
You are compelled to dispel the myth of loneliness and
the pathos of the "God" who needs no friends. You are
driven to pursue our relation. You will not leave me
alone. You are insistent in your pursuit. And you
will drive me mad before you will damn me to linger in
bondage to a "God" who enjoys my lonely worship. You

are constrained to break through the depression bind-
ing my heart.

But what makes you tick, you who
tremble as the story is told again of fearful people
who fashion a "God" who beckons us away from humanity
and lifts us above the world? What compels you to
weep and drives you mad as we lift our hearts up to
"God"? What makes you stand, rather than kneel, look
down rather than up, and scream rather than whisper,
to us rather than "God"?

Come down, sisters!

Come down, brothers!

See the world!

Know humanity!

I wonder what compels you, angry pro-
phet, comforting psalmist, terrifying friends with me
here, you who have seen that which consumes us if we
come too close, or so the story goes.[29] Dietrich and
Dorothee and Elie, others of you with names and faces
and hands, what is it that compels you to compel me,
opens you to open me, drives you to drive me to wonder
what compels you?

Kill my "God"! It would be better any-
how, because I refuse to love a "God" who does not
take me seriously, a "God" who does not love me, a
"God" whose condescension is His acknowledgement. It
is better that "God" be dead. But I am terrified of
losing Him, terrified of coming down, of seeing, of
knowing who I am without Him; terrified and compelled
to come down with you, because I am tired of meander-
ing in the chasm between loneliness and justice. I am
lonely. I am needy. I am terrified, and driven, with
you, to tremble. With you, to look down. With you,
to look closely, very closely. With you, to fix my
eyes upon the world. With you, to re-member myself as
prophet with you, and only with you.

Terrified, we see. It is terrible,
what we see. And it is good that we see together that
we are not alone. We see broken bodyselves crying to
be healed; separated people yearning for relation;
suffering humanity raging for justice; nations,
strangers, friends, spouses, lovers, children, sisters,

171

brothers, with us, we begin to remember ourselves,
compelled by a power in relation that is relentless
in its determination to break through the boundaries
and boxes that separate us. We are driven to speak
the Word that spills over among us:

"Without our touching, there is no God.

Without our relation, there is no God."

Without our crying, our yearning, our
raging, there is no God. For in the beginning is the
relation, and in the relation is the power that creates the world through us, and with us, and by us, you
and I, you and we, and none of us alone.

By this power we are pushed further
than we dare to imagine we can go. By this power, we
are en-couraged to live together. By this power we
are en-abled to see and to know that we are encouraged
and enabled constantly to god. By us, with us,
through us, the power is re-leased.

And at last, hand in hand, we are
blessed.

FOOTNOTES: CHAPTER V

¹Adrienne Rich, from "Phantasia for Elvira Shatayev," The Dream of a Common Language, pp. 4-6.

²See Chapter III, especially pp. 79ff.

³A-7713 was the number given to Wiesel upon entrance to Auschwitz.

⁴cf. Hannah Arendt, "Radical Evil," in Guilt: Man and Society, ed. Roger W. Smith, pp. 217-53. "There is only one thing that seems to be discernible: we may say that radical evil has emerged in connection with a system in which all men have become equally superfluous" (p. 252).

⁵See Phyllis Trible, God and the Rhetoric of Sexuality (Philadelphia: Fortress Press, 1978), Chapter 4, "A Love Story Gone Awry," pp. 72-143, for a rhetorical critical analysis of the Genesis story of 'ādām (whom Trible designates as "the earth creature").

⁶See Chapter IV, pp. 126ff.

⁷For Paul Tillich, this is the transition from "essence to existence." He writes, "Creation and the Fall coincide in so far as there is no point in time and space in which created goodness was actualized and had existence .... There was no 'utopia' in the past, just as there will be no 'utopia' in the future. Actualized creation and estranged existence are identical." Systematic Theology, Three Volumes in One (Chicago: University of Chicago Press, 1967), Vol. II: Existence and the Christ, p. 44. Tillich's emphasis remains largely on "the tragic element" ("destiny") in human existence, whereas mine is on human posse (which Tillich would place under the rubric of "freedom," in "ontological polarity" with "destiny," Vol. I, pp. 182-6). Tillich writes, "Destiny is not a strange power which determines what shall happen to me. It is myself as given, formed by nature, history and myself. My destiny is the basis of my freedom; my freedom participates in shaping my destiny" (Ibid., p. 185). I agree with this, but disagree with Tillich's fundamental contention that "God has no destiny because he is freedom" (Ibid.). Whereas Tillich believes in "Being-itself" or "the absolute" (Ibid., p. 239) as the ground of everything that has being, I would approach "being" from the opposite direction--

173

namely, from the function of doing (any relational act) as the
basis of any understanding we may have of an active power/God
grounded in human relation. God's destiny as well as God's freedom is in relation to human destiny and freedom. God and humanity are thoroughly relational, thus resistant to ontological
conceptualization.

[8]For contrast with Pannenberg, see Chapter IV,
pp. 130-2.

[9]See Tillich, Systematic Theology, Vol. II, pp.
369-72, for elaboration on kairos and kairoi (moment[s] in which
[God's] time is fulfilled). Tillich writes, "Awareness of a
kairos is a matter of vision ... not a matter of detached observation but of involved experience" (pp. 370-1).

[10]Charles Williams develops the theme of "the terror of good" in his novels. See especially Descent Into Hell
(Grand Rapids: Eerdmans Publishing Co., 1937; reprinted, 1973),
p. 93.

[11]This occurred in the Summer of 1972 at Sleighton
Farm School for Girls, Delaware County, Pennsylvania, where I was
a chaplain in Clinical Pastoral Education. The School has since
been closed by the state.

[12]As Simone de Beauvoir notes, "[A]mbiguity must
not be confused with ... absurdity. To declare that existence is
absurd is to deny that it can ever be given a meaning; to say
that it is ambiguous is to assert that its meaning is never fixed,
that it must be constantly won." The Ethics of Ambiguity
(Secaucus, N.J.: Citadel Press, 1972; originally published,
1948), p. 129.

[13]This is meant to be an allusion to "original sin"
in two overlapping senses: (1) its universality and (2) its collective, social character. This is where Augustine is, in my
opinion, most helpful. See, for reference, The City of God, Book
XIII; also, On Forgiveness of Sins, and Baptism in N and PNF, pp.
11-78, especially Book I, chapters 8-15; III, 7-15. The problem
with this doctrine, given classic exposition by Augustine, is
threefold: (1) It looms so large as to overshadow the possibility also of an "original good" (a theme that Schleiermacher
develops in the "relative oppositions" of sin and grace). (2)
Therefore, the Fall is experienced and interpreted as wholly evil
and destructive, rather than as a fall also into creation or the
human capacity to make creative (as well as destructive) differences in the world. (This is the theme Tillich develops.) (3)
Related to the above problems is Augustine's (and orthodox
Christianity's) location of original sin's "transmission" in

sexual intercourse. Sexuality becomes the seat of evil in human
life and thereby the fundamental human experience of that which
is anti-God, non-spiritual, sinful, and symbol of evil: "the
flesh," "the world," and "the devil." As paradigm of the non-
good, sex cannot be experienced much less conceptualized (without
a great deal of difficulty) as embracing any "original good" or
any un-mediated creativity (procreation and celibacy being media-
ting functions). As paradigm of raw human power--dunamis, freedom of will in its spontaneity--sexuality symbolizes the deprav-
ity of fallen humanity and evokes among us senses of self as
shameful and guilty. This self-image of humanity may serve
largely to insure our shameful "acting out" of fear and injustice in human relation. We act out a role we have learned to
believe is the role we are bound to play.

[14]Writing in 1960, Valerie Saiving Goldstein
challenged the equation of sin with pride (in the works of Anders
Nygren and Reinhold Niebuhr), thus forerunning my equation of sin
with the denial of our own relational power. Goldstein locates
the problem in male theologians' failures to realize the extent
to which women's experiences of ourselves in the world are very
different from men's, and that our sin, as women, is "the under-
development or negation of the self." "The Human Situation: A
Feminine Viewpoint," in The Nature of Man in Theological and
Psychological Perspective, ed. Simon Doniger (New York: Harper
and Row, 1962), pp. 151-70. This feminist theme has been
expanded by other women in recent years, especially Mary Daly
and Judith Plaskow. It is significant both in that it flags the
extent to which female experience has been denied historically
in the shaping of religious thought, and in that it proposes a
re-experiencing and re-naming of "sin" (and concomitant doctrines) on the basis of experience which is shaped, to a large
degree, by social and political reality.

[15]Frederick Perls, Ralph F. Hefferline, and Paul
Goodman speak of the "single, immediate grasp of ... differentiated unity" as a possibility for insight into friendship, painting, or other relational constellations. This is in contrast to
our tendency to fix our attention, set our minds, upon one piece
of a relational transaction (or act) as if it had a static, non-
relational character. This "grasp of differentiated unity"
approximates my sense of our "co-creative task." See Perls,
Hefferline, and Goodman, Gestalt Therapy: Excitement and Growth
in the Human Personality (New York: Dell Publishing Co., 1951),
p. 66.

[16]See Appendix D on Gustavo Gutiérrez.

[17]By this, I mean that power in relation effects
justice, not simply that it "should" or "ought to" effect jus-

tice. We choose to love or not. We ought to choose to love.
This is a moral imperative. But when we choose to love and do
so, our power makes love/makes justice--period. It is a statement of fact.

[18]See Rosemary Ruether, Faith and Fratricide: The
Theological Roots of Anti-Semitism (New York: Seabury Press,
1974), on relation between Christian messianism and anti-Semitism.

[19]The failure of religious "leaders" and "followers" to appreciate this contributes not only to sanctioned cult-
phenomena, such as the equation of the ordained priesthood with
alter Christus (hence, with a divine power), but also to the
various religious cults in our time, whose leaders assume a
deified posture in relation to their followers. Case in point:
the late Rev. Jim Jones of the Peoples' Temple.

[20]Adrienne Rich charges the social structures in
our time, structures shaped by white men of the upper classes,
with having been built and maintained upon "lies, secrets, and
silence," which can begin to be un-done only if we ask questions
we have not dared to ask before, even of ourselves. She views
lesbian/feminism as a collective attempt by women to discover the
truths of our lives, and to speak it, as women and as representa-
tives of the human capacity to "break down ... self-delusion and
isolation ...; [to] do justice to our own complexity ...; to
extend the possibilities of truth between us. The possibility of
life between us." See "Women and Honor: Notes on Lying," in On
Lies, Secrets, and Silence: Selected Prose, 1966-1978 (New York:
W. W. Norton & Co., 1979), pp. 185-94. Rich continues to be a
primary theological resource for me.

[21]Reference is to Nikos Kazantzakis' The Saviors
of God: Spiritual Exercises (New York: Simon and Schuster,
1960). Kazantzakis and I are not speaking of the same experience, although there is, in effect, some co-incidence between
what we propose. In short, Kazantzakis assumes one transcendent
God: "Abyss, Mystery, Absolute Darkness, Absolute Light, Matter,
Spirit, Ultimate Hope, Ultimate Despair, Silence" (p. 101). "We
struggle to make this Spirit visible, to give it a face, to
encase it in words ...." (p. 100). The human journey is an
ascent, an upward charge, the "transmutation of matter into spirit" (p. 106). Kazantzakis speaks of a reality that is greater
than human life in the world. In this, he and I are different.
He emphasizes human action, including choice and passion (as
depth of investment in one's immediate situation), as the
vehicle by which God is delivered from matter or flesh. It is
Kazantzakis' insistence upon human action as vital to everything
that matters (namely, God) that bears some resemblance to what I

am trying to do, although I do not share his dualistic perception of spirit and matter, creator and creation, God and humanity.

[22]See Appendix C for feminist critique of Jesus as Lord.

[23]This is in reference to the Great Commandment (Mark 12:28-31), which established love of God and humanity as Jesus' own highest value, or ethical norm. See Chapter II, pp. 48-9.

[24]Up until the present time and the work of such theologians as Dorothee Soelle and Tom F. Driver, the only major Christian theologian (of whom I am aware) who actually approached the possibility of grounding theology thoroughly in human relation was Dietrich Bonhoeffer in his Letters and Papers. Even he stopped short of suggesting that our choices, vocations, and effects are, in no essential way, different from those of Jesus but rather are shaped by the details, praxis and meanings of our own lives in our own time and place.

[25]"Perverse" is from Latin pervertere: per (completely) + vertere (to turn).

[26]Anselm's Cur Deus Homo suggests that human sacrifice--in particular, Jesus'--was vital, indispensable and necessary in order for God to be "satisfied." Anselm writes in legal terms of debt and payment. What must be restored is God's "honor," which humanity has violated (by sin). Anselm expounds the idea of sacrifice as the way to God, the only means of human communication with the divine. The assumption behind sacrificial theology is that the life and value--even "honor"--of the creature (human or other animal) is worth less than that of the creator. I find this problematic, all the more so because it legitimates human beings' lingering senses of ourselves--and others--as worth nothing, or very little, in relation to each other or to that which we have learned to call "God." See Cur Deus Homo in Saint Anselm: Basic Writings, translated by S. N. Deane (LaSalle, Ill.: Open Court, 1962), pp. 171-288.

[27]See Appendix C for feminist critique.

[28]See Appendices C and F for experiential roots of my own emphasis on "sisters."

[29]See Exodus 3:1-6. The story of Moses and the burning bush conveys a sense of danger in approaching the divine-- Yahweh said, "Do not come near ... for the place on which you are standing is holy ground" (3:5). "And Moses hid his face, for he was afraid to look at God" (3:6b). I believe there is truth

177

here. The power in relation is a consuming creative power which we choose to either claim or deny. If we claim and use it, we cannot bear to dwell upon or capture the power in what we are doing (a danger even in writing this book). It's much like staring at bright light or experiencing electrical current or sexual orgasm. It is not ours to be owned or kept, but rather only to be experienced, chosen, affirmed, and shared. If we deny the power, it still consumes us, I think, through our fear and the violation of relation that we do in our denial. The evil that we effect destroys us. In other words, the power in human relation is a terrible good, because in both our affirmations and denials, we are affected, changed, consumed. Fire is an appropriate image for this power.

EPILOGUE

ELIE WIESEL AND THE REDEMPTION OF GOD

Eberhard Bethge's suggestion that the term "'Holocaust' ... carries profound transformational qualities" may lead us to ask in what sense this is true.[1] What do we learn from the Holocaust that may transform us? We return to my earlier analysis of Elie Wiesel's experience:

> From within a world of relational expectation that human experience will be meaningful exactly to the extent that humanity values close friendship, Wiesel is plunged into its negation. Auschwitz and Buchenwald are experienced by Wiesel not simply as the antithesis to relation, out of which might be drawn some reasonable synthesis, such as an acceptance of ambiguity or of the imperfection in human relations. The Holocaust is experienced as the negation--obliteration, total destruction --of relation. To the degree that relation is that which is, for Wiesel, radically good, the Holocaust is the experience of radical evil: the extinction of the meaning and the value of human experience; the nullification of human existence; that which is utterly without relation.[2]

Wiesel asks us to re-member the Holocaust as an occasion on which evil was done by humanity so thoroughly as to destroy the power of relation in Jewish experience. Wiesel's books reflect his attempt to understand, even believe, his own experience of radical evil, as well as his attempts to persuade us that it could happen again--if we do not value ultimately human life.

We need to look first at the relational ethic implicit in Wiesel's experience of good and evil,

179

an ethic that corresponds to my own; and second at
Wiesel's questions about God which are founded on
theological assumptions about the omnipotence of a
wholly good God.

The Ultimacy of "Glances Heavy with Existence"

Wiesel's experience of friendship corresponds to my experience of relation. The further in
time Wiesel moves from the Holocaust and the longer he
struggles with his experience and questions, the more
adamantly he asserts the ultimacy of friendship, of
discovering "the real heights" at "the real depths" of [3]
relation, in exchanging "glances heavy with existence."

His early works offer a clue to the
meaning of friendship, or relation, in their [4] shatter-
ing descriptions of the absence of relation. By
showing what happens when there is no passion, no
relation, Wiesel encourages us to imagine what the
alternative to this evil might be. By unveiling the
Holocaust as an arena of non-relation between Nazi and
Jew, Allies and Jew, Church and Jews, and finally even
between Jew and Jew, Wiesel lays bare the character of
evil as a psycho-social structure of non-relation, in
which humanity effects no good.

Wiesel portrays the Nazis as having
acted on the assumption that Jews were not human, an
assumption of humanity's non-relation to humanity: no
bonding, no friendship, no relation between Aryan and
Jew. Accordingly, the Nazis attempted to construct a
world in which there would be no Jewish presence; no
pretentious claim of any Jew to be human; no need or
possibility of any Aryan to experience or remember any
Jew as sister or brother.

From this negative perspective, the
Nazi effort was grounded in a relational definition of
humanity: The essence of humanity is relation. To be
a friend is to realize one's essential bond to others.
In order to most effectively solve the "Jewish problem," the Nazis believed--and tried to convince the
Jews--that the Jews were "vermin." The Final Solution
necessitated a systematic effort to destroy the Jews'
experience of themselves as human, by breaking apart
the Jews' senses of relation to others and, finally,
to each other. [5]

In telling and re-telling the story,
Wiesel locates all that is of moral value in human
relation. Perhaps the highest value in relation is
the power to choose--finally, the power to choose not
to victimize and not to be victim, not to dominate and
not to submit, a choice available only in voluntary
relation. Where there is to be an effective effort to
destroy relation, those responsible for the destruction must eliminate the others' sense of power--to
choose, to effect, to create. The ideal victim is one
who has no sense of her power to effect anything in
relation to anyone. The Nazis had to attempt to
infuse into Jewish self-consciousness a sense of dispassion no less chilling than their own in relation to
Jews as vermin.

The Holocaust was an arena of radical
moral evil: the absence of relation. Radical moral
good is, for Wiesel, human bonding in relation, the
intense connectedness between person and person which
permits no indifference to human life and no possibility of a Holocaust.

To turn one's attention away from human
life toward something "higher" is to help cultivate
the soil for another Holocaust, the destruction of
humanity by humanity. There can be no religion or
doctrine; no ethic or moral suasion; no racial, sexual, class, or ethnic pride; no technological feat;
no end or means; nothing in heaven or earth--not even
a deity--that is any more valuable, any more important,
any better, than human love for humanity.

We are the Saviors of God?

Given his basically socio-anthropologi-
cal ethic, in what sense does Wiesel envision the possibility of a personal, transcendent, deity who may
yet redeem the world by transforming the quality of
human relation? For Wiesel, "everything is question"
--especially everything about God.6

It is, I believe, inexcusable to impose
Christian answers upon Jewish questions. It is, moreover, inappropriate to attempt to "answer" the theological questions of Elie Wiesel. He is not asking us
for answers. He is asking us to listen--and repeat--
his questions. Everything is question. I do not want
to make light of or lose the dialectical quality of

Wiesel's interrogations, his difficult suspension of both belief and disbelief in the benevolence and omnipotence of the God of Israel.

I want to name, for myself, the place in which Wiesel's theological questions have impressed me, and to explore this location on my theological terms. Having experienced the Holocaust, Wiesel knows the difficulty in affirming both the omnipotence and the goodness of a personal God. Logic alone, supported by Jewish faith-claims, demands that a God who is both all-powerful and all-good is one whose power enables Him [sic] to overcome evil in history, and whose goodness is His [sic] desire to do so. Would not such a God have done something to help the Jews? Something to prevent the Holocaust? The magnitude of Jewish suffering suggests that Yahweh was either unable, or unwilling, to effect the good that faithful Jews would have expected that He [sic] would both be able and want to do.

With Wiesel, we may make an ethical affirmation: humanity's love for humanity is good. Moreover, with Wiesel, we may recognize that this good --to which we attribute highest value, the quality of ultimacy--is, in fact, our experience of God in human life. Hence, Wiesel's theological dilemma poses for me the questions not of the goodness of what is most valuable, but rather of the omnipotence of this goodness. Wiesel does not question the goodness of human relation, but rather the power of relation to overcome non-relation. Wiesel interrogates the personal source (Yahweh) of what I call "the power in relation," the same God who has promised in covenant with Israel that goodness will be experienced as powerful, and in whose own nature goodness and power are believed to coincide.

Theodicy is a philosophical endeavor to hold together the power and goodness of God. Wiesel makes no attempt to do this. After the Holocaust, Wiesel must charge that goodness is not omnipotent in the world. What Wiesel, like Job, encounters is juxtaposed between humanity's belief in an omnipotent personal deity who can save humanity from evil, and humanity's experience of this God's apparent impotence in history. Unlike Job, Wiesel cannot accept simply the wonder and mystery of a God whose ways are incomprehensible to human beings (Job 42:1-3). In his interrogation of God, Wiesel drives us beyond the faith-claims of Israel (and of Christendom) toward the

182

possibility of an altogether different understanding of God.

The key for me to his theological sug-gestiveness is Wiesel's insistence upon the ultimacy of human relation. Whatever or wherever else God may or may not be, God is experienced in human love. But can we assume that love is victorious over evil (love-lessness) in the world--that is, can we assume that God is omnipotent? The Holocaust suggests that we cannot--unless we recognize, in the unholy alliance between Nazis, Church, and Allies, that there was very little love for Jews in the world between 1933 and 1945. Wiesel implicitly asks us, I think, to consider the possibility that our love for humanity might yet be revealed--not only as good, but also as powerful--depending entirely upon our willingness to love one another in the world.

Wiesel's message to me is that if there is to be any redemption of humanity from evil in the world, it is up to us. We can never again abdicate our responsibility to an omnipotent deity. If God is omnipotent, it is in and through the power of human love. Only if we take humanity seriously on human-ity's terms may God be delivered, with us, from evil.

FOOTNOTES: EPILOGUE

[1]Bethge, "The Holocaust and Christian Anti-Semitism," p. 153.   See Chapter III, p. 77 and p. 101, note 12.

[2]Chapter III, p. 80.

[3]Wiesel, _The Town Beyond The Wall_, p. 188.

[4]Wiesel, _Night_; _Dawn_; and _The Accident_.

[5]The common citation of the Jews' "passivity" in the Holocaust reveals both ignorance of--and insensitivity to--the depth of the anti-Semitic madness for which the Nazis were responsible: that is, the systematic effort to obliterate the Jews' experience of themselves as human, and thereby to diminish the possibility of Jewish resistance to the final assault on their humanity.   That Jews _did resist_, in fact, is remarkable, much in the same sense as the slave rebellions in the antebellum South.

[6]See Chapter III, pp. 89f.

ROOTS OF RELATION IN LIBERAL PROTESTANTISM:

SCHLEIERMACHER

For Friedrich Ernest Daniel Schleiermacher (1768-1834), the human experience of relation
was the source of faith and theology. He held that in
the experience of "consciousness," "self" and "God"
are in relation. Locating all religious knowledge in
this relation, Schleiermacher reversed the time-
honored direction of Christian epistemology in which
the absolute and non-human character of the divine had
been considered the source of Christian knowledge.
Schleiermacher thus initiated modern liberal theology's
attempt to loose human faith from the fetters of theological a prioris.

He asked people to explore their own
consciousnesses and suggested that therein they would
discover God. This theological movement inward signaled a shift in focus from heaven to earth, from
external to internal authority, and thereby from God
(as the reified and external locus of value) to the
inner human experience of "God-consciousness" as the
source of all that is valuable in the world.

In this schema, faith becomes an
"entirely inward" experience of a God who is neither
subject nor object of the human capacity to worship.
Rather, God is co-subject with the person in her own
self-consciousness. Her self-consciousness reveals
her God-consciousness, which in turn enables her to
realize that God-in-herself upon whom she is "absolutely dependent." A person is unable to objectify
God as "something" totally other than herself.
Together relationally, self and God, creature and
creator, are co-operative agents in the world.

Schleiermacher was a son of Prussian
privilege; child of the Enlightenment; pastor,
teacher, and theologian to and among and for "cultured despisers" of Evangelical piety. His early work
was on behalf of individuals who took seriously the
autonomy and rationality of the person, and yet who

sought something other than that which could be contained within boundaries of pure reason. Schleiermacher inspired people by naming their capacities for exploring their own untapped, mysterious and free-floating, possibilities. In later years, Schleiermacher's interest shifted from the individual to community and from religion in general.

Throughout his theological development, feeling (Gefühl) was, for Schleiermacher, religion-- "not simply a sense-experience, but a feeling ... elevated to the nature of community and rationality" (W. A. Johnson, On Religion: A Study of Theological Method in Schleiermacher and Nygren [Netherlands: Brill, 1964], p. 52). Human experience reveals God as the "divine causality," upon which human life depends. God is not a personal figure, not someone who gives. "God-consciousness" is not something given externally to humanity but rather is revealed within "self-consciousness" as the fundamental, most basic, dimension of the human experience of relation--specifically, the relation of "self" to "God." God is apersonal, universal, and natural (as opposed to supernatural), the absolutely spiritual and free cause of history itself. Rejecting the idea of a personal God, Schleiermacher does not present a God who "acts" in history. His position is that because God is the cause of history, history is a consequence of God. Schleiermacher's doctrine of God is also a doctrine of humanity, in which human beings are held to be ultimately responsible for our own actions in the world.

But what of evil? If God does not act in history except insofar as God participates in human self-consciousness, bound radically within the confines of human consciousness, human judgment, and human activity, what is to prevent humanity from acting in the world on the basis of unconsciousness and misjudgment? Nothing--except humanity itself.

This answer is, I believe, both correct --and dangerous. It is not difficult to imagine some relation between Schleiermacher's Prussia and Hitler's Germany; a connection between enlightened people inspired with a confidence in their own creative capacities and their heirs obsessed with a compulsion to create a world in their own image, exclusively for themselves.

186

In the early twentieth century, the Schleiermacherian theology of humanity was cross-examined by theologians who were shaken by their experience of evil in the world. Disturbed by the violent effects of World War I, these "crisis" theologians, persons such as Barth and Brunner, accused their liberal forebears of having falsified basic Christian claims. Contrasting crisis theology with liberalism, Barth wrote:

> [When we spoke of God], we did not speak in the light of results of any self-knowledge or self-estimate of human reason or existence. We did not speak with reference to any observations and conclusions in respect of the laws and ordinances which rule in nature and human history. We certainly did not speak in relation to any religious disposition which is supposed to be or actually is proper to man. There is only one revelation. (Church Dogmatics [Edinburgh: T. & T. Clark, 1961], IV.1, p. 45).

Only one revelation: something given; something not internal; something other than human, extrinsic to human consciousness, human reason, human capacity to seek and find. Only one revelation of God. Barth's conviction is that God, not humanity—God alone, not with humanity—initiates and accomplishes all knowledge of God, all faith in God, and all that is godly—good or just—in the world. Such a God, and human faith in God, together constitute the answer to the problem of evil in the world. Evil is rooted in human sin, which for Barth bears close resemblance to Schleiermacher's celebration of self-consciousness, or humanity's celebration of itself.

I see my work in continuity with liberal relational theological tradition as informed (1) by the Barthian critique of its failure to acknowledge the depths of human sin; (2) by a Marxian critique of its bourgeois individualism; and (3) by a feminist critique of its indifference to structures of male dominance which themselves constitute the social basis for all (including theological) experience and its articulation.

187

Despite his own shortcomings, Schleier-macher is one of few modern Christian theologians who not only has given explicit serious attention to female characters (<u>Christmas Eve</u>, 1804) but also has suggested a theological alternative to divine-human alienation--namely, a theology of "relative opposition." I realize that the roots of much of what I am attempting to do lie in the Irenaean (later Schleiermacherian) tradition. (See Chapter IV for full discussion; also, for reference, Schleiermacher's <u>On Religion</u>: <u>Speeches to Its Cultured Despisers</u>, trans. John Oman with intro. by Rudolf Otto [New York: Harper and Row, 1958]; and <u>The Christian Faith</u>, Eng. trans. of the second German edition, ed. H. R. Mackintosh and J. S. Stewart [Edinburgh: T. & T. Clark, 1928, latest imp., 1976]).

APPENDIX B

CHALCEDON'S ONTOLOGY

Chalcedon (451 A.D.) attempted to state
the relation between the divine and the human in Jesus
Christ:

> Our Lord Jesus Christ is ... truly
> God and truly man [sic] ... made
> known in two natures without con-
> fusion, without change, without
> division, without separation, the
> difference of the natures being by
> no means removed because of the
> union, but the property of each
> nature being preserved and coales-
> cing in one prosopon and hypostatis.

In this formula, Chalcedon produced what has been
regarded as the definitive dogmatic foundation for
subsequent christology.

From the experience of Jesus' own con-
temporaries of his resurrection up to the Council of
Chalcedon, Christians had believed that Jesus of Nazareth had lived, died, and risen in a particular and
significant relation to God. Subsequent generations
of Christians were left heirs to this mystery and the
formidable task of attempting to articulate polemi-
cally, apologetically, and evangelically the relation
between the human and the divine in Jesus. This is
the christological task.

During the first three centuries of the
church, facing political, religious, and philosophical
animosity which had the weight of both reason and
institutional power on its side, Christian mission was
to issue, on the one hand, defensive polemic against
paganism and heresy and, on the other, doxological
affirmation for the benefit of community cohesiveness.
Early Christian theology grew in response to the needs
of the church for survival and strength with which to
endure political opposition, and for reason with which
to combat these heresies, such as Gnosticism, perceived

(rightly or wrongly) to be infringing from the outside on right-thinking Christians.

When in the fourth century the church found accommodation within the state and was no longer in an adversary position to the Empire, doctrinal questions of a speculative nature began to crystallize within the church, albeit along lines politically expedient to the Emperor (Constantine) whose first interest, one might guess, was the unity of the Empire rather than the unity of Father and Son. In any case, christological questions, as orthodoxy has asked and answered them, were first officially set forth at the Council of Nicea (325).

Against the Arians, Nicea asserted with Athanasius that Jesus was divine, the Son co-equal, co-eternal, and consubstantial with the Father. The relationship between Father and Son was homoousios. Nicea thus set the stage for what would follow logically: How could this be so? How can a human being have divine substance? This became the central doctrinal question.

The two groups whose rivalry precipitated Chalcedon (and Ephesus twenty years earlier) were the Alexandrians, whose central figure was the Patriarch Cyril; and the Antiochenes, whose figurehead was Nestorius, deposed Patriarch of Constantinople. The dispute between these factions is significant to all that has followed Chalcedon in the history of christological thought.

The Alexandrians were proponents of a Logos/sarx (Word/flesh) christology, which had developed around the Logos-christology of Origen and had received authoritative impetus from Athanasius. Logos/sarx thought found its biblical mandate in the Johannine literature: "The Word became flesh" (John 1:14). For Cyril of Alexandria, the key to the Incarnation (on the Platonic analogy of soul and body) was that the Logos was the animating--life-giving-- principle of the flesh; the Logos was the principle of unity--uniting itself with the flesh, thereby forming one nature (that of Logos) out of two different natures (Logos = divine; human). (See Richard A. Norris, "Christological Models in Cyril of Alexandria," in Studia Patristica, Vol. XIII, ed. Elizabeth A. Livingstone [Berlin: Akademie-Verlag, 1975], pp. 255-68).

Although Alexandrian apologists cite Cyril's emphasis on the unity of the divine and human natures in Christ, it is a unity-by-takeover: The unity is the result of the human nature's having being subsumed by the Logos; a unity initiated by the divine and incarnate in a divine prosopon.

The Antiochenes emphasized, rather than the unity of divine and human natures, the differences between the two natures in a Logos/anthropos (Word/man [sic]) christology. Nestorius represented an extreme Antiochene position, proposing not only the separation of the two natures in Christ but also lending himself to the charge that he asserted two prosopa (a charge he denied). The earlier and less dualistic Antiochene position was established by Theodore of Mopsuestia (d. 428), whose insistence on the distinction between the two natures was grounded in his belief not only in the rational possibility, but moreover in the moral necessity, of a human being's relation to God involving the person's free choice. Human nature encompasses the freedom to choose. (Richard A. Norris, Manhood and Christ [Oxford: Clarendon Press, 1963], p. 237). The Incarnation is not a "hypostatic union" (Cyril), but rather a union "by good pleasure" --initiated by the divine but including the human being's decision to respond and enter into the union (Ibid., pp. 237-8).

Grillmeier and others (certainly the Monophysites, whose reaction against the Chalcedon formula precipitated the next Council meeting in Constantinople) have perceived the Chalcedon formula as an Antiochene victory. This is true up to a point: the formula's statement that Christ is "in (not "from") two natures--without confusion and without change--is an Antiochene contribution. But the heavier implications of the formula, it seems to me, abound from its affirmation of the Nicene declaration of the homoousios of Father and Son; the acceptance of Mary as Theotokos--affirming thereby that Mary gave birth to God, not simply to Christ, as Nestorius had proposed; and the Council's refusal to grant the human nature its own hypostasis (that which is real and concrete) or prosopon (that which is experienced as identity).* To have a divine hypostasis and prosopon is

---

*These definitions were offered by Richard A. Norris in correspondence with me, January 7, 1980.

to have the realized, concrete identity of God. Chalcedon affirms Christ's identity as that of God the Son, born into the world as God, with a pre-existent and on-going eternal life in God. An Antiochene victory? Theodore's assertion of the role of human freedom in the Incarnation is eliminated, if not explicitly, then implicitly, by the Council's metaphysical presuppositions of the absolute and all-consuming role of the divine in relation to the human.

The primary Chalcedonian motif is anchored by the weight of the Council's emphasis on the unity of Christ's person on the terms of, and at the initiative of, the divine, irrespective of the role of the human. The motif, established at Chalcedon as the foundation of christology and, hence, as central to Christian theology, is that all life exists within an ontological structure of hierarchical dualism, in which the higher essence is the valuable essence. In order to take Chalcedon seriously, or christology itself as it has been shaped traditionally, theologians must examine the suitability of ontological dualism as the basis for Christian faith. To say, with Grillmeier, that the Chalcedonian definition "may seem to have a static-ontic ring" (Aloys Grillmeier, Christ in Christian Tradition [New York: Sheed and Ward, 1965], p. 491) is like saying that an apple may seem to be a fruit.

The implications of this motif have been plentiful. Various overlapping ontological dualisms have been fastened in it. For example, in philosophy: divinity over humanity; infinite over finite; essence over existence; supernatural over natural; revelation over reason; ontology over function; permanence over change; in christology: Jesus the divine Son over Jesus the human being (i.e., reflections on what Jesus did while he lived on earth); the kerygmatic Christ over the historical Jesus (as authority for the church); Jesus Christ over the rest of humanity; in anthropology: divine activity over human passivity; impersonal/anhypostatic humanity over the value of each person; authority of the past over that of the present, and expectations for the future over serious engagement with the present; in ecclesiology: church over world; priest over laity; faith over works (doxology over discipleship); security over risk; and in methodology: dogma over development; answers over questions; polemics over engagement; abstract over concrete; and theoria over praxis.

192

APPENDIX C

JESUS: LORD OR BROTHER?

A FEMINIST CRITIQUE*

I. Introduction

           Shortly before my ordination as an
Episcopal deacon in 1973, I had several long talks
with friends about how uneasy I was about taking the
vows and making the promises that would be required of
me. I had begun to doubt that I believed much of what
I assumed deacons, priests, and bishops believe about
the relationship of God to the world, especially in
terms of Jesus Christ, a figure that puzzled me. One
of the most problematic symbols of my discomfort was
the Nicean Creed: "God the Father Almighty"? "One
Lord Jesus Christ, only Son of God, eternally begotten
of the Father"? "Begotten, not made"? "Who became
incarnate from the Virgin Mary"? It was not that I
knew these things to be untrue--theologically or
philosophically--but rather that I had serious reservations about them, grounded in a suspicion that such
dogmatic formulations as these bear some relationship
to the negative valuation of women in Christian ministry.

           My friends advised me not to take so
literally the dogmatic propositions that troubled me.
It is possible, after all, to know in one's own heart
and head, as one repeats the creed, that one does not
really mean that God is a male-figure or principle,
but rather that God has father-like "qualities"; it is
possible to realize that one does not really mean that

_____

           *This is a sermon I gave on November 8, 1978, in
James Chapel, Union Theological Seminary, New York City. I have
included it here, with a few minor revisions, for two related
reasons: (1) In it, I raised certain themes (such as relation)
which, six months later, I decided to explore more fully here.
(2) It is a feminist critique of Jesus Christ and, as such, may
help set the thesis itself in an explicitly feminist cast: for
example, it indicates in what way the issue of Jesus' full humanity is a woman's issue, whatever else it may be.

193

Mary was a woman who had no sexual intercourse, but rather that she was a "young maiden"--and moreover, that the theological significance of the Virgin Birth has nothing to do with sexuality but is rather intended to convey divine initiative in the Incarnation. It is possible even to know deep inside that one does not really mean that the Incarnation was the supernatural intervention of divinity in history but rather that Jesus was the culmination of a natural evolutionary process or that "Christ" is the archetypal cipher of "essential personhood" in history. I was told, and have discovered, that it is entirely possible to participate in communal recitation of a creed in full awareness that neither I myself, nor perhaps many others, really mean what we are saying.

Still today, I participate regularly in this kind of equivocation, because I do not know yet what else to do in the context of the Episcopal and other Christian communities in which I live and work. But I have misgivings about this. For I have begun to doubt that it is healthy or helpful either for the individuals like myself, who are willing to equivocate, or for the world-church for which we are responsible. I think we must go further, meeting our linguistic heritage on its own terms, recognizing and accepting the fact of the sexism of the tradition.

Ours is a patriarchal tradition. The church is sexist. To try to find ways of justifying it--or glossing it over to pretend that it does not really mean what it says, or that it isn't really as bad as it seems, or that it never was intended to denigrate women--is to fool ourselves, and is only to delay the processes or change and transformation within it. And so, I think, we cannot pretend that "God the Father" does not really mean that God is a Father; or that the Virgin Birth does not really mean that Mary was sexually inactive; or that Jesus as "Lord"--the only Begotten Son of God--does not really mean that Jesus is utterly unlike human beings.

Rather than equivocate ourselves deeper and deeper into a theological doublespeak which serves primarily to confuse us and others and to postpone significant institutional change, those of us who are troubled by the sexism and the blinding aura of unreality around dogmatic propositions such as these must push as responsibly as we can at the parameters of dogma, stretch the boundaries of faith and theology, and interrogate Christian language and its meanings, precisely because we are committed to a church that will take seriously its responsibility in and to a world which is its context and its membership. Hence, realizing the very basic patriarchal assumptions of our religious and cultural heritage, we need to pour ourselves into the re-creation of religion on the basis of a re-experience of reality itself.

II. "Who do you say that I am?"

Laying aside for the time being the Fatherhood of God and the Virginity of Mary, I want to focus today on christology, the person of Jesus: to attempt a response to the question put to his disciples by Jesus on the way to Caesarea-Philippi, after they had told him that others believed him to John the Baptist, or one of the prophets: "But, my friends, who do you say that I am?"

a. History and Community

No answer can be reached in a vacuum, as if history and community were of no account. An answer must reflect both its historic and communal context--which is to say, the experience of people in history: our experience, informed by that of our forebears, like Peter, whose response to Jesus was, "You are the Christ"; and including Nicea's affirmation of the homoousios (the consubstantiality of Son with Father), and Chalcedon's doctrine of two-natures (fully human, fully divine) and the reformulations of these orthodox propositions within our various denominational traditions. Such history provides the continuity and momentum of the questions and answers by which we seek meaningful ways of expressing what is real for us. If it were not for Nicea and Chalcedon, this sermon would be utterly unintelligible and impossible to give or to receive. But we must realize that history gives us not only continuity, but also discontinuity: the source of both rage and humor, rebellion and surprise, alienation and the possibility of reconciliation. What we experience and what we express does not have to be new, but it does have to be real, insofar as we mean to be faithful people.

195

b. Why Christology concerns me

Christology has become important to me for two primary reasons: (1) First, I am hooked on Jesus. I could no more pretend that the Jesus-figure, indeed the Jesus Christ of the kerygma, is unimportant to me than I could deny the significance of my parents and my past in the shaping of my future. As a "cradle-Christian"--a person who came to know the storybook Jesus long before I sat down and thought about God--I have no sane or creative choice but to take very seriously this Jesus Christ who is written indelibly in my own history.

(2) The second reason christology is important to me is that there is no more fundamental and problematic an issue for feminists than the person of Jesus. The centrality--the Lordship--of this male god, has been employed--doctrinally, politically, psychologically, structurally--in the service of a fellowship of brothers and fathers--the Church--whose female members have been auxiliary or, in special cases, perceived to be enough "like men" ("the exceptional woman," "one of the boys") to be relatively welcome in the fellowship of men. This is the locus of Mary Daly's legitimate analysis and critique of Christianity and of her reservations about the entry of women priests and ministers into an all-male society of clerics.

c. Feminist approach

Rosemary Ruether has asserted that christology is intrinsically anti-Semitic. Anti-Semitism, she says, is the "left-hand of christology," an unavoidable corollary to the Jews' rejection of the full, perfect, and final revelation of God in Christ. So, too, is christology, for all practical purposes, anti-female. In a related way, christology has been fundamentally anti-human. It is the latter problem that I want to lift up here: christology as anti-human. I approach this dilemma as a feminist woman. By "feminist," I mean one who values and attempts to relate to people as human beings irrespective of whether they are women or men. Furthermore, as one who believes that there is no higher value--no greater good, no other God--than that which enables human beings to love all people as themselves, to do what is just, and to share the earth and its resources as a common home and heritage. My religious heritage, Christianity, has compelled me to be feminist: to search incessantly for ways to effect justice. Yet, it has been despite the most vocal articulations of dogma, worship, and discipline within our traditions, that many women (I am one) have begun to believe that Jesus Christ is not what he has been cracked up to be. He is more remarkable than we had realized. More remarkable, more helpful, because he is more truly human than he has been made out to be in orthodox-- both catholic and reformed--christology.

d. The "divinization" of Jesus

The two most explicitly-christological councils of the church took great pains to stress the divinity of Jesus: the divinity of a human being. What was at stake, they believed, was redemption. It was deemed absolutely necessary to assert the divinity of Jesus if, in fact, Jesus had been, and was, the Redeemer of humanity--the savior of humanity from god-lessness--and this was not up for dispute at either Nicea or Chalcedon. Jesus had to be conceptualized as divine because patristic anthropology could make no allowance for the possibility that an ordinary human being could have done for others what Jesus had done. Hence, the divinity of Jesus was cemented in a low and static view of what it means to be human.

e. Jesus in relationship

This is what feminist theology must challenge: the passivity and powerlessness of human beings in relation to an active and omnipotent God who has no need of us. Surely, human beings do not choose and act entirely on our own--that is, without one ano-ther and without God--but human beings do choose and we do act--for the good or the ill of a God who needs us. And so we ourselves must share responsibility for the world, share credit for what love and justice there is, and share blame for what injustice and fear there is. God is here for us, but it is we who choose to open ourselves to this relationship, whereby the world is affected by this voluntary conjunction of human and divine activity. To insist that the sole and lonely agent of redemption is "not I, but God," is, I think, to miss the point of our being human and of God's being God, which is for us to be able to affirm that, "It is I--and God is with me." "It is God--and I am with God." Neither one nor the other, neither alone, but both together in relationship. It is, I believe, the secret that Jesus knew: what it means to be human in the fullest and most open way to God: an understanding of reality, relationship, and redemption (liberation) that Jesus attempted to convey to those who had hands and hearts and heads with which to follow his lead in the doing of God's work in the world. "They who have ears to hear, let them hear."

f. "Lord?"

             Now, the problem of thinking of Jesus as "Lord" is rooted not in the earliest christological tradition, but rather in the later historical and cultural development of christological dogma. Reginald Fuller notes that while the Aramaic term Mari, "My Lord," was used in reference to Jesus by the early Palestinian Christians, as well as by his disciples, its use was analogous to the term Rabbi. Fuller writes, "The important thing to notice ... is that the term Mari does not connote divinity: it is simply a recognition of human authority. Even when used of equals, it is always a term of politeness." (Foundations of New Testament Christology, p. 50). Today, however, the term "Lord" connotes more than politeness. It implies divinity; it is to say that this son of God is God the Son, an eternal person with a Trinitarian Godhead. And to affirm the divine Lordship of Jesus is, I think, to negate the full and the simple humanity of this person who was born--like us all--with a choice to make regarding his acceptance of relationship to God. To assume, or to imply, that Jesus was God, God the Son, is not basically to affirm "paradox" or "mystery" but is rather to project our own personal and communal responsibilities as participatory agents of redemption and liberation onto a mythical construct. It is, I think, to render Jesus ineffectual--to render his life, our memory of his life and death and resurrection, and the power of the Spirit which he told us would be in our midst--impotent in our world today.

             I myself am coming to realize that I do not find it helpful to think of Jesus as Lord. I may call him "Christ," but it is not because he was divine, different from us, in any way superhuman or supernatural, but rather because he was exactly human, like us. As Jon Sobrino says, Jesus showed us the way to God;

as J.A.T. Robinson suggests, Jesus lived God; as Dorothee Soelle writes, in the life and work of Jesus, God
voluntarily identified with the non-identical (a human
being) and the human being (Jesus) voluntarily identified with the non-identical (God).

g. What was revealed in Jesus' life

Following Soelle's line, I would suggest
further that in this dialectic of identification both
God and Jesus were changed--as is always the case in
mutual relationship--revealing to us thereby something
new about both God and being human. And the something
new--the revelation--is that when God and humanity act
together in the world, human action and divine action
are the same action, the same love, the same justice,
the same power, the same peace. Hence, it may be possible to assert--with some care and in tremendous awe--
not only that God is love (I John 4:8), but also that
love is God--which may be a clue, in the form of a
bridge between theism and humanism, between Christianity and other religions, to the problem that many
feminists have with the person of Jesus Christ.

h. Jesus our brother

Jesus is to be remembered, not revered.
Remembering Jesus does not warrant Jesusolatry or
Christolatry, the idolatry of a male God. Remembering
Jesus does not warrant the worshipping of Jesus, but
rather compels us to be open to the God of Jesus, the
one whom Jesus called "Abba": Daddy. Moreover, to
remember Jesus does not mean that we "imitate" Jesus,
but rather that, like him, we seek to act with God in
our own time, under the political, social, psychological, physical, and institutional conditions of our own
place. Jesus' "Daddy" may be our "Mama," or "sister,"
or "friend," or "lover," or simply the "Holy Spirit,"
which Christians have always believed is the active
power of God in our own time.

It is important for us to remember that
Jesus was not unique in and of himself. The so-called
"scandal of particularity" is exactly that: a scandal,
a mistaken doctrine. Other men and women can live--
and have lived--in an open, trusting, active, and
finally revolutionary relationship to God. Jesus is
the person whom we, as Christians, are able most com-

monly to remember. It is a matter of our particular
history; our particular community; our collective
memory. It is not that Jesus was unique; rather, that
his relationship to God was uniquely and singularly
the only liberating relationship a person can have to
God. In the life of Jesus, we are able to see that
the way to God is not by rote prayer and fasting; not
by ritual; not by credal statements; not by ecclesiastical obedience or membership. Rather, the way is a
relational, active life in the world; it is a just
way; an urgent way; a hard way; an unpopular way; a
costly way; a way of trust and hope; the way of the
cross: of suffering for others not for the sake of
suffering but for the sake of what is right and just
for others; and what is right and just is always that
which is vulnerable to the love of God, which is, in
fact, the love of humanity.

III. Feminism

        I believe that it is tremendously
important for women to seek female points of reference
for relationship to a God who has, at times and
places, been experienced as a mother or a woman. I
affirm this search and am part of it. And although I
can understand why women would leave the church which
so offends us, I am troubled by the movement of many
women out of Christianity into an all-female context
in which they seek a female 'God. They may be right.
And I may someday join them.

a. On leaving the church

        But, at this time, I am troubled on two
counts: (1) First, I am troubled by the implicit
assumption that "maleness" or "femaleness," in this
case--should be awarded such an essential status as to
provide a rationale for either men or women to idola-
trize sex or gender. This is dangerous--a delusion
that leads to hatred, fear, discrimination, and, in
time, disillusion, such as is the case with racism in
the United States among whites who have revered
"whiteness." Needless to say, this kind of gender-
idolatry is exactly what has been done by men on
behalf of their "maleness." It is exactly what is
done today by most churchmen and many churchwomen who
refuse to consider such symbols as the Fatherhood of
God, which is cemented in the tradition and in urgent

need of being cracked open. To say that God is Father
is to mean what we say. For many of us, it is not
enough; it is inadequate; it is alienating. The
resistance of churchpeople and theologians to an over-
hauling of doctrinal assumptions is, I believe, intel-
lectually shallow and emotionally deep. We must challenge this with intellectual and emotional depth, with
reason and with passion. There is good reason for
women to research, find, and name ourselves and God,
and to search for female leadership among past and
present women to help show us the way to God as women
have experienced and lived in this relationship. But
Christian women cannot, I believe, reject Jesus solely
on the basis of his "maleness" or Jesus' "Father" on
the basis of God's bondage to patriarchal projection
without strengthening the tenet that is so oppressive
to us: that biology is destiny.

          (2) The second reason that I am trou-
bled by women's departure from the church bespeaks my
own self-interest. We who are here need our sisters
here with us. I am troubled that the departing women
may be taking far more seriously the sexism of the
tradition than the revolutionary possibility of who we
together are as makers of tradition that will be revo-
lutionized only if we fasten ourselves uncompromisingly
within it to be reckoned with. To be sure, we are in
a difficult and, more often than not, a disheartening
position: in our churches, seminaries, jobs, and
relationships. It is not an easy way. It is costly,
and it is a way of trust, for I do not believe that we
today will live to see many of the fruits of our
labors.

          Any feminist whose vocation is to be a
Christian needs to be aware also that her vocation is
to be a prophet. For if she herself is unwilling to
be feared, trivialized, distanced, despised, rejected,
or ignored in her own time and home; if she is unable
to see the humor--the incongruities of her situation;
if she is unwilling to struggle for herself as well as
for others--in the familiar words of Mother Jones, to
"pray for the dead and fight like hell for the living"
(among whom she is one), she cannot be both feminist
and Christian. She will have to give up one or the
other: either the church, or herself and her sisters
and brothers.

b. On staying in the church: God and power

If she stays and chooses to struggle, what might be her lot? To trust that God is God and that she is with God. And that just as she is justified by God in the act of her openness to God, so too is God justified by her in the active presence of God in her life, her work, her choices, her death. God is, and will be, for the world what she chooses to do with God and for God in the world.

She will learn, she will know, that when God acts, it is with power. And that God's power is that which equalizes human power--redistributes it--whereby there is neither Jew nor Greek, slave nor free, male nor female, Christian nor non-Christian, gay nor straight, rich nor poor, white nor black, teacher nor student, but rather people together on the earth. She will know that God's power is that which gives to the President of the United States and to the prisoner at Riker's Island what each needs to live and choose and love and learn and repent and forgive and act. God's power equalizes the President and the prisoner, the mighty and the weak. To equalize is not to neutralize; it is to make equal; to make just; to overthrow, if necessary, the racist, classist, sexist, dehumanizing structures and attitudes that impede the growth and livelihood of all people. If, as Soelle maintains, our hands are God's hands in the world, our power is God's power in the world--if we choose to do what is loving and just.

Martin Buber wrote: "We cannot avoid using power, cannot escape the compulsion to afflict the world, so let us, cautious in diction, and mighty in contradiction, love powerfully." To the extent that we love humanity powerfully, we are those in whose lives today the realm of God is coming with power!

IV. Conclusion

A matter of no small faith! No small risk! No small promise! Thanks be to God, and to our brother Jesus, whose restraint from making or accepting magnanimous claims for himself has enabled us to discover that we are, like him, simply human, and are, like him, able to affect the course of events in the world.

202

In the words of Elie Wiesel, we are here to "re-create the universe." We are here with God--our Bakerwoman Mama, our tender Papa, our sister-brother-lover God who, when she comes, comes with power! Alleluia! Amen.

APPENDIX D

A LATIN AMERICAN VOICE: GUSTAVO GUTIERREZ

          Peruvian priest Gustavo Gutierrez's
theology reflects his conviction that "when the
wretched of the earth awake, their first challenge is
not to religion but to the social, economic, and
political order oppressing them and to the ideology
supporting it."[1] The Latin American liberation theology which Gutiérrez articulates is a new theology of
humanity, specifically an expression of faith rooted
in the populist movements for economic and political
liberation among the Latin American poor. Theology is
"the second act"; commitment to revolution, the first.
He is Irenaean in his rejection of the Augustinian-
Lutheran doctrine of the "two Kingdoms," believing
rather that "history is the locale where God reveals
the mystery of his person,"[2] and that "without liberating historical events, there would be no growth of
the Kingdom."[3] Gutiérrez's wholly good God is in the
world, a God whose advocacy of the poor is apparent in
Christ and is revealed in Scripture, as in Isaiah:

          Is not this the fast that I choose:
               to loose the bonds of wickedness,
               to undo the thongs of the yoke,
          to let the oppressed go free,
               and to break every yoke?

          Is it not to share your bread with
               the hungry?
          and bring the homeless poor into your
               house;
          when you see the naked, to cover him,
          and not to hide yourself from your own
               flesh? (58:6-7)

          Like Irenaeus, Gutiérrez emphasizes the
creativity, rather than the fall, of humanity. He
faults traditional Western (Augustinian) theology for
"a curious omission of the liberating and protagonis-
tic role of man, the lord of creation and copartici-
pant in his own salvation."[4] The operations of God
and those of "natural" humanity--human beings uncor-

rupted by unjust social structures--are the same operations in history. Eschatologically, God and humanity have the final word, a word of love and justice.

What is new in Gutiérrez's theology, or what distinguishes it from earlier theologies of humanity such as Schleiermacher's, is that Gutiérrez (1) is interested in classes, rather than individuals, as his primary theological resource; and (2) equates natural, or uncorrupted, humanity with "the poor," a materialistic distinction, contending on the basis of a Scriptural hermeneutic that "the poor person for the gospel is the neighbor par excellence."[5] This departure from liberal theology is significant, in that it serves in a fundamental way to signify a shift from the individual's preoccupation with her own faults to a thoroughgoing analysis of social, economic, and political structures in which "sin is not considered as an individual, private, or merely interior reality." Rather, for Gutiérrez and Latin American liberation theology,

> Sin is regarded as a social, histori-
> cal fact, the absence of brotherhood
> and love in relationships among men,
> the breach of friendship with God and
> with other men, and, therefore, an
> interior, personal fracture.[6]

Passivity in the face of social oppression, whether it be the passivity of rich or poor, is sinful and is responsible for the evil of injustice in history.

Humanity, specifically poor humanity, becomes responsible for coparticipation with God in human redemption from evil. God is with humanity on the earth. "It is not enough to say that love of God is inseparable from the love of one's neighbor. It must be added love for God is unavoidably expressed through love of one's neighbor."[7] "Conversion to the Lord implies conversion to the neighbor."[8] Moreover,

> The neighbor is not an occasion, an
> instrument for becoming closer to
> God. We are dealing with a real love
> of man for his own sake and not "for
> the love of God."[9]

This is, emphatically, a theology built upon human experience, a theology that can be legitimated only in and by its effects in praxis, or the circular movement between practice and theory. It is a theology that begins with the poor, those whose "epistemological privilege" it is to know God, and who are the spokespersons for all humanity. Gutiérrez's methodology applies Marxist social and economic analysis to a Biblical hermeneutic founded upon the faith-claim that God is love. "To live love is to say yes to God."[10] To live love is to be responsible for justice in society. "Christ is not a private individual; the bond which links him to all men gives him a unique historical role."[11] Christ reveals God in history as the love which binds humanity to humanity. "When justice does not exist, God is not know; he is absent"[12] (underlinings mine).

For Gutiérrez, God is love, God is wholly God, God is active in history through the poor and oppressed, whose task is to construct a "utopia" in history, which is not synonymous with the Kingdom promised by God at the eschaton but which is rather humanity's responsibility in the building of the Kingdom.[13] Gutiérrez works on the assumption that evil--that is, unjust social structures--can, and must, be undone by humanity and God in partnership, or "in Christ."

Nowhere does Gutiérrez question the goodness of God. What Gutiérrez does question is God's omnipotence, thereby marking his most radical departure from traditional Western theology. He joins Bonhoeffer in suggesting that "religion," as opposed to gospel, is bound to the concept of an omnipotent deity, a God who maintains control over direction. With Bonhoeffer, he concurs, "The God of Christians living in a world come of age--meaning a world without God--must share God's suffering."[14] We are met here by Wiesel's image of the boy hanging: "Where is God? God is hanging on these gallows." (Chapter III,

It strikes me as remarkable that Gutiérrez, having come this far in his acknowledgement of a God who is in trouble, goes no further toward the suggestion that humanity is, in fact, responsible for the redemption of God in history. Perhaps it is because he sees no need to focus attention on God's problem, given the urgency he experiences of humanity's problem; perhaps also because his faith has led him to a realization that in and through the liberation of humanity from evil, God too is liberated in the world.

Gutiérrez and the liberation theology he represents present a constructive and dynamic corrective to the Irenaean theological tradition of "development." Gutiérrez's momentum is engendered by class struggle and the "privilege" of the poor to find meaning, and take heart, in the possibility--even promise--of their own liberation from material oppression, a liberation that they themselves can and must effect. This Latin American liberation theology is steeped in a political realism infused by faith in a just God. It is, thoroughly, a theology of the oppressed, in which the question of God's goodness or love can be experienced and envisioned in the context of God's powerlessness. This is especially true inasmuch as such a God is believed to be not only identified with the poor, but also close to poor humanity in history, a God both "like" and "with" humanity, both good and powerless.

To the extent that, in theology, we seek to express the meaning of our own lives in the world, Gutiérrez's theology is not simply transferable to middle and upper classes in society, not even by the process of "identification with the oppressed."[15] What of non-poor humanity? To the extent that we too seek intimate relation with God, we encounter a particular theological difficulty: Our God does have power, just as we do, in Gutiérrez's analytical schema. What then is the relation of our God--both to us and to the poor--in the context of unjust social structures? More to the point, where are we in relation to the poor? This is the issue with which I wrestle in the Epilogue (pp. 179-83), employing Wiesel's questions as a vehicle.

208

FOOTNOTES: APPENDIX D

[1]Gustavo Gutiérrez, "Liberation Theology and Progressivist Theology," in The Emergent Gospel: Theology from the Underside of History, ed. Sergio Torres and Virginia Fabella, M.M. (Maryknoll, N.Y.: Orbis Books, 1978), p. 240.

[2]Gutiérrez, "Liberation Praxis and Christian Faith," in Frontiers of Theology in Latin America, ed. Rosino Gibellini, trans. John Drury (Maryknoll, N.Y.: Orbis Books, 1979), p. 16.

[3]Gutiérrez, A Theology of Liberation: History, Politics, and Salvation, trans. and ed. Sister Caridad Inda and John Eagleson (Maryknoll, N.Y.: Orbis Books, 1973), p. 177.

[4]Gutiérrez, A Theology of Liberation, p. 173.

[5]Gutiérrez, Praxis de liberacion y fe cristiana (San Antonio: Mexican American Cultural Center, 1974; rev. ed., 1976), p. 15.

[6]Gutiérrez, A Theology of Liberation, p. 175.

[7]Ibid., p. 200.

[8]Ibid., p. 205.

[9]Ibid., p. 202.

[10]Gutiérrez, "Liberation Praxis and Christian Faith," p. 20.

[11]Gutiérrez, A Theology of Liberation, p. 201.

[12]Ibid., p. 195.

[13]"Utopia ... a historical plan for a qualitatively different society, and the aspiration to establish new social relations among men ... is characterized by its relationship to present historical reality ..., a denunciation of the existing order ..., an annunciation of what is not yet, but will be ..., praxis, and rationality." A Theology of Liberation, pp. 232-4.

209

[14]Gutiérrez, "Liberation Theology and Progressivist Theology," p. 233.

[15]The problem with "identification with the poor" is that we have the option <u>to choose not to be poor</u>. This precludes total identification by the non-poor with the poor.

APPENDIX E

SOME CHRISTOLOGICAL POSITIONS IN

RELATION TO MY OWN: A SUMMARY

Dietrich Bonhoeffer's transcendent
hermeneutic, as evidenced in Christ the Center (1933),
renders his early christology abstract and other-
worldly. As he fleshes out this christology in his
Letters and Papers (1943-1945), Bonhoeffer's christology comes to life for me. His insights which serve as
christological foundation for Jürgen Moltmann, Dorothee
Soelle and Jon Sobrino are intimated in Letters and
Papers on the basis of urgent praxis.

Bonhoeffer suggests that we are living
in a world in which we not only must get along without
"God" but moreover need to rejoice and celebrate
because this is so. The "world come of age" is no
cause for despair, or repentance, but rather is a
world in which humanity is grown up.

The attack by Christian apolo-
getic upon the adulthood of the world
I consider to be in the first place
pointless, in the second ignoble, and
in the third un-Christian. (LP, p. 327)

No longer adolescent children who need to depend upon
a projection of good order and protection, personified
as an omnipotent and wholly good God, humanity lives
in an occasion--contemporary history--in which humanity itself is responsible for the world. "[T]he
world's coming of age ... has done away with a false
conception of God ...." (LP, p. 361). Indeed,

God would have us know that we must
live as men who can manage our lives
without him. The God who is with us
is the God who forsakes us (Mark 15:
34). The God who lets us live in
the world without the working hypothesis of God is the God before whom we
stand continually. Before God and

211

with God we live without God. God
lets himself be pushed out of the
world on to the cross. He is weak
and powerless in the world, and that
is precisely the way, the only way,
in which he is with us and helps us.
(LP, p. 360).

Bonhoeffer's christology is set here in a vision of
"religionless Christianity," the personal presence of
Christ in history as "the man [sic] for others," and
the help rendered by a "powerless and suffering God."
The shift in Bonhoeffer from the biblical conservatism
of dialectical theology to the biblical radicalism of
a proto-political theology has transparent roots in
his own experiences in Nazi Germany.

        Throughout his Letters and Papers,
Bonhoeffer continues to bring a transcendent hermeneutic into christology. In other words, he continues
to speak of Jesus Christ in terms that convey a meaning of "something" above, or other than, human experience in the world:

        [Jesus'] 'being there for others' is
        the experience of transcendence. It
        is only this 'being there for others'
        ... that is the ground of his omnipo-
        tence, omniscience, and omnipresence.
        (LP, p. 381).

        Thus, Bonhoeffer himself never proposed
a theology or christology of "radical immanence"
(Driver). By his own insights, however, about God as
"a working hypothesis" and humanity's need to "manage
our lives without him," Bonhoeffer laid groundwork for
others of us to take seriously his insights.

        I have similar difficulties with Jürgen
Moltmann that I do with Bonhoeffer. Moltmann expli-
cates a christology in The Crucified God (1973).
Despite the fact that he seeks an alternative to theism, Moltmann's central doctrinal reference for God is
the Trinity, especially the inner-trinitarian relation
between the Father and the Son. Attempting to articulate a kenotic christology (Phil. 2:5f), which takes
humanity seriously, Moltmann trips himself (and his
reader) up by beginning and ending on the assumption
that what is of greatest value is what is happening
within God. Humanity is in God. History is in God.

But the emphasis throughout is on God--not humanity,
not history. The appropriate relation of humanity to
God is that of "openness," which suggests to me a
"passive-aggressive" stance toward the future. God's
inner life is conceptualized as a three-person cadre
within which we live on a promise that someday we will
be assumed fully into the divine and mysterious cadre
of fellowship. What is significant is that, whereas
we are in God, God is conceptualized as "outside" of
us (this is the distinction between the "economic" and
the "inner" Trinity). One gets the feeling that it is
in the latter that all that is worthwhile and valuable
happens. The crucifixion is, most importantly, an
event between "God and God," rather than between God
and humanity, humanity and humanity, or even moral
good and moral evil. It is as if Moltmann wraps a
mythological blanket around history as a promise of
history's value and ultimate redemption from apparent
meaninglessness. I do not mean to be overly harsh,
and if I were writing a full essay on Moltmann, I
would speak with appreciation for many of his insights.
For example, in his treatment of Jesus' historical and
eschatological "trials," he presents more fully than
in any christology I have encountered the specifics
and the various hermeneutics of Jesus' life, death,
and resurrection--as a human being. But Moltmann does
not develop this human emphasis. Rather, he draws us
continually back to what feels to me like a spectator-
box to observe God in relation to God. I find myself
unclear as to what this has to do with either the
human Jesus, or us.

          Jon Sobrino's Christology at the Cross-
roads (1976) is a splendid effort at constructing a
"christology from below." Sobrino begins and ends
with an emphasis on Jesus, the person who taught and,
later in his life, became the way to God. Christolog-
ically, Jesus becomes the Son. Adoptionism? Perhaps.
This is "gradual Sonship." Even after the resurrection, Jesus' Sonship or Christ-function is that of
providing the way to, not the essence of, God in history. For Sobrino, christology is rooted in communal
experience, or social praxis. Faith and obedience--
which constitute together the mandate of discipleship
("Follow me"--Mark 1:17-18)--lead to the transformation of power from sin to love. Sobrino draws exten-
sively from Moltmann in the presentation of his doctrine of a Trinitarian God who suffers. Ironically,
the doctrine makes better sense in Moltmann's tho-

213

roughgoing Trinitarian hermeneutic of reality than as
an insert into what is otherwise, for Sobrino, an
anthropological Christology.

Sobrino emphasizes the role of human
freedom and responsibility in redemption, including
the Incarnation as one of moral union. He believes
that God suffers, and intimates a doctrine of thoroughgoing immanence which he does not develop. Like
Bonhoeffer and Moltmann, Sobrino seems to be wedged
between, on the other hand, a sense (intuition? commitment? passion?) of humanity and an immanent God
and, on the other hand, a belief in a divinity whose
essential being is above, beyond, or something wholly
other than creation and human experience.

Dorothee Soelle has a stronger sense
than Sobrino of the centrality of human will and
choice in everything that matters. She does not
articulate clearly a doctrine of God, which reflects,
I believe, her ambivalence about theism. I am closer
to Soelle than to Sobrino (Moltmann, or Bonhoeffer) in
this way. Soelle relies heavily on experience and
contemporary praxis as parameters for her work. Like
me, she is a white female member of the First World.
Although unfortunately Soelle does not pay much explicit attention to the significance of her sex, her
theology wells up from her racial- and especially her
class-consciousness as a mandate to do theology that
will be not simply explicative of, but transforming
in, the world.

The impetus for her christology--from
Christ the Representative (1965) to her most recent
book Death By Bread Alone (1975)--is the frightening
magnitude of alienation and evil in human life. However she might attempt to spell this out theologically,
Christ is her God. By Christ, Soelle means a number
of things: (1) Christ is provisional representative
(not replacement) of both God and humanity. Where
human activity is Christ-like, it is divine activity.
In history there is no gulf between humanity and
divinity insofar as Christ is operative. At some
point, both God and humanity will be able to dispense
with representation. And who or what is this Christ?
(2) Christ is political, concerned with power. The
abuse of institutional power is the manifestation of
evil in history. Christ is the historical Jesus who
stood unaccountable to the powers of religion and
society. Human relationship redefines power. Rela-

tional power is ultimately stronger than institutional
oppression (Christ the Representative [London: S.C.M.
Press, 1967; German, 1965], p. 105).   Christ demytholo-
gizes power (Ibid.).   (3) The historical Jesus is
Christ for us in a mystical way.   "Mystical love ...
transcends every God who is less than love" (Suffering
[Philadelphia: Fortress Press, 1975; German, 1973],
p. 94).   For Soelle, Christ is the on-going historical
presence of the Jesus who loved.   As such, Christ is
love--political love that suffers and knows itself as
God (God's representative?) suffering for justice.
"That is why, in the Christian understanding of suffering, mysticism and revolution move so close to one
another" (Ibid., p. 102).   (4) Christ is the one whose
life revealed, and presence evokes, phantasie--imagina-
tion, freedom to risk, the aim of which is to discover,
make visible, and disclose that which is invisible"
(Beyond Mere Obedience [Minneapolis: Augsburg, 1970;
German, 1968], p. 80).   Presumably, this is to make
visible the possibilities of relationship and justice.
(5) Christ means liberation.   "For Jesus, 'God' meant
liberation, the unchaining of all powers which lie
imprisoned in each of us, powers with which we too can
perform miracles no less significant than those we are
told Jesus performed" (Ibid., p. 79).   (6) Christ is
truth--and the truth is concrete.   "Truth ... cannot
tolerate abstraction, naked theory, pure doctrine, or
the abrupt, unexpected, and therefore dogmatic kerygma.
The truth of Christ exists only as concrete realization ....   The verification principle of every theological statement is the praxis that is enabled for
the future" (Political Theology [Philadelphia: Fortress Press, 1974; German, 1971], p. 76).   (7) Christ
is the one who "identifies with the non-identical."
(Hegel).   Christ's identity with both God and humanity
is on the basis of non-identity.   (It is unclear in
what sense Christ is non-identical with humans except
insofar as he is only one person and not all of us,
which I take to be Soelle's point).   On the basis of
Bonhoeffer's suggestion of the powerless and crucified
God, Soelle is able to employ Hegel's method to assert
that, in Christ, God "put himself at risk, made himself dependent upon us, identified with the non-identical" (Christ the Representative, p. 152).   It seems
to me that Soelle is straining to assert (but does
not) that in Jesus' life and death--God's identification with the non-identical, and a human being's
identification with the non-identical--both God and
the human being are changed; and that in this mutual
relation, something new emerged: the actualized

215

identity of God and human being in history, a "synthesis" that was passed on to other persons--Jesus'
friends, disciples, Christians, others, creating a
christological basis on which it is possible to say
not only that "God is love" (I John 4:8), but also
that love is God. Soelle does not make this claim
unequivocally, because she continues to struggle with
theism. I share this struggle. Soelle has been as
significant an influence on my work as any theologian.

APPENDIX F

LOVE AND SEXUALITY*

Consider the words of James Baldwin:

> The role of the artist is exactly
> the same as the role of the lover.
> If I love you, I have to make you
> conscious of the things you don't
> see.

The role of the artist. Lover.
Teacher. Counselor. Christian priest--lay or
ordained. If I love you, I have to make you conscious
of the things you don't see. I understand this to be
our common vocation.

I stand here as one whose own understanding of herself continues to evolve--often
roughly, sometimes abrasively even to myself, peppered
with surprises about myself and others. A changing
sense of self that is never finished. I do not understand myself primarily in categories that suggest that
anything about me is static. Even those categories
that most of us assume to be basic--such as female or
male sex, or human identity itself--seem to me more
elusive, less still, than we often assume. I am
tempted to say, and will for now, that nothing is
fixed.

And yet, there is something basic among
us, something evolutionary--and revolutionary; something more basic than femaleness or maleness, whiteness or blackness; gayness or straightness; something
more basic than Christianity or any religion. Something that is unchanging, stable, constant, precisely

*My address to Integrity (Gay Episcopalians and
their friends) Convention, September 7, 1979, Denver, Colorado.
Edited and abridged transcript, ©️ 1979 Integrity, Inc. This
appendix is included because it uncovers the core of my book as
I have been attempting to share it in the church. The Integrity
Convention provided an opportunity for this.

in its dynamic, revolutionary movement in the world. I am speaking of the human experience, and perhaps also the experience of other creatures, of love--or, our experience of God in the world. And so, if there is one fundamental category that can be appropriately descriptive, even definitive, of who we are--of what we are here to do in the world--it is that of lover.

Because the word "love" has become a catch-all for sweet and happy feelings; because we have learned to believe that love stories are warm and fuzzy stories about dewy eyes and titillating embraces; because love has been romanticized so poorly, trivialized so thoroughly, and perverted--turned completely around--from its Gospel meaning, we find ourselves having to begin again to re-experience, re-consider, re-conceptualize what it means--to say "I love you." What it means to believe that God is in the world, among us, moving with us, even by us, here and now. What does it mean--to be a lover? Indeed, as Baldwin notes, to make those whom we love conscious of the things they don't see; but first to become conscious ourselves of the things we don't see.

It occurs to me that it may be our special privilege to take very seriously what it means to love. Homosexuals have had to fall back on the category of "lover" in order to speak of some of our most meaningful relationships. Deprived of categories that are steeped in the tradition of romantic love-- categories like husband and wife, masculinity and femininity, bride and bridegroom; deprived of the symbols of romantic love, such as rings and weddings and public displays of affection; deprived of the religious legitimation of romantic love--the blessing of our relationships; deprived of celebration, acceptance, even acknowledgement of our relationships, we have had no other common word for ourselves, and for those whom we love, except the word "lover." Deprived of civil and religious trappings of "love," we may well be compelled to plumb the depths of what it really means--to love. Our deprivation becomes an opportunity: to become conscious of the things we have not seen, and to make others conscious of these same things.

What might it mean--to love? I want to tell you what I am discovering, in the hope that you will be moved to consider carefully your own experiences. There is a time, occasionally, for us to come to a consensus for the purpose of corporate action.

218

But I am not here this morning to gather a consensus on what it means to love. At this point, the last thing we need is a new set of commandments writ large in stone. I believe it is a time, in the words of Nelle Morton, to "hear each other into speech." It is a time to tell our stories, to listen carefully, to begin to experience our experience, to risk realizing and sharing our senses of confusion, fear, frustration, anger, even rage, about what is done to us, and about what we do to ourselves and others, all in the name of a "love" that is too often not love at all, but only a sham.

And so I speak personally, as a lesbian feminist Christian priest and teacher. I use these words to describe myself, because each of them has grown out of my evolving sense of how I might best be a lover of sisters and brothers in the world today. Lesbian. Feminist. Christian. Priest. Teacher. Either these dimensions of my identity enable me to love or they are destructive, dysfunctional dimensions of who I am and would best be somehow discarded. For now, these overlapping senses of myself infuse me with a sense not only of what love means, but also that who I am--and who you are, and who we are together--matters. If I love you, if we love, we matter. Lovers make all the difference in the world.

. . .

I am discovering that <u>love is justice</u>. Love does not come first, justice later. Love is not a "feeling" that precedes right-relationship among the persons in a family or the people of the world. We do not feel our ways into right-relationship: with other races, other people. We do not feel our way into doing what is just. We act our way into feeling. This was, by the way, the raison d'être of the Philadelphia ordination: a conviction shared by many that we act our way into new feelings, new emotions, new ideas. And the act is love. The act is justice. "Good feelings" may come later. I am discovering that this is true in friendship itself. Increasingly, I see that the more just a personal relationship, the more loving this relationship, the more mutual, honest, beneficial, and creative for both my friend and me, the more intensely I experience feelings of love between us. Speaking sexually, the better the

friendship, the more sustained and precious to me is
the erotic flow of energy that bonds us together.

I find this terribly confusing in the
context of a social order in which there is historically a great divide between "friendship" and "sexual
love"--between philia and eros. Most of us have been
out of touch, from the beginning, with the eroticism
that does, I believe, draw us toward friendship with
persons of both sexes. Sexuality is our experience of
moving toward others: making love, making justice, in
the world. It is the drive to connect; movement in
love; expression of our desire to be bonded together
in life and death. Sexuality is expressed not only
between lovers in a personal relationship but also in
the work of an artist who loves her painting; a father
who loves his children; a revolutionary person who
loves her people. I see love, justice, and the sexuality which makes them, in close friendship; in the
victory salutation of a Sandinista rebel in Nicaragua;
in the poetry of E. E. Cummings, Emily Dickinson,
Adrienne Rich; in the celebration of a Maundy Thursday
Eucharist on behalf of Maria Cueto and Raisa Nemikin;
in the genital pleasure of two women, or two men, or a
woman and a man, who are doing their best to make justice in their relationship. Where there is no justice
--between two people or among thousands--there is no
love. And where there is no justice, no love, sexuality is perverted into violence and violation--the
effects of which include rape; emotional and physical
battering; relationships manipulated by control, competition, and contempt; even war itself. Love is justice. Sexuality is our means of making love, justice,
in the world.

. . .

I am discovering that love is passionate.
Passion is willingness to suffer--not masochistically--
but rather, in the broadest sense of the verb "to suffer"--to bear up who we are, to endure both the pain
and the pleasure of what it means to love, to do what
is just, to make right our relationships. A person of
passion, a lover of humanity, is she or he who enters
seriously and intentionally into the depths of human
experience, insists upon its value, and finds God, to
quote Elie Wiesel, in "the exchange of glances heavy
with existence"; or in the testimonies of Sarah Grimké,
by refusing to live any longer with "someone's feet

upon our necks"; or in the spirit of Martin Luther King, Jr., in the vision of a promised land in which we are "free at last"--a land in which love as justice is our common experience.

Our passion as lovers is that which fuels both our rage at injustice--including that which is done to us--and our compassion, or empathy with those who violate us, hurt us, and would even destroy us. Rage and compassion, far from being mutually exclusive, belong together. Each is an aspect of our integrity, for just as our rage is appropriate to our experience of lovelessness in the world, so too is our compassion the on-going acknowledgement and confession of our own refusals to make love in the world--beginning in our own homes, in our own beds, at our own altars. How, in the name of either God or humanity, can we hear an Anita Bryant (or the hidden voices of men in corporate power who use her as a frontispiece); or the frustrated and fear-laced protests against us raised by bishops, priests, and laypersons of our own church, without experiencing both rage at what is being done to us in the name of "love," and compassion for those who--like us--act out of fear, projection, denial, scapegoating, and contempt for persons who threaten us?

I am not suggesting that we be marsh-mallows. To the contrary. I would like to continue to toughen up. I believe that the way to do this is to realize and accept my own participation in fear and denial, in injustice and lovelessness. And to do what I can each day "to go and sin no more." I know that, regardless of good intention, my own feet will always be placed squarely on someone's neck and that it is the loving vocation of those whom I am putting down to ask me to remove my feet from their neck; if need be, to tell me; and, finally--if I refuse--to knock me off.

We, who are lesbians and gay men in the Church, are asking ecclesiastical authorities to remove the feet of a predominant theological tradition --both sexist and heterosexist--from off our necks. Some of us are telling these institutional authorities. And, if it is not done, our vocation is to knock it off.

Both as oppressor (white, male, upper middle-class people, capitalists in a world yearning

221

for common resources, unjust lovers in one-to-one relationships) and as oppressed (female, homosexuals, the poor, blacks, other colors of minorities, victims of domination in personal relationships), we need to remember that it is the oppressed--women, lesbians, gay men, black people, poor people, victims of domination and control--who set both the timetable and the agenda for liberation. If we say now is the time, now is the time!

In a society, a contemporary world-order, built upon sex roles; an economy, capitalism (although Marxism has a similar set of sex-role problems), maintained upon sex-roles; a religion, Christianity, thoroughly patriarchal and rooted in sex-roles, the deepest currents of women's liberation and gay liberation merge in radical feminism and threaten to bring down the entire social/economic/religious structure of reality.

Many fear that lesbian feminism poses a threat to the nuclear family; the economic order; and religious assumptions about marriage as the blessed state, the fatherhood of god and the motherhood of women, the procreative norm of sexuality, and the high value of dominant-submissive relationships beginning with male property-rights and extending to God the Father. Those who fear that this is what we are about fear rightly. As lesbian, feminist, Christian, I believe that our vocation is to bring down the sacred canopy that has heretofore prevented our active realization of love and justice in human life as the only sacred--godly, right, and normative--dimension of our life together.

As first offspring of sexism, hetero-sexism is the ideological underpinning of gay oppression. Heterosexism is rooted in men's fantasies about what it means to be female and male and what it means to have sex, fantasies that rigidly delineate male from female, masculine from feminine, animus from anima, top from bottom, initiator from receiver, and power of the phallus from gratitude of the womb. Heterosexism is structurally pervasive in our culture and worthy only of being un-done.

. . .

222

And yet, to participate in its un-doing is to feel a little crazy. We have been raised and instructed in heterosexist values. Since my "coming out" articles, I have begun to realize that heterosexist assumptions all but complete our senses of who we are in the world. To reject them privately is difficult, tedious, and tends us toward strange senses of schizophrenia. To reject them publicly is to take a step none of us is ever prepared to take. It is to begin to act our way into what we trust will be new ways of feeling and thinking about ourselves and others in the world. To state publicly that we are lesbians or gay men is to enter, for a time at least, into a sense of oneself as crazy. This has been my experience. By "craziness," I mean that my own sense of what is important, of who I am in relation to others in the world, of what my vocation as priest and teacher is, even my sense of what is happening in my closest relations is called into question, often as much by me as by others. To feel crazy is to wonder if I am concocting a reality meaningful only to me and to a few folks who are crazy enough to agree with me. It is to feel as if I have stepped outside the arena of what is not only acceptable, but also intelligible --even to myself. My decision (years in the making) to state publicly that I am a lesbian was a decision central to my vocation as a teacher (of students, for whom sexuality is usually a primary concern); as a priest (of a church, in which sexuality is a bedrock of the entire corpus of theological tradition and praxis); as a feminist (in a society founded upon unjust assumptions about female and male roles); as a Christian (who believes that the command to love neighbor as self has as much to do with eros and philia as with agape, and that such love knows no sex- or gender-confines); and indeed as a lover--a person in pursuit of friendship, justice, and co-creativity in the world, including our most immediate and intimate relations.

To say I am a lesbian is to make a statement at once personal and political. It is to acknowledge the fact that, in our present social order, equal sexual relationships--relationships truly mutual--are available largely in same-sex relationships. I have come to believe that it is unwise to expect mutuality between women and men in a sexist society. While I can appreciate--and affirm--the efforts of women and men toward this end, this is not where I choose to invest my self, my passion.

223

The lesbian relation, as I experience it, can be mutual, and as such, may offer a glimpse into a way of being in the world that is as instructive for women and men in relation, as for women and women, or men and men. To be a lesbian is for me the best way to be a lover. It is to begin to untangle myself from the "lies, secrets, and silences" that have been draped as a shroud over our lives together on earth. It is to invite projections onto myself, to trigger anxiety, to learn to bear up--with others--common pain, common yearning, common responsibility to make each other conscious of the things we don't see.

Lesbian sexuality can be expressed intimately between peers who have work to do together in the world--specifically, the liberation of women. It is to "linger on the detail" of being woman in a patriarchal society. Adrienne Rich speaks of lesbianism as a "primary intensity" between women--an intensity, it seems to me, that is vital (at least for some of us) if we are ever to take ourselves, and our sisters, as seriously as were born to believe we should take church fathers, natural fathers, employers, husbands, sons, the Sonship of a Redeemer, and the Fatherhood of our Creator. Lesbian feminism is a protest against the structures of male dominance.

They who resist us have good reason. The stakes are high. True sexual liberation--for homosexuals and for women--will happen only when our economic, religious, educational, business, and other social structures and customs do not operate on the assumption that men will lead and women follow; that men work away from home and women in the home; that only a man and a woman constitute a creative couple; that only procreation is truly creative; and that in order to have a social order, someone must be on top and someone else on bottom: economically, religiously, sexually, otherwise. To challenge these assumptions is, in some very real sense, to go mad: The "fathers" are not with us. Our families do not know how to be with us. Our church believes it must be against us. The Bible admonishes us. Jesus was silent about us. The authorities that be despise the threat that we pose, and they despise it all the more if we appear to be wise and happy people. It is much easier to tolerate a sad and pitiful homosexual than a proud and creative gay man or lesbian. If we affirm ourselves, we are seen as sick; if we renounce ourselves, we are called healthy. And we think we are crazy.

All of which is to say that, for me, lesbianism is a delightful, tedious, and important way of my learning to love myself, my friends, my God. Lesbianism means justice for women. Lesbianism means passion by women for women. Lesbianism means creative cooperation among women, on behalf of a humanity of women and men in which cooperation often gives way to competition; and love, to coyness, manipulation, and contempt.

. . .

To say I love you is to say that you are not mine, but rather your own.

To love you is to advocate your rights, your space, your self, and to struggle with you, rather than against you, in your learning to claim your power in the world.

To love you is to make love to you/with you, whether in an exchange of glances heavy with existence, in the passing of a peace we mean, in common work or play, in our struggle for social justice, or in the ecstasy and tenderness of embrace which we believe is just and right for us and others in the world.

To love you is to be pushed by a power/ God both terrifying and comforting, to touch and be touched by you. To love you is to sing with you, cry with you, pray with you, and act with you to co-create the world.

To say "I love you" means--let the revolution begin! God bless the Revolution! Amen.

225

The ultimate most holy form
of theory is action. Not to look
on passively while the spark leaps
from generation to generation, but
to leap and to burn with it!*

*Nikos Kazantzakis, The Saviors of God, p. 99.

BIBLIOGRAPHY

Resources Cited

Altizer, Thomas J.J., and William Hamilton. Radical Theology and
        the Death of God. Indianapolis: Bobbs-Merrill,
        1966.

Anselm. Cur Deus Homo. In Saint Anselm: Basic Writings.
        Trans. S.N. Deane. LaSalle, Ill.: Open Court,
        1962. pp. 171-288.

Aquinas, Thomas. Introduction to St. Thomas Aquinas. Intro.
        Anton C. Pegis. New York: Modern Library, 1948.

Arendt, Hannah. "Radical Evil: Total Domination." In Guilt:
        Man and Society. Ed. Roger W. Smith. New York:
        Doubleday and Co., 1971. pp. 217-53.

Augustine. The City of God. Vol. 18 in Great Books of the
        Western World. Chicago: Encyclopedia Britannica,
        1952. Also, ed. Vernon J. Bourke. Garden City:
        Image Books, 1958.

_____. Confessions. Trans. with intro. by R.S. Pinc-
        Coffin. Harmondsworth, Middlesex, England:
        Penguin, 1961; rep., 1977.

_____. "On the Forgiveness of Sins, and Baptism." In
        Nicene and Post-Nicene Fathers of the Christian
        Church. Ed. Philip Schaff. Vol. V: St. Augus-
        tine: Anti-Pelagian Writings. Grand Rapids:
        Eerdmans, rep. 1971, 1975. pp. 11-78.

_____. "On the Spirit and the Letter." In Nicene and
        Post-Nicene Fathers. Vol. V. pp. 83-114.

Baeck, Leo. Judaism and Christianity. Trans. with intro. by
        Walter Kaufmann. Philadelphia: The Jewish
        Publication Society of America, 1958 (5719).

Barth, Karl. Church Dogmatics. Edinburgh: T. & T. Clark, 1961.

_____. Dogmatics in Outline. New York: Harper & Row, 1959.

Battenhouse, Roy W., ed. A Companion to the Study of St.
          Augustine. New York: Oxford University Press,
          1955.

de Beauvoir, Simone. The Ethics of Ambiguity. Secaucus, N.J.:
          Citadel Press, 1972; orig. pub., 1948.

Berger, Peter. The Sacred Canopy: Elements of a Sociological
          Theory of Religion. Garden City: Doubleday &
          Co., 1967.

_____, and Thomas Luckmann. The Social Construction of
          Reality: A Treatise in the Sociology of Knowl-
          edge. Garden City: Doubleday & Co., 1966;
          Anchor Books, 1967.

Bonhoeffer, Dietrich. Christ the Center. Intro. Edwin H.
          Robertson and trans. John Bowden. New York:
          Harper & Row, 1960.

_____. Letters and Papers from Prison. Ed. Eberhard
          Bethge. New York: Macmillan, 1953; first
          Macmillan paperback, 1972.

Bradley, John P. "The gentle, vital art of learning to think."
          Charlotte [N.C.] News. Friday, July 14, 1978.
          p. 4A.

Brown, Peter. Augustine of Hippo. Berkeley: University of
          California Press, 1967.

Brown, Robert F. "Irenaeus' Two Schemata of Salvation." M.A.
          thesis. Union Theological Seminary and Columbia
          University, New York City, 1967.

Brown, Robert McAfee. In class ("Theological Themes in the
          Writings of Elie Wiesel"). Union Theological
          Seminary, New York City. February 15 and March
          15, 1978.

Brunner, Emil. The Mediator: A Study of the Central Doctrine
          of the Christian Faith. Philadelphia: West-
          minster Press, 1947.

Buber, Martin. I and Thou. A new translation with prologue and
          notes by Walter Kaufmann. New York: Charles
          Scribner's Sons, 1970.

Bultmann, Rudolf. Jesus Christ and Mythology. New York:
          Charles Scribner's Sons, 1958.

Bultmann, Rudolf, and five critics. Kerygma and Myth. Ed. Hans
          Werner Bartsch. New York: Harper & Row, 1961.

Burnaby, John. Amor Dei: A Study of the Religion of St.
          Augustine. London: Hodder and Stoughton, 1938.

Cadbury, Henry J. The Eclipse of the Historical Jesus. Haver-
          ford, Pa.: Pendle Hill Publications, 1963.

de Chardin, Teilhard. The Divine Milieu. New York: Harper &
          Row, 1960.

Christian, Meg. Face the Music. Olivia Records, Inc. 1977.

Clement of Alexandria. "On Marriage." In Alexandrian Chris-
          tianity. Ed. J. Oulten and H. Chadwick. Vol. II
          in Library of Christian Classics. Philadelphia:
          Westminster Press, 1954. pp. 40-92.

Cochrane, C.N. Christianity and Classical Culture. London:
          Oxford University Press, 1940.

Collins, Sheila D. A Different Heaven and Earth. Valley Forge:
          Judson Press, 1974.

Cross Currents, XXVIII:3. Fall, 1978. (Special issue on the
          Holocaust).

Cullman, Oscar. Christ and Time. London: SCM Press, 1962.

Daly, Mary. Beyond God the Father: Toward a Philosophy of
          Women's Liberation. Boston: Beacon Press, 1973.

Desert Fathers. Trans. with intro. by Helen Waddell. Ann Arbor:
          University of Michigan Press, 1957.

Dillenberger, John, ed. Martin Luther: Selections from His
          Writings. Garden City: Doubleday & Co., 1961.

Dostoyevsky, Fyodor. The Brothers Karamazov. Vol. 52 in Great
          Books of the Western World. Chicago: Encyclo-
          pedia Britannica, 1952.

Driver, Tom F. Patterns of Grace: Human Experience as Word of
          God. San Francisco: Harper & Row, 1977.

Eliot, T.S. "The Hollow Men." In Collected Poems, 1909-1962.
          New York: Harcourt, Brace, and World, 1970.
          pp. 79-82.

Engels, Friedrich. The Origin of the Family, Private Property
    and the State. New York: International Pub-
    lishers, 1942.

Fey, Harold E., ed. How My Mind Has Changed. Cleveland: World
    Publishing Co., 1961.

Fleischner, Eva. Auschwitz: Beginning of a New Era? Reflec-
    tions on the Holocaust. New York: KTAV Publish-
    ing House, Cathedral Church of St. John the
    Divine, and Anti-Defamation League of B'nai
    B'rith, 1977.

Fuller, Reginald H. The Foundations of New Testament Chris-
    tology. New York: Charles Scribner's Sons, 1965.

Galligan, Michael. God and Evil. New York: Paulist Press,
    1976.

Gilkey, Langdon. Naming the Whirlwind: The Renewal of God-
    Language. Indianapolis: Bobbs-Merrill, 1969.

Goldstein, Valerie Saiving. "The Human Situation: A Feminine
    Viewpoint." In The Nature of Man in Theological
    and Psychological Perspective. Ed. Simon Doniger.
    New York: Harper & Row, 1962. pp. 151-70.

Griffin, David R. A Process Christology. Philadelphia:
    Westminster Press, 1973.

Grillmeier, Aloys. Christ in Christian Tradition. London:
    Mowbray, 1965.

Gutiérrez, Gustavo. "Liberation Praxis and Christian Faith."
    In Frontiers of Theology in Latin America. Ed.
    Rosino Gibellini. Trans. John Drury. Maryknoll:
    Orbis Books, 1979. pp. 1-33. Also pub. as
    Praxis de liberacion y fe cristiana. San Antonio:
    Mexican American Cultural Center, 1974; revised,
    1976.

_____. "Liberation Theology and Progressivist Theology."
    In The Emergent Gospel: Theology from the Under-
    side of History. Ed. Sergio Torres and Virginia
    Fabella, M.M. Maryknoll: Orbis Books, 1978.
    pp. 227-55.

_____. A Theology of Liberation: History, Politics and
    Salvation. Trans. and ed. Sister Caridad Inda and
    John Eagleson. Maryknoll: Orbis Books, 1973.

Harrison, Beverly Wildung. Conversation. New York City, March 20, 1979.

Hartshorne, Charles. A Natural Theology for Our Time. LaSalle, Ill.: Open Court, 1967.

Hick, John. Evil and the God of Love. Glasgow, Scotland: William Collins Sons & Co., Ltd., 1968.

Howes, Elizabeth Boyden. Intersection and Beyond. San Francisco: Guild for Psychological Studies, 1971.

Irenaeus. Against Heresies. In Vol. I, The Ante-Nicene Fathers. Ed. the Rev. Alexander Roberts and James Donaldson. Grand Rapids: Eerdmans, 1975. pp. 307-567.

_____. Fragments from the Lost Writings of Irenaeus. From the Catena on St. Paul's Epistles to the Corinthians. In Vol. I, The Ante-Nicene Fathers. pp. 568-78.

Jerome. Against Jovinianus. In A Select Library of Nicene and Post-Nicene Fathers. Ed. Schaff and Wace. Vol. 6. Grand Rapids: Eerdmans, 1955.

Johnson, W.A. On Religion: A Study of Theological Method in Schleiermacher and Nygren. Netherlands: Brill, 1964.

Kazantzakis, Nikos. The Saviors of God: Spiritual Exercises. New York: Simon and Schuster, 1960.

Kee, Howard C. Community of the New Age: Studies in Mark's Gospel. Philadelphia: Westminster Press, 1977.

Kelly, J.N.D. Early Christian Doctrines. New York: Harper & Row, 1958.

Knox, John. Criticism and Faith. London: Hodder and Stoughton, 1953.

Lehmann-Haupt, Christopher. Review of The Dancing Wu Li Masters: An Overview of the New Physics by Gary Zukar. New York Times. Wednesday, March 28, 1979.

Levin, Nora. The Holocaust: The Destruction of European Jewry, 1933-1945. New York: Schocken Books, 1973.

233

Madden, Edward H., and Peter H. Hare. Evil and the Concept of God. Springfield, Ill.: Charles C. Thomas, 1968.

May, Rollo. Power and Innocence: A Search for the Sources of Violence. New York: Dell Publishing Co., 1972.

Mill, John Stuart. "Mr. Mansel on the Limits of Religious Thought." In God and Evil. Ed. Nelson Pike. Englewood Cliffs, N.J.: Prentice-Hall, Inc., 1964. pp. 37-45.

Moltmann, Jürgen. The Crucified God. New York: Harper & Row, 1974.

Moule, C.F.D. The Gospel According to Mark. Cambridge: Cambridge University Press, 1965.

Murray, James A.H., ed. A New English Dictionary on Historical Principles. Oxford: Clarendon Press, 1901.

Near, Holly. Imagine My Surprise! Redwood Records, Inc., 1978.

Niebuhr, R.R. Schleiermacher on Christ and Religion. New York: Charles Scribner's Sons, 1964.

Nineham, Dennis. "Epilogue" in The Myth of God Incarnate. Ed. John Hick. Philadelphia: Westminster Press, 1977.

_____. "Some Reflections on the Present Position with Regard to the Jesus of History." In Historicity and Chronology in the New Testament. Theological Collections #6. London: S.P.C.K., 1965. pp. 1-18.

Norris, Richard A. "Christological Models in Cyril of Alexandria." In Studia Patristica, Vol. XIII. Ed. Elizabeth A. Livingstone. Berlin: Akademie-Verlag, 1965. pp. 255-68.

_____. Manhood and Christ. Oxford: Clarendon Press, 1963.

_____. In class ("Irenaeus and the Gnostics"). Union Theological Seminary, New York City. May 1, 1978.

Outka, Gene. Agape: An Ethical Analysis. New Haven: Yale University Press, 1972.

Pannenberg, Wolfhart. Theology and the Kingdom of God. Ed.
    Richard John Neuhaus. Philadelphia: Westminster
    Press, 1969; fifth printing, 1977.

Pearce, Jane, and Saul Newton. The Conditions of Human Growth.
    New York: Citadel Press, 1969.

Perls, Frederick, Ralph F. Hefferline, and Paul Goodman.
    Gestalt Therapy: Excitement and Growth in the
    Human Personality. New York: Dell Publishing
    Co., 1951.

Perrin, Norman. Rediscovering the Teaching of Jesus. London:
    SCM Press, 1967.

Ragni, Gerome, and James Rado. Hair. United Artists Corp.,
    1979.

Rich, Adrienne. The Dream of a Common Language. New York:
    W.W. Norton and Co., 1978.

_____. On Lies, Secrets, and Silence: Selected Prose,
    1966-1978. New York: W.W. Norton and Co., 1979.

Robinson, James M. A New Quest of the Historical Jesus.
    London: SCM Press, 1959.

Rosenfeld, Alvin H., and Irving Greenberg, ed. Confronting the
    Holocaust: The Impact of Elie Wiesel. Blooming-
    ton: Indiana University Press, 1978.

Ruether, Rosemary. Faith and Fratricide: The Theological
    Roots of Anti-Semitism. New York: Seabury
    Press, 1974.

Schillebeeckx, Edward. Jesus: An Experiment in Christology.
    Trans. Hubert Hoskins. New York: Seabury
    Press, 1979.

Schleiermacher, Friedrich. The Christian Faith. Ed. H.R.
    Mackintosh and J.S. Stewart. Philadelphia:
    Fortress Press, 1928; latest impression, 1976.

_____. On Religion: Speeches to Its Cultured Despisers.
    Trans. John Oman with intro. Rudolf Otto. New
    York: Harper & Row, 1958.

235

Schweitzer, Albert. The Quest of the Historical Jesus: A Critical Study of its Progress from Reimarus to Wrede. New York: Macmillan, 1961.

Sobrino, Jon. Christology at the Crossroads: A Latin American Approach. Maryknoll, N.Y.: Orbis Books, 1978.

Soelle, Dorothee. Beyond Mere Obedience: Reflections on a Christian Ethic for the Future. Minneapolis: Augsburg Publishing House, 1970.

_____. Christ the Representative: An Essay in Theology After the "Death of God." Philadelphia: Fortress Press, 1967.

_____. Death by Bread Alone: Texts and Reflections on Religious Experience. Trans. David L. Scheidt. Philadelphia: Fortress Press, 1978.

_____. A poem for Sydney and Robert McAfee Brown. Read at Union Theological Seminary, New York City. May 18, 1979.

_____. Political Theology. Trans. with intro. by John Shelley. Philadelphia: Fortress Press, 1974.

_____. Suffering. Trans. Everett R. Kalin. Philadelphia: Fortress Press, 1975.

Struik, Dirk J. Intro. to Karl Marx's The Economic and Philosophical Manuscripts of 1844. Trans. Martin Milligan, ed. by Struik. New York: International Publishers, 1964.

Tillich, Paul. Love, Power, and Justice: Ontological Analyses and Ethical Applications. London: Oxford University Press, 1954.

_____. Systematic Theology. Three Volumes in One. Chicago: University of Chicago Press, 1967.

Trible, Phyllis. God and the Rhetoric of Sexuality. Philadelphia: Fortress Press, 1978.

Union Seminary Quarterly Review, XXXII:3 & 4. Spring & Summer, 1977. (Special issue on the Holocaust).

von Rad, Gerhard. Old Testament Theology. New York: Harper & Row, 1962.

Wainwright, Geoffrey. <u>Eucharist</u> <u>and</u> <u>Eschatology</u>. London: Epworth Press, 1971.

Warfield, B.B. "Introductory Essay on Augustine and the Pelagian Controversy." In <u>The</u> <u>Nicene</u> <u>and</u> <u>Post-Nicene</u> <u>Fathers</u>, Vol. V, xiii-lxxi.

Wiesel, Elie. <u>The</u> <u>Accident</u>. New York: Avon, 1961.

_____. <u>Ani</u> <u>Maamin</u>: <u>A</u> <u>Song</u> <u>Lost</u> <u>and</u> <u>Found</u> <u>Again</u>. New York: Random House, 1973.

_____. <u>A</u> <u>Beggar</u> <u>in</u> <u>Jerusalem</u>. New York: Avon, 1970.

_____. <u>Dawn</u>. New York: Avon, 1960.

_____. <u>Four</u> <u>Hasidic</u> <u>Masters</u> <u>and</u> <u>Their</u> <u>Struggle</u> <u>Against</u> <u>Melancholy</u>. Notre Dame: University of Notre Dame Press, 1978.

_____. <u>The</u> <u>Gates</u> <u>of</u> <u>the</u> <u>Forest</u>. New York: Avon, 1966.

_____. <u>A</u> <u>Jew</u> <u>Today</u>. Trans. Marian Wiesel. New York: Random House, 1978.

_____. <u>Night</u>. New York: Avon, 1969.

_____. <u>The</u> <u>Town</u> <u>Beyond</u> <u>the</u> <u>Wall</u>. New York: Avon, 1964.

_____. <u>Zalmen</u>, <u>or</u> <u>The</u> <u>Madness</u> <u>of</u> <u>God</u>. New York: Pocket Books, 1974.

Williams, Charles. <u>Descent</u> <u>into</u> <u>Hell</u>. Grand Rapids: Eerdmans, 1937; rep., 1973.

Williamson, Chris. <u>The</u> <u>Changer</u> <u>and</u> <u>the</u> <u>Changed</u>. Olivia Records, Inc., 1975.

Wink, Walter. <u>The</u> <u>Bible</u> <u>in</u> <u>Human</u> <u>Transformation</u>: <u>Toward</u> <u>a</u> <u>New</u> <u>Paradigm</u> <u>for</u> <u>Biblical</u> <u>Study</u>. Philadelphia: Fortress Press, 1973.

Selected Related Works

Bellah, Robert N. *Beyond Belief:* *Essays on Religion in a Post-Traditional World.* New York: Harper & Row, 1970.

Boesak, Allan Aubrey. *Farewell to Innocence:* *A Socio-Economic Study on Black Theology and Power.* Maryknoll: Orbis Books, 1976.

Brown, Robert McAfee. *Theology in a New Key:* *Responding to Liberation Themes.* Philadelphia: Westminster Press, 1978.

Buber, Martin. *Eclipse of God:* *Studies in the Relation Between Religion and Philosophy.* New York: Harper & Row, 1952.

Cone, James H. *A Black Theology of Liberation.* Philadelphia: J.B. Lippincott, 1970.

Daly, Mary. *Gyn/Ecology:* *The Metaethics of Radical Feminism.* Boston: Beacon Press, 1978.

Davis, Charles. *Body as Spirit:* *The Nature of Religious Feeling.* New York: Seabury Press, 1976.

Dawidowicz, Lucy S. *The War Against the Jews, 1933-1945.* New York: Bantam Books, 1976.

Fackenheim, Emil L. *God's Presence in History:* *Jewish Affirmations and Philosophical Reflections.* New York: Harper & Row, 1970.

Jones, William R. *Is God a White Racist?* *A Preamble to Black Theology.* Garden City: Doubleday, 1973.

Kaufmann, Walter. *Existentialism, Religion, and Death:* *Thirteen Essays.* New York: New American Library, 1976.

Klein, Charlotte. *Anti-Judaism in Christian Theology.* Philadelphia: Fortress Press, 1978.

Kramer, Heinrich, and James Sprenger. The Malleus Maleficarum. Trans. with intro., bibliography and notes by the Reverend Montague Summers. New York: Dover, 1971.

Milgram, Stanley. Obedience to Authority: An Experimental View. New York: Harper & Row, 1974.

Miranda, Jose. Being and the Messiah: The Message of St. John. Maryknoll: Orbis Books, 1977.

_____. Marx and the Bible. Maryknoll: Orbis Books, 1974.

Nelson, James B. Embodiment: An Approach to Sexuality and Christian Theology. Minneapolis: Augsburg, 1978.

Niebuhr, H. Richard. Christ and Culture. New York: Harper & Row, 1951.

Ogden, Schubert M. Faith and Freedom: Toward a Theology of Liberation. Nashville: Abingdon, 1979.

Phipps, William E. The Sexuality of Jesus: Theological and Literary Perspectives. New York: Harper & Row, 1973.

Pittenger, W. Norman. The Word Incarnate: A Study of the Doctrine of the Person of Christ. New York: Harper & Brothers, 1959.

Robinson, J.A.T. Honest to God. Philadelphia: Westminster Press, 1963.

Rowbotham, Sheila. Woman's Consciousness, Man's World. Harmondsworth, Middlesex, England: Penguin Books, 1973.

Ruether, Rosemary. Liberation Theology: Human Hope Confronts Christian History and American Power. New York: Paulist Press, 1972.

_____. New Woman New Earth: Sexist Ideologies and Human Liberation. New York: Seabury Press, 1975.

Segundo, Juan Luis. The Liberation of Theology. Maryknoll: Orbis Books, 1976.

Wiesel, Elie. The Oath. New York: Avon, 1973.

_____. One Generation After. New York: Avon, 1965.

Wiesel, Elie. _The Trial of God (as it was held on February 25, 1649, in Shamgorod)_. New York: Random House, 1979.

Wiles, Maurice. _The Remaking of Christian Doctrine: The Hulsean Lectures, 1973_. London: SCM Press, 1974.